A SKEPTIC'S CHRISTIANITY

A Skeptic's
Christianity

Mark Holmes

Belleville, Ontario, Canada

A SKEPTIC'S CHRISTIANITY

Copyright © 2002, Mark Holmes

ISBN: 1-55306-331-7

**For more information or
to order additional copies, please contact:**

Mark Holmes
150 Yeovil St.
Port Hope, ON L1A 1W8
(905) 885-2084

Essence Publishing is a Christian Book Publisher dedicated to furthering the work of Christ through the written word. *Guardian Books* is an imprint of *Essence Publishing*. For more information, contact:
44 Moira Street West, Belleville, Ontario, Canada K8P 1S3.
Phone: 1-800-238-6376. Fax: (613) 962-3055.
E-mail: info@essencegroup.com
Internet: www.essencegroup.com

Printed in Canada
by

Guardian
B O O K S

CONTENTS

Acknowledgements

Thanks go first to Nora, who has generously lived through most of the events and all of the book (more than once). Henry Regehr and David Royal kindly read the first draft and made constructive suggestions. Susan Blaine and John and Marianne Goertzen have given me frequent encouragement along the way. Numerous members of St. Mark's, Port Hope, Bob and Ruth Stephens of Christ Church, Campbellford, other friends, and numerous preachers in Anglican churches have had an unwitting influence—although they may wish to dissociate themselves from the outcome. Posthumous thanks go to Bill MacKenzie and Tom Rooke.

INTRODUCTION

This book was originally intended for two groups of people, people who are generally moving towards the spiritual, and those moving away. Either way, while not being determined atheists, they have no strong attachment to a religious faith. Having been rejected by mainstream publishers, *A Skeptic's Christianity* is now addressed to friends and family. If it had been accepted, changes would probably have been made. The first, personal chapter would likely have been reduced to a couple of pages. Chapters 4 and 6, being illustrative more than part of the central argument, might have been substantially deleted. Readers may want to skip those chapters.

According to the media, Christians are naïve, confused, and sometimes intolerant. They are frequently labeled as ignorant, self-righteous, or hypocritical. Fundamentalists are painted as (usually insincere) believers in all kinds of ridiculous things that no sane and educated person—such as a journalist—would accept. Mainline Christian leaders are shown using their religion as a bat to attack government policies of which they disapprove from a self-appointed position of moral superiority. Then there are the nominal Christians approved by the media, for whom church is an occasional event, marriage or baptism, perhaps, and a Christmas carol service, who make sure that church does not ever interfere with whatever they want to do.

A fundamentalist Christian group attacks the teaching of evolution in the schools. A bishop attacks a government for not building more public housing for single parents. A nominally Christian political leader supports publicly-funded abortion on demand, arguing that one's private religion (unlike one's secular ideology) should not influence the legislation one approves. The picture of Christianity presented in the media is neither coherent nor attractive; it is discouraging to the person yearning for spiritual meaning. None of those caricatures is entirely fair to the media (and less so to Christians), but those images do emerge from television and newspapers, and they contain a grain of truth.

Many people who have grown up like me, without religion, feel emptiness; they seem to need something to justify their lives other than personal pleasure. Not all those people will be attracted by my message. After all, there are many substitutes for religion in the contemporary world. Most obvious is the materialistic worship of more, or mammon. There are liberal rationalists who contort themselves impressively as they derive all kinds of odd beliefs to guide their own and others' lives, based on a belief in what is often conveniently called "enlightened" self-interest.

Many connect with fashionable causes: environmentalism, anti-racism, universal human rights, and child poverty. Although the environment, racism, and poverty are important problems requiring vigorous response, their isolation from a grounded set of beliefs and values can easily lead to unwise, emotional action that may do more harm than good, however well-intended. For example, some groups call for massive cutbacks in our use of energy to stave off global warming, without: knowing how clearly established the pattern really is; extensively researching overall effects (both positive and negative) on our country and the world; understanding the implications of the lack of commitment on the part of the fastest-growing energy users in the developing world, China being the prime example; and addressing ignorance of the potential damage to our economy, together with its effects on those least able to sustain increasing impoverishment.

Clearly, we human beings are the greatest threat to the environment, and the richer we become, the greater the harm we cause. But how many of us really oppose anyone getting richer? How many parents with young families want to freeze their incomes? The problem of the environment demands serious scientific study and intelligent consideration of what is possible and what is in everyone's best interests. Too often, enthusiasts, lacking any central meaning in their lives, invent a religious enthusiasm for their cause.

At one time, anti-racism in North America meant integration of blacks and whites. But today, many blacks choose their own company, their own schools, and their own interpretation of Islamic religion. Does anti-racism mean treating people of different races differently, or the same? Today, in Canada, it is fashionable to view any different treatment of blacks as wrong; at the same time, attempts to treat First Nations people the same as other Canadians are considered equally heinous. We need a deeper appreciation of human equality than implied by quick-fix programs for "us" to do something to or for "them," whether it be equal or unequal treatment. Those who exhort everyone to think and act globally often end up imposing their own versions of "universal" human rights, democracy, and capitalism on peoples and cultures for whom those ideas are meaningless or even corrupting.

At the same time, those who believe that such problems are best addressed without considering the moral and ethical basis for human behaviour—that is, to be defined as technical problems simply requiring new government policies and programs—may well not be interested in my overall argument.

I am not suggesting, however, that all we have to do is learn from devout Mennonites or Jehovah's Witnesses to obtain the solution to the problems afflicting Western society and the world (although there are worse places to begin). As long as the religious illiterate can keep busy, captivated by work or leisure (and Western society is nothing if not busy), the hole of gnawing despair can be ignored. But there are quiet moments in most of our lives when we confront where we are, who we are, and where we are going; the confrontation is not always reassuring.

Understandably in the context, many Christians, the second part of my original audience, have drifted away from the church—perhaps as adolescents rejecting incredible stories of virgin birth, miracles, and a man-god arising from the dead; as young parents, far too busy with children and work to think about the meaning of life; or as mature adults, finding prayers unanswered, and spiritual longing for certainty unsatisfied. The reasons for the drift are many. There is an enormous gap between those who describe themselves to Statistics Canada as having a religion and those who attend religious services on a regular basis; in Canada, much more than half the population falls in the former category, perhaps a quarter in the latter.

One reason for the drift is that ours is a secular society. Religion is no longer a part of most young people's schooling. Religious symbols are less and less a part of our celebrations, even at Christmas and Easter. The Salvation Army choir was forbidden to sing in the Oshawa hospital at Christmas, 1997, on the grounds that the singing carried a religious message. However inhumane it may seem, the ruling is not without logic. There is, nevertheless, a danger that the proliferating arm of the state will embrace those who have no wish to be embraced in a version of spiritual harassment. Children in state schools, too, are reasonably not expected to participate in religious rituals or receive religious instruction, but with a virtual state monopoly, that leads to mandatory secularization.

The pluralist societies of Canada, the United States, and Britain must (and substantially have) come to terms with the new secular reality. But that reality, however neutral and fair-minded the leaders of the new regime, makes it easier for people to shed their religion. In the 1940s and 50s, a great many people still attended church out of habit and social custom, with little grounded religious belief beyond habit and tradition. The Enlightenment had opened the door to religious disbelief two hundred years earlier, a disbelief even more firmly grounded in the nineteenth century with the birth of Marxism, the development of science (notably geology and evolution), and a realization in announcements of the death of God. Those ideas had significantly permeated Western society by the beginning of the twentieth century. My paternal grandfather was a non-believer, my grandmother a suffragette. I see, admittedly dramatically, my parents' generation of middle-class, agnostic, Fabian socialists, as spending the religious and moral capital accumulated over thousands of years. Their values were largely Christian, but they despised Christianity. They believed in science, progress, and a benevolent state.

There are various reasons for the decay of Christianity as its versions of historical truth became increasingly implausible in the light of new knowledge. Intermarriage among denominations, sects, religions, and systems of non-belief confronts spouses with conflicting ideas and decisions concerning the raising of their children. Religion is not taught in public schools, and when it survived after World War II, it was more inoculation than inculcation.

Some years ago, when I was moving towards formal baptism in the Christian faith, I met an old friend. Stuart (not his real name) and his wife had been strong Presbyterians who had grown up in the faith in Scotland. Stuart is a highly educated man in all senses of the word. At the time of our meeting, he had recently lost his faith. He had read some of the narratives derived from the discovery of the Dead Sea Scrolls and had come to the conclusion that the story of the Virgin birth, the miracles, and the physical resurrection were simply unbelievable in the context of the numerous competing narratives of Jewish sects of the time. He had gone to talk over his growing unbelief with his minister. Rather than try to shore up Stuart's lost faith, the honest minister simply confirmed the doubts, saying that he himself and many other Presbyterians shared them.

Although the supposed conflict between science and faith is no longer a problem to some, religious and secular, to many others, it remains an important barrier. If much of the New Testament story of Jesus is not factually accurate, at least in its key points, where does that leave Christianity? That is the starting point for this book. For many nominal and ex-Christians, the problem Stuart faced is crucial. Some simply leave the church in disgust. More drift away, perhaps retaining the name of their denomination, but lacking an anchoring commitment. Others vigorously denounce the back-sliders to re-affirm their own faith.

It may well be this crucial point that explains, more than any other, the steady decline of the mainline churches, while the more doctrinally faithful churches manage to maintain or even augment their congregations. The mainline churches try to balance on a knife edge. If they lean too far towards fundamentalism, they lose the Stuarts and many more liberal than he. If they lean too far towards "liberal Christianity," based on emotion perhaps, or on a deification of a "happy-clappy" Jesus who virtually replaces God as a human, accessible idol, they alienate not only traditional believers, but the social conservatives who form a significant proportion of churchgoers even in the mainline churches.

Social conservatives, some of whose beliefs involve metaphor and allegory when they interpret doctrine, cannot abide the attempt of many mainline leaders to turn the church into an ideological movement in opposition to an evil capitalism and the traditional values of family, sexual fidelity, and humility.

Some readers may be most interested in the chapters devoted to Christian belief. Others will find the later application of Christianity to one's life more interesting.

Yet others, however, will see little connection between the two themes, belief and behaviour. I believe there is a vital cord between coming to the terms of Christian truth about the nature of God and determining how to live one's life; indeed, a core theme of the book is that the strongest faith in traditional dogma is of little value if it does not carry over into how one lives one's life. I have little sympathy with those who say they fully believe dogma, but who at the same time act on the assumption that secular leaders, usually politicians and the promoters of current causes, can best tell them how to live their lives.

Some Christians have founded their faith in sudden conversion following an important event in their lives, death of a loved one, disease or disaster, or a divine moment. They have found their own way, and my message may be unnecessary or unhelpful; they will be more certain of their newfound truth than I am. There are many roads to truth.

But it should not be imagined that the only way to Christianity is through a charismatic experience of Jesus or God. Members of my audience are more likely to feel they face a dilemma. On the one hand, they feel a yearning for some spiritual meaning in life. On the other, they fear the tight bonds of religious doctrine and a demanding community. While they like, at a time when our society is increasingly atomized, the idea of a religious community, they wonder if too much will be expected of them—too much time, too much commitment, too much belief, and too much money.

Therein lies the spiritual crisis of our age. We want to belong. Most of us want family and community. But we want to conserve our own individual identity. We, and I include myself here, want it both ways.

In the following chapter, I describe where I am coming from—my own path to Christian belief. Some will skip the chapter, on the grounds that my arguments for belief in a non-believing age either stand or fall by themselves. I take the time to trace my own path to help others appreciate the place where I have landed, the point I have reached in my search for God. I do not suggest for a moment that others can, will, or should follow the same track or reach the identical milestone. If the metaphor of the spiritual path makes sense, it would hardly be surprising if my own location, five years from now, is different. There cannot be a single entirely satisfactory, universally acceptable explanation of spiritual truth; my hope is that my search will help others, just as that of others, some frequently mentioned in the book, have helped me.

Whether we wish it or not, we live and breathe individualism. Most of us do not have the choice of becoming an integral part of a collective journey; our very independence and freedom deny it. We follow different routes and, unsurprisingly, end up in different places. To expect there can be a hard, fast, complete, widely acceptable, and rational divide between reason and unreason in the search for truth is itself unreasonable. Far from condemning Christians whose views are more orthodox than mine, I respect them—to the extent that they are constant and consistent. I envy the serenity and certainty of those good people with a deep and abiding faith. There is no longer, if there ever was, one expression of religious truth on which to rest. On the other hand, I am no naïve innocent; it is absurd to proclaim that there is truth in everything and everybody, that one person's opinion is just as valid as any other. There is falsehood and evil. If no one is privy to complete truth, equally there are expressions of truth and untruth. If there is no single right answer, there are many wrong ones.

CHAPTER 1

FROM ATHEISM TO HOLY BAPTISM

CHILDHOOD

Born to non-believing parents, I was never baptized as a child. Nevertheless, I had two early contacts with the Church of England. One was at school, the other through my maternal grandparents. While neither had a significant impact at the time, it is possible that seeds were sown.

When I was three, my father, mother, elder sister, and I moved from the industrial city of Middlesbrough, in the north of Yorkshire, the county in northern England where I was born, to the smaller industrial town of Sowerby Bridge, in west Yorkshire. Sowerby Bridge is only four kilometres from the large industrial centre of Halifax, but that distance was much greater in 1938 than it is today, both because I was a child and because travel was less common and more difficult.

My father had taught in a grammar school in Middlesbrough. His promotion to headmaster of Sowerby Bridge Secondary (soon to become Grammar) School was quite a coup for a young man of thirty-one. He had achieved a rare double first in classics at Cambridge University. Equally rare at that time was it for an unusually brilliant Cambridge graduate to decide, on ideological grounds, to work in the state rather than in the private system.

His children's education was a problem. By salary, educational background, and level of employment, he was clearly now in the upper middle class. His own father had owned a chemist's shop in London, a lower (but still middle-class) status occupation in the acutely class-conscious England of that time, but one sufficiently rewarding to allow his two sons to attend a private day school of some prestige, before the days of universal access to an academic education. Private education was obviously a problem for my father's egalitarian and socialist conscience; he also doubtless begrudged spending money on a cause which he opposed.

Although my father was skeptical of private schools in 1938, the local, working-class state primary schools in industrial Yorkshire must have been difficult for him to accept for academic reasons. In any case, my sister and I both initially attended a private girls' day school in Halifax. It was not unusual for private girls' day schools to have a primary section for both boys and girls, because private preparatory (frequently boarding) schools typically enrolled boys from the age of eight.

Following my eighth birthday, I was placed in Trinity School, also in Halifax, run by the Church of England but financed by the state. England has long had parallel state, Church of England and Roman Catholic state schools; today, it also has Muslim schools. I assume that by this time (1943), my father had learned something of the reputations of the local state schools. Although I was a fish out of water (being shy, non-Christian, and upper-middle-class by culture and accent), I do not have memories of being unfairly treated in what today would be called an inner-city school. I do remember being firmly grounded in the basic skills, of being strapped frequently for talking (which I am sure many people wish had had more effect), but have little recollection of the religious instruction.

Two memories testify to some religious teaching taking place. We lived in a rented section of a large house owned by a local industrialist. It had spacious grounds, of which we had use of a significant portion; the mill owner was an officer in the army during the war, while my father, having an essential occupation and poor eyesight, served in the air force reserve. My sister's and my time was not filled with organized activity as is that of my grandchildren. We read a lot and played together. We had no friends living close by—we both traveled to school by tram, until it was replaced by the bus. Despite the general poverty of wartime and early post-war industrial, northern England, the streets were safe (except from some local bullies who would take the opportunity to beat up a toff, easily identifiable by his appearance, were it not for his formidably aggressive sister). I explored alone quite frequently and on Sunday mornings I would occasionally go to the local parish church, wandering around, not daring to enter, fantasizing that the rector would talk to me and invite me in.

At the age of ten, I transferred to a local state grammar (academic) school, up the valley in Hebden Bridge, another small industrial town, already attended by my sister, Janet. For good reason, my father did not want us attending his school, which would be embarrassing both for us and for him; in those days, the distance between teachers and students was much greater than today (and greater than in North America). Religious instruction was a part of the school program, but it was taught in such a detached and anodyne manner that its function was mainly prophylactic, certainly in my case. I only recall one religious instruction teacher. We read parts of the Bible, but purely as narrative; she made no attempt to discuss truth, morality, or ethics. In fairness to her, the quality of most teachers I experienced in those early post-war days was equally low.

Home life was entirely non-religious. I have no recollection of religious discussions of any kind during this period of my life. My father, with a demanding job and responsibilities as a member of the air force reserve, had little time for family life. In those days, it would in any case have been unusual for a middle-class father to be much involved in the raising of children. Such children (the middle class was much smaller than today) typically attended private—often, in the case of boys, boarding—schools. Access to grammar school on the basis of competitive examinations only began in 1945 (the year I transferred). It was mainly attended by bright children from working-class or lower middle class (often upwardly mobile) families; indeed, its intended function was to permit children from the poorest backgrounds to gain the highest level of education. Even in the grammar school, most left school either at age fourteen or after gaining their "school certificate" at age fifteen or, from 1950, sixteen.

My mother was a Christian in almost every way except one. She had been brought up in a strong, Christian home and this showed in her values and character. She was totally honest, to the point of being blunt, tactless, and occasionally thoughtless. She was humble and modest to an unusual degree for the twentieth century. Hers was not the self-conscious self-deprecation of the sophisticated, who draw attention to the qualities they believe that they possess by disclaiming or demeaning them. She went beyond an admirable (in my opinion) humility to less-admirable self-sacrifice. Fanny, Jane Austen's unlikely (to the modern mind) hero in *Mansfield Park*, is the finest portrayal of a Christian in fiction, and my mother is the only person I have come across who even faintly resembles her. This may seem like cloying praise from a favoured son for his mother, but it is not; she was universally admired by relatives and others who knew her well for the qualities I have described. She had become, however, a non-believer and never attended church on her own account as an adult. While my sister, being the first-born, female, and more outgoing and amiable than I, was, in hindsight, given special attention by my father as a young child (Janet was six when the war began), none of the three children, my brother John being born in 1944, claims to have had an especially close relationship with my mother. If she seems a paragon of virtuous rationality, I should mention that she told Janet and me after the war that she had planned to drown us if the Germans had successfully invaded England. She was to deny it later in life.

Although my mother and I never had an emotionally close relationship, it was strong and positive. The harshest criticism that I heard her make of another child was that he was spoiled. She avoided spoiling by being reluctant to praise (and almost as slow to criticize). None of us was spoiled in the conventional way, and I soon learned not to take any complaint or worry to my mother. She would remark that I was being "silly" or that I had got out of bed the wrong side that morning (the latter, at least, often being the case). So I learned to keep personal thoughts and problems to myself. I learned not to boast of having done well on a test ("If you had done any work, you would have done much better"), or of scoring, most unusually—I was always physically inept—a goal in soccer ("I hope you didn't get your trousers all dirty again").

My mother thought of herself as being plain and unattractive. Perhaps for that reason, together with her self-consciousness, modesty, and humility, she disapproved of mirrors, still more of permanent images. My photograph was taken as a baby (for my paternal grandparents), but there is no other photograph until I was given a second-hand camera at about the age of twelve. My father owned a camera for a time, but avoided taking photographs of people; his only interest was in historic buildings and, vary occasionally, scenery. He soon changed to collecting guides and picture postcards. Interestingly, his informal memoir dwells on events, and says little of people. On the few occasions when he mentions my wife and family or me, he is apt to be factually inaccurate; that may be the case with others, and with himself.

I was uncomfortable in my skin from an early age, and have unsurprisingly had a strong aversion to being televised in adult life. A chance sight of myself in a mirror, or reflected in a shop window, is still sometimes occasion for momentary discomfort.

Although we were held at a distance emotionally (particularly the two boys), we were all spoiled in a less obvious way. My mother lived for my father and her three children. She always put herself last—to a fault. One should live one's own life, and one should not give one's children and spouse a feeling of being more important, a sense they will be only too ready to assume. She hid her feelings, and I at least responded by not understanding that she had any. Although she set high standards of moral behaviour herself, she made it easy for the rest of us, my father and the three children, to be thoughtless, unhelpful, and selfish.

Those characteristics of our upbringing, the superficial social and emotional indifference, the distance from our father, the absence of spiritual nurture, the strong Christian moral background by example, and the sheltering from personal responsibilities around the home, all contribute to an understanding of the children's characters as adults. All three have become baptized Christians as adults (I was the last); all have had to face, often submit to, inclinations to selfishness.

It would be incorrect to see our benign neglect as being entirely by default, necessity, or custom. My parents were progressive, atheistic socialists. They believed that children should become independent, particularly in the sense that they should be intellectually and morally autonomous. Their central faith, notably my father's, was in science and rationality. Although he would often announce the superiority of classical thought to Christian humbug, I never heard him develop an opinion based on classical philosophy, except perhaps his claim to being tolerant and temperate, which he might, if asked, have attributed to Aristotle.

He was more a child of Rousseau. Formal teaching of values or ideologies was wrong. Children should be educated objectively and left to determine their own values and choices. Obviously, there was a great deal of indirect and unintended teaching in the household, but that only became apparent to me in late adolescence and adulthood. Middle-class children were far less entertained in those days than today. What was unusual was our comparative social isolation, absence of friends and relatives outside school other than siblings, an absence that resulted from the social-class gap between our working-class and lower-middle-class neighbourhood and schools and our upper-middle-class home environment; by not attending neighbourhood schools, we also faced a physical gap. While my sister, more gregarious by nature, has managed to compensate for that lack, my brother, John, and I remain uncomfortable in many social situations.

It is in this context—an absence of formal instruction in religion or values; an absence of personal conversation of any kind (although general discussion of books and current events was plentiful); a disapproval of the display of emotion (except for laughter)—that a single, significant conversation took place when I was nine or ten. Unremarkable, even banal, in itself, it stands out as being the only personal or spiritual conversation with my father or mother that I remember while I was growing up. "Do you believe in God?" I asked my mother. "I don't believe in a God sitting up in the sky wearing golden sandals," she replied, "but I do believe there is a spirit of good." End of conversation. Those words, however, stayed with me, even during my dreariest days of adolescence; they survive in the world view developed in this book. The journey from atheism to baptism may seem to indicate a reversal, perhaps rebellion, but there is a strong thread of continuity. I told a Christian friend, David Russell, about my baptism and confirmation, with some pride perhaps, and certainly with some expectation of pleasure. His comment, meant kindly, was, "Well, it won't make any difference, will it? You always lived a Christian life." I like to think he was wrong, that it *has* made a difference, at least when I do not think and act spontaneously.

My mother's character clearly developed from her Christian childhood. That may sound like a truism or platitude; after all, I have also indicated that aspects of my own upbringing have influenced my adult life; but I do not see much of a parallel. (An observer might remark that I have taken on the form of a Christian, while my mother was one). While she had indeed developed a character by young adulthood that survived relatively undisturbed in adult life, my own character was only dimly formed by early adulthood, and has changed, for better or for worse, during my adult life, in the early years of marriage and, to a lesser extent, in my fifties and sixties. My mother was morally and religiously educated; I had minimal moral or religious instruction. One can, of course, observe that I was as surely indoctrinated in atheism, rationality, science, humanism, and socialism as my mother had been in Christianity—and neither form of indoctrination completely took.

Two of my three daughters have developed characters as adults very different from those they had as children and, in one case, as an adolescent. None of my four children's future adult character and manner could have been neatly characterized at the age of ten. I reject the notion that the adult can be predicted from the young child. After the event, one can always trace some enduring traits, but prediction from age six or even, or in many cases, sixteen, would be generally inaccurate. British film-makers have followed a sample of six-year-olds into their forties. They claim that the adult is formed by the age of six; "Give me a child until six and...." But their own project refutes them. While some in their sample do follow predictable lives, many more do not. Those who believe in that kind of scientific determinism use faulty logic to bolster their case; if children follow their upbringing, then that is proof of cause and effect. If they do not, then their rebellion is equally proof of cause and effect. By that account, the three Holmes children, Janet, Mark, and John, all simply rebelled against their atheistic parents. In fact, the conversion of the three children to Christianity took place in entirely different circumstances, none apparently linked to rebellion. Further, I am the only one to have taken a very different political course from my parents (being conservative as distinct from socialist); even in that case, rebellion seems an unlikely cause. There are many plausible causes of changes in our spiritual and ideological commitment, besides the effects of home environment and rebellion against it. They include: the effects of influential others, friends, and, particularly, spouse; individual will; school; genetic predisposition; chance circumstance; occupation; one's individual character or daemon; and, I have come to believe, God's spirit.

After the death of my maternal grandfather at the beginning of World War II, my grandmother continued to run the private hotel they had rented just after World War I, in Dunster in the west of England county of Somerset. She was helped by her sister, my great aunt, who joined her at the hotel after the death of her own husband. Aunt Gertrude was a favourite relative of mine, particularly in adolescence and early adulthood. As a young child, I had generally preferred my father's family to my mother's. My paternal grandfather, who died when I was about five, was, in my memory, a kindly, generous old man whom I remember reading my favourite books to me, sitting on his knee. My paternal grandmother was always pleasant to me, and generous financially at Christmas and birthdays, but there was little opportunity for interaction between us.

Looking back, the greater influence, direct and indirect, came through my mother's side; I suspect the two sisters' religious influence on Janet was greater and more direct. My happiest memories of my youth today, other than of the occasional family holiday away from home, are of days spent at the hotel in Somerset.

While it was customary in those years for the middle classes to take holidays away from home, the opportunities were obviously more limited during the war and immediate post-war years. Overseas travel was impossible during the war years, and the seashore, including Dunster beach, was heavily defended. Even so, my grandmother's hotel stayed open for the entire period, with some summer visitors and several permanent guests. As is the way with small family-run hotels, there were staffing and other crises; their frequency increased as the two sisters aged and found it more difficult to cope.

During the 1940s, our family, often without my father, and occasionally my mother alone in time of crisis, visited the hotel quite regularly. Part of my affection, then and now, for The Old Manor arises from its guests, young and old, who were people of my own social class, whom I could talk to, to whom I was not alien. This enjoyment was a sign of growing independence; my parents looked down on regular visitors to the Old Manor as being unimaginative and bourgeois. By the 1950s, my parents' upper-middle-class generation was looking for "undiscovered" places in Europe, unsullied by vulgar crowds, by both the upper and (unspoken) the lower class, or by "loud" and "wealthy" Americans; in other words, like most people, they approved people like themselves. Unlike most people, they would have fiercely rejected the idea—tolerance was a prominent value. The guests at the Old Manor were generally conservative in politics, as were my great aunt and grandmother. My sister, in 1945, remarked at the dinner table, when talk turned to Winston Churchill, the Conservative prime minister who went down to crushing defeat to socialist Clement Attlee in that first post-war election, "My daddy says Churchill ought to be shot." It should be borne in mind, in fairness to my father, that the colloquial expression of the time was not to be taken literally. Even so, the effect on the guests, seated mainly around one large dinner table, was electric.

My grandmother seemed to me to be harsh and tough in the early days (I always adored my great-aunt, equally tough, but with a soft spot for boys), but that fear turned later to respect and affection—perhaps love. On a number of occasions, I accompanied one or other of the sisters to church. It is difficult now to recall my feelings at the time with accuracy. Situated in one of England's most picturesque villages, Dunster's parish church is a beautiful building, and my memory of it remains vivid. The well-attended Sunday morning 11 a.m. service, as best I can recall, was always Morning Prayer—my favourite service to this day. Communion sometimes followed for the small numbers remaining. When my mother suggested that I attend (for my grandmother's sake), I know I objected, but it may have been the *pro forma* objection of the young male. It was rare for my mother to direct me to do anything—even a direct suggestion or request was unusual. I believe that I secretly enjoyed going, particularly the singing of hymns and the organ music. Church music has remained throughout my life a particular joy, even—perhaps especially—at times when I felt no affiliation with any church or religion. My children tell me that they remember the boredom of their childhood Sundays when I played recordings of organ music. One does not have to imagine what a psychiatrist would make of that.

ADOLESCENCE AND YOUNG ADULTHOOD

My childhood—sheltered, lonely, and favoured, by the standards of the times—ended abruptly in 1948. My father was appointed headmaster of one of the first large comprehensive high schools in the British Isles. The later decision to "go comprehensive" by a Labour government was one of the greatest causes for rejoicing in his life, for reasons both personal and ideological. The old academic grammar schools for those who passed their 11-plus, and the secondary modern schools for the 75 or 80 per cent that failed, were to be combined into one egalitarian secondary school for everyone, along the lines of the idealized and "democratic" American high school. The secondary modern school had only been introduced in 1945, but it was immediately under attack, and for good reason. It was to be a Deweyan school, without tests or examinations, where experience was all. The experience, as it turned out, was largely negative. The comprehensive high school may have been the only aspect of North American culture that my father liked (ironically, because it turned out to be even less enduring in England than in its home country). When I, and later my wife, emigrated to North America, inveterate traveller as he was, my father preferred to visit remote parts of Europe, or Latin America.

The prospect of moving to Douglas, on the Isle of Man, in 1948, excited me as much as it appalled my sister. The idea (as distinct from the reality) of moving has never ceased to attract me, and upset her. My mother's true feelings, as usual, were never made known, and never sensed—at least, not by me; insofar as our life was more rural, she was likely pleased by the change. She also found some friendship, of which she had little or none in Sowerby Bridge. The Isle of Man experience was to prove to be the least professionally satisfying of my father's career; it also proved to be the least happy period of my own life.

My father, to my chagrin and misfortune, decided I should attend his school, Douglas High School for Boys. He had asked me if I would like to attend a private school, Prince William College, in the south of the island as a weekly boarder, but had decided against it after I had said I would; he felt that it would be hypocritical to send his son to a private school while touting the virtues of the comprehensive for others. He had also paid six thousand pounds for a house, expensive in 1948, a change from the sixty pounds a year rent he had paid, for a nicer place, in Sowerby Bridge. Quite apart from the social problems in Douglas High School, aggravated by my awkward shyness, Nordic features—the Manx are Celtic in origin—and being the head's son, the academic education I received there was mediocre, even by the standards of post-war Britain. There was no religious instruction. My only continuing thread to religion was to my grandmother and her sister in The Old Manor.

In 1953, I was admitted to Cambridge University, where I initially studied geography, of which I tired. I changed to anthropology and archaeology in my last year, and found the social anthropology most appealing. That teaching influenced my later ideas about education, and to some extent, my ideas about religion and tradition. I was particularly struck by the significance of myth and social convention to the civil order and meaning of primitive (and by analogy, advanced) society. I developed ideas about community which have continued to interest me. Community was to me then, and has continued to be, like a light to a moth: an almost irresistible attraction, but one that would be fatal if fulfilled. I was to hover around the light, but always withdraw when it came to the sacrifice of will.

At Cambridge, I was a consciously deliberate outsider, joining many groups and societies, but always unwilling to be drawn into the centre. Partly, I was accustomed to it, and partly I expect that I feared rejection. It was characteristic that my major sport at Cambridge, rowing, required commitment, self-discipline, and determination, but neither social communication nor physical dexterity.

There were four major political clubs; the Conservative, Liberal, and Labour clubs represented the three British political parties, the Liberal being a minor third party at the time (as it is today under the name of the Liberal Democrats). In addition, there was a Socialist club, which was more radical than the mainstream Labour party. My parents were strong Labour supporters; I joined the Liberal and the Socialist clubs.

If not rebellion, my choices did represent a fierce independence from my relatives and peers. In the first place, most people who joined political clubs, chose—reasonably enough— one that represented their ideology or their family background, usually both. The large Conservative and Labour clubs were training grounds for future mainstream politicians. Having an equal lack of respect for the aristocracy and the big trade unions, I chose two venues where independent ideas would be welcome. An outsider in both clubs, I felt closer affiliation with the Liberal party, which in those days was more like a moderate, middle-class, conservative party of today, similar to the Canadian Progressive Conservatives and moderate Republicans of the time. By 1956, despite my membership of the Socialist club, I was probably already moving to the political right of my parents. In educational terms, however, I remained a believer in the comprehensive school, only dimly aware that my own had provided me with a poor secondary education. I, reasonably enough, blamed myself for any deficiencies in my level of learning. Only in later life, I realized that good teaching in school and clear, demanding expectations at home would have overcome my difficulties in mathematics, for example, to which my mind is well suited.

Two seminal events took place in the summer of 1956, between Cambridge and the army. First, I fell madly and uncontrollably in love just after the end of my final term, when I traveled to Durham, in the northeast of England, to row in a college boat in a regatta. From the age of five, I had had a series of crushes, of varying intensity and longevity—more often than not unknown to the recipient of my affection, but this emotion was of a blinding, once-in-a-lifetime intensity, perhaps because it appeared to be reciprocated. Nora, the sister of a fellow student (but not friend) at my college, was to become, after some travails, my wife.

Second, my father found me work for a few weeks as a supply teacher in south-west London, where he was by then the head of one of London's first big comprehensive schools. There was a great shortage of teachers, particularly in the remaining secondary modern schools (for those who failed the 11-plus) in the less desirable parts of London. After a few days teaching in a chaotic school with only a handful of permanent teachers, I became briefly engrossed in teaching in one of the better secondary moderns. Although I could not have foreseen it at the time, two of three blocks forming the foundation and self-determination of my life had been put in place. Nora and I would carefully and deliberately build our own lives together, and the lives of our children, alone in the New World. Education would become my job and central interest throughout my working life.

At the time, however, I had little sense of future, a characteristic that stayed with me for another forty years. Major decisions were made quickly, even impulsively. During adolescence, my sense of the good, based on that single conversation with my mother, and what I had picked up by osmosis, had been corrupted by temptation, opportunity, greed, lust, laziness, and lack of active support. In conversation at home, if religion were mentioned, it would be with contempt, derision, or condescending humour. Religious people were seen either as poor, innocent dupes, who had been taught nonsense at home or church and had never thought for themselves, or as hypocrites, who pretended to values they never acted upon.

The new religion was socialism, whereby government would provide equal opportunity in education and subsequently a fair distribution of jobs and money, free health care so none would suffer from unattended illness, full employment by means of nationalization of the economy, and individual autonomy in a classless society. Perceived enemies included: Winston Churchill in particular, conservatives in general, the upper classes and the landed gentry, the churches, any vestige of empire, financial corporations (especially banks and insurance companies), charity (standing in the way of the government agencies which would abolish condescending pity), and the conventional middle classes.

The last category may seem surprising, considering that my parents were quite typical of a growing segment of the upper-middle-class (the more so when they moved to London in 1955 and found a circle of fellow-thinkers). My mother told me that she did not mind what I did for a living, as long as I was not a bank clerk or salesman. Just as Marxist academics today distinguish between those few liberated working-class members (who agree with them) and those still enslaved to traditional beliefs, my parents, consciously or not, distinguished between the agnostic and left-wing liberated middle class (mainly upper middle class) and those unenlightened creatures who still attended church, worked in insurance offices, washed their cars on Sunday afternoons or went for sedate walks, took holidays in the same seaside resort every year, and, worst of all, voted Conservative. There is nothing quite like the contempt we have for those who are rather like us, but have not made it in the ways we have. Those from the working classes, who have struggled to success and acceptance, are particularly disdainful of those who did not attempt the upward class struggle, or who attempted and failed.

My parents' admiration, at a distance, for the working class did not extend to entertaining its members in their home. The women cleaners whom they employed were treated with affectionate condescension. That may sound unfair to my mother, who was generally liked except by those whom she considered pompous; she took people as they were. But she was no more able to cross class boundaries in the building of friendship than anyone else; her working-class acquaintances would have felt just as uncomfortable with the idea as she. She was not a snob and had no objection to our being entertained by these kindly women to afternoon tea. Her affection was genuine, the condescension entirely lacking in malice. Her ideology, or perhaps it was my father's, denied the separation of their worlds, but my mother was ever a practical woman.

In 1956, I began two years of mandatory National Service in the British army. This turned out to be a period of waiting—literally, in the sense that the two years contained precious little activity; metaphorically, in that my authentic life began in 1958, when I undertook a life determined by my own deliberate will (admittedly with a substantial boost from chance and the proverbial silver spoon). Until then, I had been following a path that I believed, rightly or wrongly, my parents wished; this was more subconscious than conscious, for I received almost no direct instruction. When I had announced, however, at the age of seventeen, that I thought I would not go to university, the quick response was, "Don't be silly. Of course, you're going." And this from "non-interfering" parents!

In many ways, the patterns (not the details) of my adolescent and early adult life will be familiar to those males of that time coming from an educated, well-read, middle-class background: the passing enthusiasms for various sporting activities; an obsession with sex; a search for women; a desire for some pure and romantic liaison based on passion rather than physical sex; and the exploration of various ideological paths. It is no more unusual that any spiritual and religious element, which had been at best a flickering candle, was put aside and excluded.

My connections with the Old Manor in Dunster had been strengthened in my university years; I often spent the long university vacations (summer, Christmas, and Easter) there, rather than make the long, expensive trip back to the Isle of Man, which I remembered as a place of prolonged torpor. It would be untrue to claim any religious conversion, or even awakening, from the Old Manor experience. I declared myself an atheist when I entered the army, only partly because I naïvely thought I would thereby avoid Sunday church parade—I did, but got to peel potatoes instead. Nevertheless, I did receive a little religious or moral education at Dunster, which I had effectively ceased to receive from my mother by that time. At close quarters, over long Easter and Christmas vacations, when there were few other residents at the hotel, I observed the strong Christianity of the two sisters.

One incident remains clearly in my mind. The hotel often used young European women as staff; they were paid little, but were given their board and the opportunity to learn English. According to my aunt, one of these, whom I did not much like, was seeing an older man, I assumed married. This was rather a wicked thing to do at the time, although she must have been in her twenties and certainly no business of mine. I deliberately enmeshed her in lies about how she had spent an evening off. I told my aunt about the dishonesty, only to be frozen with disapproval. As I thought about it, I realized how obnoxiously priggish I had been, although it was only later that I could judge my behaviour in Christian terms. My aunt would observe, disapprove, but she would not make a formal judgment or condemnation, and she would certainly not accept entrapment.

Our daily newspaper at home was the *Guardian,* which I was to discover decades later to be a left-wing organ, believing in my youth that it was fair and objective, in the centre of rational, intelligent, right-minded opinion. Far from being a rebel, I adopted my parents' left-wing ideas and rationalism. I heard without interest that my sister had been baptized in the Church of England after leaving home, probably attributing it to her employment by the National Children's Homes, run by a Protestant denomination. Janet's faith has always been of that personal and private kind found within mainline religious denominations. She does not wear her religion on her sleeve. Janet has remained vaguely on the political left. My brother John and I similarly do not announce our religious beliefs; on most social occasions, it is unlikely an observer would know we were Christians. I write this descriptively; for my part, I feel some shame. I do believe that Christians should proclaim the gospel, should evangelize, not implicitly accept the secular reasoning prevalent in educated discourse. It is a fault of mainline Christians that we usually fade into the woodwork, rewarded by secular acceptance or praise for "tolerantly" not "imposing" our beliefs on others. There is no comparable social disapproval of strong secular statements and persuasion, concerning, as examples, abortion or divorce on demand. Listeners may disagree, openly or not, with the frequently pronounced opinions of left-wing intellectuals, but they do not denounce them as inappropriate. In the secular world, religion has displaced homosexuality in the closet.

If there were seeds of betrayal of my parents' faith, they were not obvious either in university or in the army. At Cambridge, I never attended a service in my college chapel (or anywhere else in Cambridge). If any of my friends at that time were religious, I was unaware of it. I had one Jewish friend (my first contact with Jews), but his world view was more obviously socialist than spiritual. Despite my parents' claim of tolerance, I had inferred a degree of hostility towards Roman Catholics and Jews (as well as, of course, fundamentalists, who were less in public evidence in those days). I remember my mother repeating the saying, "How odd that God should choose the Jews," in the context of a general dismissal of the Bible, and the expression, "You dirty Jew," was used on occasion. Tolerance was extended to those mainline Protestants who would joke about their religion while sharing my parents' secular politics. I can say without pride that I felt no prejudice against Jews, Catholics, or Muslims; without pride, because there is no virtue in being tolerant of ideas and beliefs about which one knows almost nothing and cares even less. I doubt that Pontius Pilate discriminated between Pharisees and Essenes.

There was one additional attitude I had learned at home: a dislike—even contempt—for things British. Janet and John deny this part of my recollection, as would no doubt my parents, were they alive. That I learned it is not in doubt, although perhaps I misinterpreted the signals. What I inferred, in the *Guardian* and in my parents' conversation, was an extension of the dislike for all things conservative and Conservative. The too-slow dismemberment of the empire (empire was assumed to be a secular evil); the superiority of Italian and French life, food, and character;

the relatively slow recovery of Britain after the war; the inefficient transport, particularly rail, system in Britain—public transport being a particular interest of my father and one inherited by my bother and me; and the inefficiency of local government (compared with that of France) were opinions contributing to that conclusion. That attitude, more assumption than carefully determined belief, was reinforced by my parents' and their friends' frequent travel to continental Europe, where everything was apparently superior to British holiday resorts; everything notably included the local people, who seemed to be uniformly kind, generous, and honest as well as being endowed with a superior sense of humour; any untoward events were treated as trivial or the subject of humour.

That disavowal of things British was to lead to the third building block in my adult life. My mother frequently remarked that she would not be able to stand having any of her children living close by. When my father retired in 1967, my parents moved to a small two-bedroom bungalow not readily accessible to either my sister or my brother and their families. By that time, I lived in Canada with a wife and four children.

THE PRIME OF LIFE, 1958-1975

Two of three blocks in the foundation of my adult life were initiated in 1956, but it would have been impossible to foresee their significance in those early years of adulthood. In the army, I served in the educational corps, but there was nothing in that tedious experience that would predict a strong future involvement in education. I never hated the army (lack of hate, the avoidance of expression of strong feeling, being one thing I learned from my parents and have not completely lost). Army life was too easy and vacuous to hate; it was a waiting-room— with the date of the appointment for a new life, "demob," clearly etched on the calendar.

A few months after joining the army, I was upset to receive a letter from Nora terminating our relationship. She told me, many years later, that my father had advised her to sever our relationship so as not to ruin her university social life. While I was too engrossed by then in my own life and family to be angry, it did confirm the emotional distance between my father and me, another example of unwanted interference. It must be understood that neither when he sacrificed me to his ideology by consigning me to his school, nor when he sought to terminate my relationship with the only girl I had truly loved, was he exercising conscious malice. Rationally, he simply thought that he was doing the right thing, my personal feelings and immediate interests being less important than his view of the general good.

Neither block (a career in education and marriage to Nora) was visible at the end of 1956, when the army gave me an opportunity to exert my independence. British and French forces invaded Egypt, to "save" the Suez Canal. My regimental group of conscripts was consistently lied to by officers, who claimed that the closing of the Suez Canal would be an economic catastrophe for Britain, doubling the price of the imports on which the country so heavily depended. A handful of "educated idiots" decided that the invasion was morally wrong and determined to refuse service in the invasion forces, i.e., to mutiny. Fortunately, the United Nations intervened. In retrospect, I am doubtful today that we were right (to make up our own minds which wars we would fight), but the dilemma did sensitize me to the importance of taking moral stands on what one believes to be right; it was the foundation of the motto that I carried through my working life: "There is some shit I will not eat," from a poem by e e cummings that I came across later.

Towards the end of my national service, I managed to find a teaching position in an English comprehensive school, to begin in September 1958. I had also applied for teaching positions in Addis Ababa, Ethiopia, Izmir in Turkey, and Saint John, New Brunswick. Shortly before I was due to begin teaching in England, I received a telegram from Saint John offering me a job there. I quickly resigned the job I had never begun.

The third block of my life, a new beginning in Canada, was put in place by that telegram. A single incident illustrates the extent to which I had misread my mother, and perhaps my father, too. I remember vividly my amazement when I left for Canada. I was in London's Waterloo station, on a boat train leaving for Southampton, where I would board the immigrant ship *Seven Seas* bound for Quebec City. Waving to my parents on the platform, I was shocked to see tears pouring down my mother's face and tears in my father's eyes. I was shocked. Exhibition of emotion was disapproved, and tears were rare indeed. I had thought that they would be pleased that I should be setting out to see the world. My mother said, later, that she thought she would never see me again.

I had truly believed I was fulfilling their expectations: I was going to teach, an approved occupation; I was not going to live next door; I was expressing independence and autonomy, their first goals; and I was leaving the despised Britain. And they were, of all things, crying. Naïve stupidity on my part, but a clear demonstration of how well I thought I had learned my part. I was to be surprised again later, when I was to discover that neither of them thought much of Saint John, New Brunswick in particular, or North America in general, compared with Britain, let alone the continent.

In spiritual terms, the next thirty years may be seen, in retrospect, as a very gradual movement towards Christianity. There were advances, stagnation, and retreats, but overall the movement was forward. Spiritual development accompanied a more general growth, at work, in my world view, in family life, and in character.

In Saint John, I first rented a room and ate meals in a board-ing house near my school. Most of the others at table were itin-erant manual labourers, but there were a bank clerk from Prince Edward Island and an immigrant, a surveyor working for the giant construction firm, Bechtel. Larry Tasker and I became friends, sharing complete isolation, an excited wonder at North America, and an English background. Larry persuaded me to go to church. Once again, it seemed almost as if I needed an excuse to go to church; I never knew Larry's true motivation. Our declared purpose was to find the opposite sex, and perhaps it was as simple as that on both our parts. By going to church, Larry assured me, we would be able to join young people's groups and meet available women. Once again, there was an Anglican connection. We attended the old Trinity Church in the heart of Saint John, just a few steps from my rented room and the school where I taught. The plan was successful, by means of the church volleyball club. I found the church services enjoyable, aesthetically attractive, but, as the old saying goes, the great thing about the Church of England is that it does not interfere with one's religion, or, in my case, lack of it.

One thing about that time is certain. I was far from sure that I wanted to stay in Canada. I had immigrated techni-cally—it was the only way to accept the job—but not emo-tionally. I was seeing the world, not choosing new citizenship. Canada, could as easily have been Ethiopia or Turkey. Neither was I sure that teaching was my ultimate career; in the mean-time, I found it fascinating, fulfilling, and exhausting. I had made up my mind, however, to marry and have a family. My central search was still less for women, although I was obvi-ously driven by sexual desire, but for a true love; that central focus of my life had not changed since adolescence, perhaps earlier. As well as my church and volleyball friends in Saint John, I was continuing a correspondence with a young German woman who had worked at the Old Manor, and whom I had visited while in the army.

In the fall of 1959, Nora re-entered my life. My mother sent on a letter from her, and our correspondence flourished. Unusually for a schoolteacher of that time, I flew to England for Christmas at The Old Manor, where Nora and I became engaged, my mother producing a family engagement ring, a need which she—not I—had typically foreseen. I returned to England, by sea, in July of 1960, and we were married in Nora's parish church in Houghton-le-Spring, in the county of Durham. I would have married her in a mosque if that had been required to tie the knot. Her parents, particularly her mother, had misgivings about the marriage, while my parents thought their son was extremely lucky, as indeed he was. I was fortunate in marrying the only true and whole love of my life. Our agreement was that we would both return to Saint John for one year, to see out my contract, and Nora would also teach, but that we would settle in Britain the following year.

This autobiographical sketch is intended to trace my religious growth, not tell my life story. My mother died in 1977, my father in 2000. I have attempted truth and clarity in my treatment of my parents, but am not prepared to do that, in this context, for my wife and children. There are minimal references, because I do not want to presume on their willingness to have parts of their lives opened to the public and because I do not want to paint a perhaps unbelievably golden picture. Nevertheless, I often said, before my experience with cancer five years ago, that not a single year of my life before I was married was happier than any year following.

Nora had been raised in the Church of England, but neither of her parents was strongly religious. We were not churchgoers in the early years of our marriage, either in Canada or in England, a result of my indifference.

By the summer of 1961, when, for my fourth time, we crossed the Atlantic by boat en route for a life at home in England, the third block of my life—a career in education—was well in place. I never considered myself a natural, charismatic teacher; my strengths as a junior high school teacher were my broad general knowledge (I could teach most subjects with minimal formal preparation), a strong commitment to the students, and a determination that they learn. I did not want to teach the way I had been taught, whereby lessons were presented on a take-it-or-leave-it basis, without life, relevance, or humour.

There could have been no better initiation for me than teaching in Prince Charles School in Saint John. The principal, Ernie Whitebone, was an intelligent, largely self-educated, and independent man totally indifferent to bureaucracy and regulations, but strongly supportive of learning, and fortunately, of me. The school was unusual even for those days in that it served a real cross-section of society: children of professionals, the then-thriving Jewish community, and the crumbling slums, some with earth floors, in Saint John's South End. The superintendent of schools, Dr. W.H. (Bill) MacKenzie, became almost a father-figure to me, one of the finest people I have known. He was totally dedicated to education, and education for him included, as it has for me, the traditional disciplines of knowledge, the arts, and physical education and sports, all within a moral framework.

I was taken by surprise when one father came to thank me for the job I had done with his son (as a homeroom teacher, I taught most subjects); he particularly emphasized the moral training I had given him. I had not thought of myself in that light. Morning Bible reading was compulsory and I always went out of my way to relate any story or teaching to students' daily lives. It just seemed common sense to me; similarly, I was always careful to pull out the moral ambiguities and lessons from any story we, or I, read in class. I discovered that fifteen-

and sixteen-year old adolescents from the slums, with few academic skills themselves, loved to be read to. Again, we would talk over the moral choices taken by characters in the book.

About this time, my own beliefs were coming more into focus. Similar processes occurred in the cases of English grammar and morality; I had never had formal teaching in either area (I had been taught Latin, French, and Spanish, but not English grammar), but when it came to teaching them, I developed an interest myself, and learned from having to pass on far more than I had ever gained from my own education.

We returned to England determined to settle. I, however, was unwell and remained so for several months. I remember assuring one doctor that I did not smoke and drank very little, to which she replied, "And that's your problem." In a way, she was right; in hindsight, the persistence of my illness (originally caused by a combination of overly fatty food and a strong reaction to blackfly bites at an end of school-year party) was psychological, resulting from my separation from Canada, Saint John, the school, and the teaching which had, for the first time in my life, given me a strong sense of belonging and purpose. I got a job in a grammar school in Clacton-on-Sea, a holiday resort in the south-east. We bought a small house and Nora gave birth to our first child, a son, just after the start of term. But strangely, back "home," I was once more lost.

By late winter, I could no longer hide from myself and from Nora my longing for Saint John and Canada. Socially, I liked the familiar role of outsider in Canada, not being pegged as a conventional, middle-class grammar school teacher (a role which I would not willingly assume), the absence of social class; educationally, I valued the opportunity for every child to succeed. Nora's life had changed, too, from busy working wife, to mother and housewife, and she readily accepted a return to Canada, where the horizons and opportunities seemed greater. Observers doubtless thought we were motivated by the higher standard of living in Canada, and perhaps we were, but we were not aware of feeling poor in England. We had returned from Canada with some capital. Perhaps if we had settled in a more pleasant physical environment than Clacton, and I in a more welcoming social and educational environment than Clacton High School, things would have been different; but I doubt it.

Back in Canada, we quickly had to adjust to starting a permanent life on our own; we both had distant relatives outside New York, and I also in Toronto, but for all intents and purposes, we were isolated from family.

Three daughters followed our son, at two-year intervals, and we consciously determined the way in which they were to be raised. We had agreed we wanted a large family (for people like us in those times) before we married. I felt that my parents had many unspoken expectations of me. They claimed to be non-interfering, but at crucial times did interfere. More often, I was supposed to infer what they wanted; but their disapproval, however silent, was obvious when I made the "wrong" choice. Sometimes I knew very well what they wanted, but determined not to do it unless they explicitly asked. I had reached the conclusion that it would have been better if they had laid out their expectations, values, and demands clearly, for me to consider or obey where relevant.

We decided that we would make crystal-clear our expectations and demands, with respect to school, to manners and behaviour, and to work around the home. We would also lay out our overall values (which were, intentionally or not, traditional Judaeo-Christian), and tell them they would be responsible for their own choices when they became adults. It is hard to distinguish what we decided then from what we did over the years, but I have no sense of any great change while the children were growing up. Nora thinks I had the greater influence in determining the pattern, but, if so, it was a pattern closer to her upbringing than to mine. There were times when we had differences in interpreting the application of our ideas in practice, particularly with one rebellious daughter. Our greatest principled disagreement concerned conflict between truth and caring. If a child brought something proudly home from school—a piece of homework the teacher had particularly admired, perhaps—Nora would be inclined to praise it too, while I would more likely apply my own, more demanding, standards (my own parents had rarely displayed any interest in my performance at school, positive or negative). Overall, however, we shared a sense that our children should become decent people, independent, family-oriented, and personally responsible. By declaring the values that we wanted our children to live by, we were also declaring the values that we ourselves ought to model, although I do not think either of us thought of it in those terms at the time.

Feeling a need for some spiritual and moral education for our children, we decided to join the Unitarian Fellowship in Saint John. Unitarianism can be seen as a compromise between Nora's background in the Church of England and mine as a non-Christian. I don't think I would have used the term "atheist" at that time. I never liked the term "agnostic"; it seems to me that one either believes in some form of god, or one does not. At the same time, I was careful to disclaim a Christian label. My spiritual yearning was by then very much in force. Although the reason for becoming Unitarian was a concern that we provide a moral framework for our children, I also read a wide range of religious and philosophical literature, an interest that I have maintained at intervals throughout my life.

Unitarianism began as a heretical offshoot of Protestant Christianity; it rejected the Trinity and the divinity of Christ. It became relatively strong in nineteenth-century England and in late-nineteenth-century New England. Perhaps I would still pass as a New England Unitarian. Unitarianism changed drastically in the second half of the twentieth century. Christianity, too, has generally moved away from a literal interpretation of biblical events—today, many mainline Protestants hold beliefs not very different from those of nineteenth-century Unitarians. Meanwhile, Unitarianism has also moved further to the religious left. Our Fellowship in Saint John (members provided joint leadership with the help of an occasional visiting minister) consisted mainly of people who had left Christian denominations, i.e., those moving away from Christian belief, while I, in contrast, was struggling towards the light. Nora and I were at the conservative end of a liberal (in the context of the early 1960s) congregation. The conservative wing of Unitarianism was distinct in two ways: it favoured more formal and spiritual services, and it was less left-wing in political ideology. Our children were all "dedicated," the Unitarian equivalent of baptism.

In 1963, I was appointed principal of a new elementary school. Being neither Protestant nor Catholic, I may have been more acceptable for the first joint Catholic and public elementary school in the city. Decades later, I was to become an advocate for separate denominational schools (for those who wished them). At that time, however, the Catholic schools were being secularized, and I was an inadvertent agent. While I cooperated with the parish priest, we got on well, I never used my authority to support the Catholic program; I left attendance to the priest and teachers.

In 1967, we moved to Chicago for fifteen months when I entered a doctoral program at the University of Chicago, strongly encouraged by Nora. I loved my work and would probably not have made the move without her pressure. The youngest of our four children was only a few weeks old when we moved. There was a strong and vibrant Unitarian church in the campus area and Nora joined the church choir. The university experience, surprisingly, strengthened my developing social conservatism, and particularly my standing as a conservative in the educational world. As an innovator in Saint John, a non-church member with a commitment to the disadvantaged, I would have been placed by many on the educational and political left. But that would never have been entirely valid; my concern was for academic achievement, combined with excellence in the arts, moral development, and a high level of physical fitness; I was at no time interested in high self-concept and a narrow, Deweyan relevance.

My own minor doctoral research in Saint John, as well as the most recent body of American empirical work in education, favoured a strong academic climate rather than the increasingly popular, progressive, "child-centred" approaches. That was not new on my part; there was no conversion at Chicago, merely reinforcement. In 1965, I had taken over as principal of a junior high school in Saint John, succeeding a man who had been strongly imbued with progressive ideas at Columbia University's Teachers College, where Kilpatrick, Dewey's strongest disciple, had a lasting effect (still evident today). Ironically, Chicago, the home of Dewey, was not at that time particularly imbued with progressive ideas; indeed, it was less favourable to Dewey than most North American and English faculties of education, where, since the late 1930s, Deweyan progressivism has gradually become a widely-held dogma. My first reform was to introduce formal examinations in an attempt to strengthen what I saw as widespread desultory teaching. My rejection of progressive ideas in education went hand-in-hand with a rejection of philosophical pragmatism, the idea that truth is based on experience; my first refereed journal article (and my responses to progressive critics), based on my thesis, shows this clearly (published in *Interchange* in 1971).

I returned to Saint John from Chicago to open a new high school. This stay lasted only three years. Bill MacKenzie retired as superintendent. The new administrative regime, combined with the effects of provincial centralization in 1967, reduced my freedom as an educational leader and inevitably entailed a period of general educational decline in the Saint John system, which had been outstanding in the Maritimes, perhaps in Canada. In addition, this was the one period in my life where I was strongly influenced by personal ambition; I had a doctorate, and felt I was capable of greater things. The longer I was a school principal with a doctorate, the more, I thought and was told, it would look as though I had some defect. The boom in educational doctorates was just beginning, and I knew that their value would soon fall. Today, most universities' doctorates in education have little intrinsic value and Chicago's once-outstanding graduate school of education has been closed.

The decade of the seventies was one of professional success (in terms of career—I suspect that my value as an educator was as great or greater in the sixties). It was equally a time of spiritual stagnation. Nora returned to full-time teaching in 1973; we had four growing children to look after. There was little time left to tend the soul, not for those lacking religious commitment. The next decade was devoted heavily to work and family, not always in that order of precedence. There had been no deliberation required for my previous promotions; I was simply promoted by the school board. Future changes, after 1971, were to be complex and never again a simple matter of will and ambition.

In 1971, I became a senior administrator for a suburban school board north of Montreal, where I was to become director two years later. At no other time have I worked as hard, but the stress was to be surpassed later. We joined the

Unitarian church in Montreal, a church whose teaching meshed closely with our own beliefs. The trip to downtown Montreal, however, was too much for us after a busy week. I worked three or four evenings except in the summer, and we attended irregularly.

Quebec was in turmoil at that time, as it has been for most of the last thirty or so years. The passage of Bill 22 (restricting choice of enrollment in English- or French-speaking schools) triggered my realization that English-language schools and the English-language population were in for a continuous and permanent decline. The Bill spoke the louder because it was passed by a Liberal, not a separatist, government. In practical terms, it meant the dismantling or decay of my proudest achievements—the development of bilingual schools (grades seven to eleven) where we could place children in varying levels of instruction in both languages, irrespective of their actual grade level; we could accommodate francophones and anglophones taking both English and French as first languages, for example. In 1975, I decided that I had to leave Quebec, not at any cost, and not necessarily immediately.

The move to Toronto was more difficult for me and the family than had been the move to Montreal. Whereas I had become frustrated in Saint John, work was settling down in Laval. We had no money problems; our children were all in school and doing well. Nora led a full life, now teaching in an English-language Catholic high school, with interesting but not excessively demanding work; we greatly enjoyed life in Quebec. Housing was much more expensive in Toronto, and my day was to be lengthened by a commute from Mississauga to downtown Toronto. Nora particularly missed Quebec, and has always preferred Montreal to Toronto. I retained a vestige of Maritime prejudice against the smug superiority of Torontonians—a prejudice that has never been erased.

1975-1993 FAILURE AND FULFILLMENT

My appointment to The Ontario Institute for Studies in Education (OISE) in Toronto was administrative rather than teaching, but I made a practice of teaching at least one course every year. I soon learned that administrative tenure at the post-secondary level, OISE in particular, was likely to be nasty, brutal, and short. My move to OISE was a lateral one, in terms of salary and prestige. Ambition no longer played a part; I vaguely thought I would have a foot in each camp—the university and the school system. When I accepted OISE's offer, I was also on the short list to become superintendent of schools in Winnipeg, so there was no determination to move into the post-secondary sector. But the move to the university was not a spur-of-the-moment decision, either; I had considered it while still in Saint John, but balked at the low salary offered.

In retrospect, the move to post-secondary administration (as distinct from academia) can be seen as a mistake; of all my jobs, I would judge my involvement least successful and least fulfilled. In a rare personal conversation with my mother, I was later to remark that I had doubts as to whether OISE provided a net benefit to education, implicitly stating that I was in a moral quandary by working there. She reverted to my childhood mode, and told me I was being silly. But she was wrong.

My five-year contract, as an administrator of field development with responsibility for links between academia and the school system, was renewed in 1980, on a very close vote; I was in two minds as to whether I wanted another term. A newly appointed director, Bernard Shapiro (whom I had helped select and whom I respected), quickly terminated all the senior administrative contracts, my second term had only just begun, with the stipulation that only those who applied unsuccessfully for one of the positions in the new administrative structure (in which there was to be no coordinator of field development) would have their administrative salaries red-circled for the remainder of their term, in my case, four years. With some misgiving, I decided to apply for the position of assistant director of administration, undecided as to whether I would really prefer the job or the red-circled salary as an unsuccessful candidate working as a full-time academic. In the event, I was the only survivor of the purge, thanks to Bernard's support.

Anyone who knows the university scene will understand that I had made many enemies by this time, not least because I was seen as being pivotal in Bernard's selection as director, for which my new appointment was thus a favour returned. A close colleague, I was told, described me as a complete hypocrite for taking such a clearly administrative position, because I had always said my professional concern was making a difference to the student's educational experience. My private justification for taking the job (apart from not wanting a pay cut) was that Bernard and I held complementary visions of what OISE should become. He and I wanted OISE to be more directed to a standard of excellence in the university sector and to the improvement of elementary and secondary schooling. Although he was more committed to the former, I to the latter, our goals and means overlapped. I was nevertheless stung by the accusation of hypocrisy, which was not entirely invalid.

Two years later, I resigned from my position of assistant director of administration under intense and almost unanimous pressure from those attending a faculty union meeting. Neither my vision for OISE, as being of direct educational value to the school system, nor Bernard's, of high academic status, was to be realized. He left a few years later under similar but more veiled circumstances. The shame of my resignation was mitigated by the support of the Board of Governors, most of the members being furious that the union should have such power, and by my imminent promotion to the rank of full professor. A good many colleagues and other staff came to my support, after I had resigned, mostly in private.

This was the first failure in my career. My closest colleagues, with just two exceptions, carefully distanced themselves during the period leading up to my resignation, during which I was a pariah. Once the boil was lanced, I was fairly well accepted as an individual, even though my ideological world view, which I could now openly propagate as a professor, was generally despised. One of the individuals closely involved in the attack on me, a Roman Catholic, came to apologize to me some years after the event.

It was a major crisis in my life and it affected my health. The intense stress affected Nora almost as much; for the most part, she had kept carefully clear of my professional life after she became heavily involved in her own teaching career. I was at the time on the short list for the position of Dean of Education at McGill, a potential move Nora vetoed. The educational situation was the same or worse in Quebec as when we left, and the stress on me would be the same as in OISE. The move would also have been awkward for her (jobs for anglophone teachers were few in Montreal), and for our youngest daughter, aged sixteen. I was not upset by Nora's decision. I was under severe stress, because I had been drawn into the competition without ever applying, because news of the circumstances of my resignation from my administrative position in OISE, combined with my educational heresy as a non-Deweyan and conservative, would almost certainly have doomed my candidacy, and because I still had no career plan. I did subsequently apply for another position in academic administration, but I was fortunately unsuccessful.

This career turning-point coincided with another stressful, if short-lived, event. My son, now married with a young child and studying dentistry, was diagnosed as having a malignant melanoma. The two weeks I lived with that diagnosis were the most stressful of my life.

I provide some detail about this period because the conjunction of events may have had an indirect effect on my spiritual life. We had, at this time, no religious connection. I repeatedly asked myself and fate (the word God, unspoken but hovering) over those two weeks, why he rather than I should suffer this usually terminal cancer, and wished it could be transposed. Those who believe in the transfer of pain and illness will be interested that the diagnosis was changed to that of a minor growth that could be safely removed. Twelve years later, I myself was to be diagnosed, correctly, with a similar and usually fatal skin cancer. Devastated as I was by that subsequent diagnosis, it was a slight compensation to realize that I was less upset and stressed than I had been by Tom's, removing my suspicion that my request of fate had been dramatic rather than sincere.

The next ten years were spent as a professor of education in OISE, carrying out research and field development, writing, teaching graduate classes, and supervising doctoral students. Overall, those years were ten of the most professionally satisfying of my career, comparable with the decade of the 60s teaching and being principal in Saint John. In hindsight, the eight administrative years in OISE were an indeterminate pause between school and university, during which my children reached late adolescence or adulthood and I became a grandfather. In the 60s, I believed strongly in what I was doing for young people. In the 80s, I made my contribution to educational thought, at least sufficient for me to continue writing and publishing for many years after retirement.

Although we had no formal, religious connection for most of our time in Toronto, those years did see some development of my spiritual world view. The change can be seen in my writing on education, becoming more focused after 1975. By the eighties, my educational writing and my personal creed converged more strongly.

By the end of the decade, the four children had graduated from university, married, and established themselves in careers. Nora and I were, by luck, hard work, love, and good management, successful in our goals for our children. Their colleagues at work would generally agree that they are decent people. They are independent, but honour their parents. At the time of writing, they work hard and have well cared-for children, fourteen in all. None is strongly religious, but none is defiantly anti-Christian; two, married to spouses of Roman Catholic background, send their children to Catholic schools.

WRITING AS AN INDICATOR OF SPIRITUAL CHANGE

A case derived from the written word can be made for both stability and change in my spiritual life. There is no sudden turning-point in my life, no moment when I became "saved." There are, however, two pivotal markers of my claim to the Christian label.

In my first publication in a refereed journal (my 1971 article in *Interchange*), I took a moral line that anticipates my more recent writing. In a strongly critical response to Ontario's enormously influential progressive educational policy document, *Living and Learning,* I wrote,

> Far from being the negation of moral responsibility, punishment is its essence. To permit an act to continue when one knows it to be socially harmful is itself immoral... Just as it is impossible to separate success from failure so one cannot have praise without punish-

ment... Punishment fulfills an important social function... Punishment is a vital part of the development of children within modern families... just as it is in all but the simplest and most anarchic of primitive societies.

Another early piece of writing concerns moral education in the school (a 1976 contribution to *Interchange*). I argued that moral education is desirable and should be explicit and focused. Supporting the inculcation of moral norms, I wrote,

Our children are rarely asked to reflect on the values by which they are expected to live—truthfulness... abandonment of violence; deference to adults, particularly teachers; consideration for others; perseverance. Action without belief is stupid, belief without action is hypocritical... It makes sense to celebrate in the schools the inheritance of basic values, at the same time laying them out clearly... A complete moral education program... uses fundamental values as a backcloth and helps children develop values by using moral reasoning processes, engendering life goals and encouraging emotional aspects of morality that more readily transform morality into behaviour.

There is a backward look to my undergraduate education in anthropology, to my program in Chicago, as well as to my later writing.

By 1986, I was well into my most productive period of academic writing, culminating in my two most revealing books, published in 1989 (*Making the School an Effective Community*, Falmer Press—co-authored by Edward Wynne), and 1992 (*Educational Policy for the Pluralist Democracy*, Falmer Press). In my field of educational administration (policy was my particular interest), I rejected both competing modes of thought—those of scientific empiricism and subjectivism. I wrote that my

57

subjectivist colleague Thom Greenfield promotes values that:

> ...happen to be selected by each individual... I do not
> share such a belief in the relativity of all values and
> therefore cannot accept such relativity as a basis for
> work in a field which is concerned with moral
> choices.... Truth... includes the nature of the good
> life.... [Many share my philosophy of belief in a tran-
> scendent good that should govern our lives, including
> those who] believe they have a revealed truth about the
> good; others, like me, feel we only have an imperfect
> sense of the good and must be guided by reasoning
> based on traditional conceptions of it. Either way, the
> principle and many of the value outcomes are the
> same—there is a purpose in our lives. If there is a pur-
> pose in our lives, that purpose is likely to be central to
> the education of children. (In a comment on Thom
> Greenfield, published in *Interchange* in 1986.)

The narrow line separating my world view from religious
belief is made explicit. Back in 1981, Clifford Pitt, then
director of OISE and a strong Christian, had told me he
could not understand how I could write what I did without
being a Christian.

In the same article, I refer to the neo-Aristotelian
philosopher, Alasdair MacIntyre, whose major work *After
Virtue* (1981) has been most influential on my philosophical
perspective. I do not know whether MacIntyre was a Christian when he wrote the book, but I do sense that he was at
least moving, like me, from the atheism of his younger days
to a time of religious belief. I was never an Aristotelian (a
neo-Platonist, perhaps, in my time at Chicago), but his
book, in my opinion, is more a blend of classical philosophy
with the Christian ethic than an exposition of classic Aris-

totelianism. Some of my best writing has been an explicit attempt to interpret MacIntyre in educational terms. His book engrossed me because I felt, for the first time, that I was reading something which, in an erudite way, captured my own groping search for truth.

The close relationship between my own world view and the Judaeo-Christian tradition is outlined in a response to a positivist philosopher who took issue with my critique of Greenfield's subjectivism, but from a scientific (positivist) position opposed to Greenfield's subjectivism. He objected that my three examples of absolutism—Christianity, Aristotelianism, and Platonism—are internally inconsistent. I replied with an analogy that I often find useful and to which I return later in the book:

> Suppose three visitors to our world were asked to observe a particular category of feathered animals which lay eggs. None makes perfect observations and the three are not equally precise. One sees an ostrich, another a penguin, the third a hawk. The three definitions of bird they produce are mutually incompatible. But that does not prove there is no such thing as a bird. (From an article in *Interchange* in 1989.)

I applied the analogy to the conflict between rival absolutes. "Ultimately there can be only one absolute [but it can] take different forms, and apparent inconsistencies may be introduced by our inability to fully comprehend their forms and impact."

I object to the moral dilemmas produced by Kohlberg and his followers, often far-fetched and appearing to be designed to teach children there is no right, no wrong, only different values. Of course, there are situations where there is no simple, right behaviour, "Should a tortured man kill his torturer to escape, or the man trying to rape his daughter?" I return to that kind of dilemma later in the book. We are sometimes faced with a choice of lesser evils, but the denial of the existence of evil makes their resolution more difficult.

I went on to show how our language reflects the oneness of the absolute. The word "beautiful" is applied to all manner of characteristics, but we would not describe Hitler as beautiful regardless of his physical qualities; we would choose a word with a lesser moral connotation, such as good-looking, handsome, or charismatic. I concluded my response with a famous poem by George Herbert, where he uses nine words to represent his absolute, the Christian God: Way, Truth, Life, Light, Feast, Strength, Joy, Love, Heart.

That article was written shortly before the first pivotal event triggering my acceptance of Christianity. A little earlier, I had reviewed a book by the Christian philosopher George Grant, also published in *Interchange*, in 1988. A sympathetic passage illustrates either that I was drawing closer to the Christian perspective or that I was molding it into my own world view, or, most likely, both:

> While the Scottish-American Alasdair MacIntyre, who is as close a philosophical ally as Grant is likely to find in modern times, carefully constructs a modern conservatism brick by logical brick, Grant sees it, more felicitously but less precisely, as a vision of the good. His good is Platonist, MacIntyre's Aristotelian. Central to Grant's vision is the distinction between subject and object. By treating one another and our environment as subjects, we should see ourselves as part of a cosmic order built on faith and good; exchanges take place but they should not be essentially contractual and they should above all not be provisional. We should love with all our hearts—not until or unless. By searching for what is 'due' (a favourite expression of Grant's) we

should be thinking not of what is contractually owing but of what is right, of what we ought to do; "One should teach Nietzsche within the understanding that he is a teacher of evil." Christian justice is concerned with one's due as distinct from one's rights; Nietzsche centres on one's will, one's freedom.

I was trying to present Grant's perspective, but if it was not my own also, it was not far from it.

The two clear markers on the path to Christianity are my decision to attend church in 1989 and my baptism and confirmation in 1991. From that period, references to Christianity in my writing have been more frequent and positive as one would expect, but the fundamental change is not great. Spanning that period of conversion was my editorship of the publication, *Ethics in Education*, an informal publication which had a small circulation mainly in Canada and the United States. It is doubtful that a careful reader would note much change in the direction of my editorial comments over that period. My first editorial (September, 1987) argues against the ethics of denying such values as purity, marital fidelity, and humility. My last words in the final issue (May, 1990) describe research showing that young Canadians who have been brought up within strong religious traditions are less likely to become involved in pre-adult sexual activity, excessive use of alcohol, and illicit drugs.

In 1993, I took part in a dialogue with philosopher Robin Barrow on the place of religion in schools, my argument being that it should be permitted in funded schools of choice. It is the only such discussion I have come across in a refereed, general interest journal of education, where positive reference to formal religion as part of education is virtually unknown. My position is one in which there is minimal interest and less support among academics in education. While mine is an explicit, targeted defence of Christian education, the ground for my argument was laid in a chapter written for the NSSE Yearbook of 1988, published by the University of Chicago Press. Before that time, my defence of traditional values and an absolute good had largely been couched within the general context of the public school; while I had supported religious schools before, my moral and ethical arguments had applied equally to public schools. In "The fortress monastery: The future of the common core" (in *Cultural Literacy and the Idea of General Education*, eds. I. Westbury and A.C. Purves, University of Chicago Press, 1988), I argue that the kind of education I most value is only likely to survive in schools of choice, schools which will, for the most part, have a religious base.

BECOMING A CHRISTIAN

It should be clear by now that my religious conversion was not a sudden event. It was not a direct consequence of the career and family stress I underwent in 1983, six years before my regular attendance at church; it was not caused by a sudden death (my mother had died a non-believer in 1978, my father lived until 2000). It was not caused by intimation of my own mortality—my carcinoma was not removed and diagnosed until 1996; and it was not a result of being saved by a personal encounter with Jesus or God.

My reading and writing, as well as my intellectual, moral, and spiritual thought, were drawing me closer to Christianity. My intellectual ideas (on education and other policy areas) have developed roughly in parallel to my religious ideas. It could be argued that, between 1965 and 1990, I moved less to the educational right than the political centre moved to the left. I was seen as an innovator, even a radical, as a young principal. Those same ideas would be deemed conservative today. My religious views in the 60s were beyond the Christian pale;

perhaps the outgoing religious tide has swept past me, with liberal Protestant churches in Canada and the United States being close to where the Unitarian church was forty years ago.

While that interpretation is a part of the truth, it is only a part. My ideas, political, educational, and religious, have changed over the years, in some cases in important ways. I have traced some of the major influences, including that of the philosopher Alasdair MacIntyre. An idea of Christopher Lasch, to which I refer in the next chapter, helped encapsulate my own position, after my religious conversion. If the basic ideas have not changed much, they have become concrete.

None of my three eldest children was married in a traditional church ceremony. Nora and I took major responsibility for the weddings of the two older girls, and they were married in a formal Unitarian ceremony. The two bridegrooms and their families seemed happy with the arrangement. Tom's wedding had been looked after by his fiancée's parents. My youngest daughter, Sarah, and her fiancé decided to get married in an Anglican church not far from our home in Mississauga. Tom Rooke, the rector, insisted that they take training prior to marriage and that they attend church to understand its purposes and ritual. I decided to attend with Sarah to give her some support, and Nora often came with us.

St. Bride's, in Clarkson, was not a typical Anglican church. It was one of two strongly evangelical churches in the Toronto area (the other being Little Trinity). It had a vigorous congregation with a sizable membership of children and youth. It was a self-supporting church and provided generous outreach to the disadvantaged in Mississauga and overseas missions.

Tom Rooke was an important influence in my life. I was immediately impressed by the sincerity and consistency in his sermons; week after week he seemed to be saying things that struck me as being true. He often used language (religious jargon and narrative) which I either did not understand or did not believe, but the message seemed to be almost unerring truth. A cynical non-believer would explain that I had found someone who shared my socially conservative views; a strong Christian that I had previously subdued a finally-admitted spiritual yearning; and a psychiatrist that I had found another father-figure to replace Bill MacKenzie. (My own father's contempt for religion, and his enthusiastic embrace of socialism and a state monopoly in education had long since ceased to appeal). All three interpretations contain truth.

The setting of St. Bride's is aesthetically pleasing; the church itself is an unusually attractive modern church (built under Tom Rooke's guidance). Unusually, he had spent almost all his ministerial life in this one church.

After Sarah's wedding, she and her husband did not live close to the church, and did not often attend any church. I decided to continue attendance, and Nora chose to come with me. To what extent she simply wished to support me in my new tender faith, and to what extent she felt the need to find her own childhood roots, I do not know. Nora does not have my habit of analyzing thoughts and feelings (if she does she keeps her findings to herself), and we felt that religion was something we would do rather than talk.

That was the crucial decision. Obviously, if the rector had been someone whom I instantly disliked, the decision would not have been made, at least not then. The qualities of St. Bride's were important—the character of Tom Rooke, the vigour of the congregation, and the attractiveness of the church and its services. My reasons for joining were in part rational, in part spiritual, and in part aesthetic.

I mention rational reasons first because I have always been a rational person, a linear, analytical, and logical thinker. I say this as a matter of fact, not as a matter of pride. I am well aware of the weakness of an excess of logic and rationality, particularly as a result of spending eighteen years in a university setting. I have seen, in others and in myself, how easy it is to rationalize self-interest.

I have written of the various ways we learn, by logical reasoning, instruction, emotion, intuition, reading, and from the example of others. In many circumstances reasoning is indeed the best way to learn, but it is never sufficient and never independent of assumptions, even in the most rational of scientists. The most dyed-in-the-wool empiricist admits that no assertions can be made without preliminary assumptions concerning the nature of matter and the nature of knowing.

Simply, I was a ripe apple waiting to fall. I was tired of being alone, of fighting educational wars with only occasional behind-the-scenes, not-for-the-record support. My ideas had become closer and closer to Christian ideas, partly because they had developed more fully, with the notable help of Alasdair MacIntyre, partly because mainline Christian thought had moved closer to me, with an increasing de-emphasis of biblical fact. MacIntyre and Tom Rooke (with Bill MacKenzie, the most important influences on me outside the family) were complementary; MacIntyre essentially showed me how my ideas could be put together in a philosophically acceptable way (Christian if necessary, but not necessarily Christian); Rooke showed me how my belief could be expressed in Christian terms.

I had read at various times a number of "proofs" of the existence of God, notably by the liberal Catholic, Hans Küng, and C.S. Lewis, hoping they would convince me; but they (or I) failed. I told an ex-student of mine of my church attendance, thinking she, an Anglican, would be pleased. I was quite upset when she replied that the moment Tom Rooke retired or died, she supposed that that would be it for my religious phase. It was a fair comment, to which I could not answer, to her, to myself, or to God.

I put my rational impulses first, because rationalism has been ingrained in me since I was a child, and it suits my analytical mind, but in my heart I believe that what drew me to the church, after Sarah's wedding, was spiritual more than rational thirst. The rational justification was necessary for me, but insufficient.

At the time, I talked to a colleague about my church going. He had been a lifelong Presbyterian, but was much more liberal than I, at the same time more conventional. I told him that I enjoyed going to church and felt better as a result of it; I had not worked out exactly what I believed, and was not necessarily committed to the church for life. I did enjoy the services; they answered a felt need for some sort of spiritual life. He readily agreed, saying that this was what the church was for, to serve individual needs. His reason for approval, although kindly meant, displeased me; either I was finding truth or I was not; I did not care to situate religion or the church as a temporary sop for a personal need or weakness. My lack of total commitment and faith had nothing to do with a psychological crisis, I thought, everything to do with my passion to be on a sure path to truth.

Although Anglican services are often moving and beautiful, particularly when the magnificent wording of the traditional Book of Common Prayer is used, St. Bride's were not outstanding from that aesthetic perspective. It was an evangelical, and therefore low, church, suspicious of too much ornament. The choir was not exceptionally talented; the music did not compare to that in the finer churches and cathedrals (but neither did it sink to the abyss of popular guitar music or happy-clappy tunes); the services were spiritual, but not aesthetically outstanding.

I do recall an intense aesthetic experience when I was already attending church regularly. I went with a colleague to a performance of Bach's St. John Passion performed by Toronto's famous Talfelmusik orchestra and choir; it was the first time I had heard that composition and it is fair to say that, then and today, the aesthetic experience of musical expression, inside or outside a formal service, inspired by the Christian tradition is an inseparable part of my spiritual and emotional life.

When I first talked to Tom Rooke about my religious background, I mentioned my time as a Unitarian. "That's not a religion, it's a philosophy," he retorted. I doubt that today Unitarianism is either a religion or a philosophy, more a collection of left-wing causes. Some readers of this book, both religious and non-religious, may decide that my version of Christianity is, at best, nineteenth-century Unitarianism—at worst, nothing more than a heretical, personal world view. I admit that the recent movement of mainline Christianity towards nineteenth-century Unitarianism has made my conversion easier. I call myself a Christian with some hesitancy, partly because it so alien to my life experience, and partly because I recognize that many decent, sincere Christians will not unreasonably reject my assertion of legitimacy.

There is no simple answer as to why I now stake my claim. I have suggested that the change can be seen from different perspectives. One interpretation is that I tired of advocating a world view (in education and in the realm of personal philosophy) that no one else shared or seemed to understand, that I rationally saw the advantage of aligning myself with those possessed of a similar social morality, and that I recognized the virtues of a Christian life. Another is that I increasingly recognized a need for meaning in my life, particularly after my career peaked, in material and hierarchical terms, in 1983. Like many others whom I admire—C.S. Lewis, Malcolm Muggeridge, Alasdair MacIntyre, and Christopher Lasch, I moved towards traditional beliefs as I grew older.

Neither of those interpretations, although both are true enough to a point, captures the whole truth. The purpose of this book is to draw a picture of Christianity that does not consist of a simple catechism consisting of tests of faith and does not assume that believers are formed simply as a result of historical accident, crisis, and personal stupidity. I do believe in an absolute God of truth, and, as well, that it is valuable, perhaps the most important thing in life, to interpret that truth.

CHAPTER 2

GOD

INTRODUCTION

Much of this book will appear to be dogmatic to those who disagree; that is inevitable in any writing that attempts to establish a coherent sense of the meaning in our lives. Either there is some truth, which will be unproven dogma to those who oppose it, or there is no objective meaning, only the versions that individuals invent for themselves. I make no pretense that my being open to criticism from both sides, both from proponents of stronger versions of Christianity and of other religions, and from resolute atheists and relativists, gives my views more value. There is no virtue in being in the centre on any important matter; the truth may lie at either end of the spectrum, anywhere in between, or on an entirely different plane.

Readers are asked to indulge that inevitable dogmatism. Every assertion is not qualified by an "I think," "I believe" or "perhaps." In the first chapter, I used the metaphor of the extra-planetary visitors whose research led to the foolish conclusion that there can be no such thing as a bird, because the three of them identified land, sea, or air as their essential habitat, just as atheists love to announce there can be no God, no true religion, because various religions describe God differently.

Another useful metaphor is the examination of God as one might view an elephant through holes in a tent. Any view of God is based on one's own sighting.

A third metaphor is to see one's life as an ocean journey by ship. At times, everything goes smoothly; one scarcely thinks about the meaning of the voyage. The sun shines, the seas are gentle, and all goes well. At other times, there are storms and tempests; some voyagers then resort to a mysterious god that can hold them safely, while others angrily deny there can be such a god that would subject them to such trial and torment. On occasion, however, through a still mist one may dimly perceive a coastline; others see it too but describe its features differently; yet others deny there is any land there at all, claiming that the others only see what they want to see. All on board know that their journey will end at some point, perhaps tomorrow, perhaps many years in the future, and wonder if the voyage really has meaning or not; was that really land that some claimed to perceive? Is there really truth or is the ultimate meaning of life nothing beyond chimera constructed from mist and delusion?

The metaphors suggest that it is reasonable and normal for people to reach different conclusions about life's meaning. As will become clearer later, my religious perspective is significantly moral in nature; I am centrally concerned about right and wrong. Therefore, I feel particular empathy for those who come to similar moral conclusions to my own, whether they be Platonists, skeptical mainline Christians, nineteenth-century Unitarians, moderate Muslims, or fundamentalist Christians. My mother, I have said, lived most of her life and died an atheist; but observers would see her life (both before and after her renunciation of Christianity) as more Christian in character than mine (before and after my baptism), despite my claim to the label. The label is useful because it speaks to our claims and purposes, but it is not notably accurate or factual.

I do not claim some wishy-washy, universal tolerance, a value that I do not even consider a fundamental virtue, as will become evident later. There are many things that I am unwilling to tolerate, including such behaviour as lying, cheating, unprovoked violence, and the degrading of human dignity. But I am willing to tolerate a number of apprehensions of God.

Hans Küng uses Kant's formulation of the universal questions of human life:

> **What can we know? Why is there anything at all?** Why not nothing? Where does man come from and where does he go to? Why is the world as it is? **What is the ultimate reason and meaning of all reality? What ought we to do?** Why do what we do? Why and to whom are we finally responsible? **What deserves forthright contempt and what love?** What is the point of loyalty and friendship, but also what is the point of suffering and sin? **What really matters for man? What may we hope?** Why are we here? What is it all about? What is there left for us: death, making everything pointless at the end? **What will give us courage for life** and what courage for death?" (*On being a Christian*, 1977; the emphases are mine, and they are of most direct relevance to my purposes.)

C.S. Lewis gets to the point directly and simply. He first distinguishes between those who believe in God and those who do not, and then distinguishes between those believers who think God is beyond good and evil, a spirit that animates all life, and those who believe God is good (*Mere Christianity*,

71

1957). Lewis then jumps quickly from an acceptance of the second category of believers to an embrace of traditional Christianity, having first rejected the first theist alternative, which he describes as Hegelian Pantheism.

My commentary begins with Kant's first question, "What can we know?" and then leads to a slower and less determinate journey than Lewis's from good to God and then to a quite untraditional (in some ways) interpretation of Christianity.

GOOD AND GOD

I shall not try to prove God's existence because I myself, as an atheist, was alienated by the flimsy nature of the familiar arguments. To argue that God is the only possible explanation for the origin of the universe and our world and for the development of man may well be simply an indicator of human arrogance. The traditional religious answer to, "What explains the universe?" prompts the atheist's question, "What explains the origin of God?" There is clearly no reasonable way of rationally convincing a serious nihilist and atheist of the existence or value of God.

The argument that the complex design of our world demands a designer is facile sophistry, containing implausible assumptions and clever tricks with the ambiguity of language. Even if one agrees, as I do, that evolution and natural selection do not satisfactorily explain every expression of life on our planet, that hardly justifies a jump to a belief in a spiritual being with human characteristics similar to those of Jews and Christians of biblical times. If the wind makes mysterious circles in fields, if the sea etches intricate patterns of coastline, that hardly means that the wind and sea are animate and conscious pattern-makers.

A frequently-used analogy is a useful guide to the possible meaningfulness of God. An irrefutable (but not therefore valid and true) philosophical argument is that all experience is subjective and that there is no objective reality. By this account, not only does life have no meaning, but there is no satisfactory evidence of objective experience. Even scientific empiricism is entirely based on faith in the existence of an objective, external world. Bishop Berkeley used the example of the railway train to support the subjectivist argument. How do we know the train exists when we no longer see it, out of sight beyond the railway station? The common sense answer is that none of us (including Bishop Berkeley) really believes that there is no objective reality (that the train is only a part of our imagination). We all behave every day on the assumption that reality, in the form of other people and concrete objects, exists. Now, it does not follow as easily that God exists. We all behave as if objective reality exists, but do we all behave as if God exists? While many people (probably most) behave much of the time as if there were not a God, or at least their behaviour can be and often is reasonably explained in that way, we nearly all behave as though Berkeley's train were real.

That said, we all, including atheists and scientists, do make assumptions and advocate principles, examined or not, that are unverifiable. Most parents teach their children to be kind, to consider others, and not to be cruel. Yet the opposite qualities often pay off in later life.

Further, just as everyone believes that, and behaves as though, there are physical objects, almost everyone also behaves as if moral objects (or fundamental principles) exist, such as, for example, that it is wrong to kill your mother. Admittedly, there is more agreement on the defining characteristics of physical objects (but not unanimity) than there is on moral objects, but that is explicable in terms of the different methods of verification. Total unbelievers announce principles of correct and incorrect behaviour, and defend them on the basis of alleged universality—consider the proliferation of alleged "universal" human rights in recent years. We nearly all believe in the existence (and value) of abstract, moral principles just as we nearly all believe in the existence of monkeys; there is naturally more factual disagreement about the former because they are based on experience, reasoning, and perception, not refutable investigation.

My basic question to the reader is, "Do you believe in good and bad?" (If one replaces the word "bad" with "evil," it focuses the intent of the question and points more directly to my own conclusion). C.S. Lewis's pantheists (whom he peremptorily discarded) likely would answer by saying that good and bad are simply human inventions without any important referent outside the immediate personal context, that there is no objective good and evil. They will be joined by far more numerous groups—by most non-believers as well as by many mainline and lapsed Christians. Those who have seriously determined that all values are relative and that there is no underlying sense of good will not be convinced by my starting argument—that there is good and evil. They will say that whereas monkeys are empirically factual, values (usually conveniently excluding their own favourite principles) are simply matters of choice. I reply that it is not a matter of individual choice whether or not it is good to kill one's mother.

It is superficially easy (as well as convenient) to dismiss my argument at this point. Some will say, "I certainly believe that some actions are better than others, but don't tell me there is an evil force with a long tail, a Satan tempting me. I have made up my own mind about right and wrong, influenced by my family, education, and social background. But there is no absolute truth; that is why different groups fight and argue. They disagree with one another's so-called fundamental truth. Protestants fight Catholics, Muslims Christians, and so on."

C.S. Lewis does not accept that Christianity involves a dualism between two evil forces, one good and one bad; I don't entirely agree with him, but the difference between us may be one of definition of "forces." The point here is that in order to get off the hook I am extending one must reject the forces of both good and evil. It is simply unreasonable to announce one believes in a perfect God but not in evil. There can be no good without bad. I am not implying that good and bad must be parallel and equivalent (a good God and an equivalent bad Satan)—which is what I think Lewis was rejecting—simply that there can be no good without some reference to not-good, an idea which Lewis would readily accept.

The problem of relativism in values is complex. I have referred to one problem already. People who deny the existence of an absolute do not hesitate to pronounce universal values; an atheist recently told me that it is a universal principle that one should not harm one's children. (The point was used to argue for the wickedness of Islam. But I cannot see how one "universal" principle can stand outside an overarching framework).

Many who claim to reject an absolute (particularly in the form of absolute, objective values) still deny being relativists. I define relativists as those who reject absolute values. I cannot perceive any position in between, even though it may be claimed that there can be uncertainty, ignorance, or agnosticism: "I have never thought about it," or "I cannot decide." That position, of opting out, common in modern times, is as convenient (and as unsatisfactory) as simply rejecting the absolute in favour of some vague set of supposedly non-relative values; indeed it is a morally bankrupt equivalent if a vague absolute principle is to be conjured up whenever required to support a specific action. Both positions leave one free to make up and change rules as one goes along; put into practice, they are equally relativist.

Either one believes in some moral absolute or one does not One cannot logically deny all absolute truth without embracing relativism. Admittedly, there are degrees of relativism. One may, for example, accept for everyday, working purposes a conventional code of values and law without believing they have a base in absolute truth. In that way, some people whom I classify as relativist may have a stronger code of values than some whom I classify as absolutist; a belief in an absolute does not necessarily lead to a strong, positive code of moral conduct, with parallel behaviour; quite the reverse, history is filled with absolutists who murdered and pillaged in the name of a single false claim to truth. There is no inherent goodness in believing in an absolute, including a Christian absolute. For example, one may believe in an absolute God, one may believe literally in the Christian story in the New Testament, and still live a despicably immoral life, calling on God to destroy one's enemies. More often, and less obviously, some of those who profess belief in the Christian God, conveniently update Christian morality so that it does not interfere with their contemporary lifestyles. The precise nature of the absolute in which one believes and how it affects one's moral code and action are crucial.

There is a sound explanation as to why so many educated, intelligent people who reject absolutism also deny being value relativists. The logical consequence of denying the existence of an absolute good, and replacing it by some form of relativism, is severe. It logically requires that you cease to insist that any action is inherently superior to another. Every value thereby becomes a matter of individual choice, law, or convention. However strongly you may embrace your own values, it is difficult to argue logically that someone else's are inferior, except as a matter of taste, or of consequences, in given situations. Rationality alone cannot justify a good; it will readily provide a limited, but never final, justification for what is called "enlightened" self-interest.

The relativist may retreat to two sources of value, law and custom, arguing that a civic society is important for us all and that respect for local convention is required for harmonious cooperation. But that is a very restricted position.

It weakens any argument objecting to a particular law; it particularly undermines your argument if you wish to assert that a given law is morally bad, as distinct from being empirically ineffective. Suppose, for example, there existed a law against abortion except in specified circumstances (e.g., where the fetus results from rape or incest, is sufficiently damaged to prevent a life of human dignity, or may endanger the physical health of the mother). The law would be based on the fundamental belief that human life is a good, and that it should only be taken in circumstances where other goods are significantly violated. A relativist, for whom there can be no fundamental principles, is in a weak moral, ethical, and logical position to argue that a woman has a moral and ethical right to harm or kill her fetus in any circumstance at any time before birth (as currently permitted under Canadian law). The only recourse is to personal opinion or the often repeated, "Women have the universal right to control their own body." Such a right (which sounds very much like an absolute) would require the legalization of the possession of heroin and cocaine, presumably for both sexes. If a woman may lawfully kill or harm her trimester unborn baby under an unfettered right to her own body, she logically has the right to drugs. Indeed, just as abortion clinics are a corollary of the right to abort, it would reasonably be argued further that the right to use heroin implies a right of access. Indeed, there is no such fundamental right to the use of one's own body; all societies have countless laws that deny that right. That does not mean that the law is not open to criticism. An absolutist may claim that all abortion contravenes the right to life or, with greater difficulty, that everyone has a right to do anything that does not bring physical harm to another person (defined as one recognized as a living being); unlike the relativist argument I have objected to, which is not extended beyond the illegitimacy of the unborn, this one would have to be applied in other parallel areas (as many libertarians do).

A more sophisticated defence amounts to a circular dance around, "I believe," based on various other moral propositions equally bereft of a source other than personal opinion. Certainly, one has the freedom to argue any position one wants on moral grounds, including racial superiority and bigotry, but calling it right should not be very convincing to others when it becomes clear that the assertion is based on nothing more than individual taste or collective fashion. Why bother to support one's case? Why not simply list your personal preferences in morals as one would in ice cream flavours? You would not bother to try and convince others that coffee ice cream is the best, so why try to convince everyone that others should be able to kill their fetuses, if there is no basic moral foundation? Indeed, if one denies an absolute good, the fierce defence of any moral position other than individual autonomy becomes tenuous. The strongly individualist position of an Ayn Rand (disliked as much by today's dominant liberals as by most Christians) has at least the authenticity of being based logically on the rejection of all external values. It is human to be inconsistent; many relativists do write what look likes fundamental doctrine in the sand. Indeed, rights quickly multiply in the vacuum of relativism and inevitably one right conflicts with another, as it must. There is not and cannot be any fundamental justification of such rights beyond individual preference. If a right becomes fully entrenched, it is then an absolute in the eyes of its supporters.

Most non-believers and Christian relativists (but not thoroughgoing nihilists) say that they too believe in the golden rule, that one should treat others as one would like to be treated oneself. They defend that moral rule on the ground that it makes sense for society; if all people were to behave according to a passing whim or fancy, society itself would not survive. But that is strictly accurate only to the degree that people's inappropriate behaviour (stealing, murdering, and cheating) is found out. If there is no absolute good, why should one bother about breaking rules if no one will ever know? Why not steal from a rich person, who will scarcely recognize the loss, if the poorer person's children will derive considerable benefit? That form of argument is immediately recognizable today, and some readers will no doubt answer, "Why not indeed?" Much political debate centres on the belief that rich people have no "right" to so much money, and that the impoverished have a "right" to more. I return to that issue later.

In practice, because their belief in the golden rule is not grounded in any set of absolute values, it is easy and consistent for relativists to except any number of cases from the golden rule, when their own enthusiasms are at risk. Those who believe that their homes should be secure for child pornography may still object if a landowner wants to fell her own trees, arguing that the former is a private activity based on their own values, while the latter is of universal interest. Christians, on the other hand, should recognize that others may react as we do to corresponding threats to their persons or property; the golden rule derives, I shall argue, from more basic attributes of the absolute good. Helpful as a guide as it is, it derives from more fundamental virtues; standing alone, even though it is the most universal of values, it is not a robust part of a defensible absolute.

Important moral issues will be addressed later; my argument here is that only a belief in an absolute good can sustain an absolute sense of moral integrity. Most frequently, the announced values of relativists consist of a mixture of values picked up along the way; they nearly always include some of

the moral capital borrowed unknowingly from their traditional, religious traditions, to which are added a number of
currently popular enthusiasms. "The West must insist on
democratic elections if a developing country is to receive our
support." "We are destroying the environment and it is fundamentally important that it be repaired." "The first moral problem of the West is racism." "No person ever chooses to be on
welfare, so the important thing is to make life on welfare as
comfortable as the people can possibly afford." "Children are
better off with divorced parents than within an unhappy family, so divorce should be readily accessible on demand." "Fundamental human rights are universal and should be universally
applied." "Women have a fundamental right to 'pay equity.'"
"Democracy" (variously defined to include any of a number of
subjective preferences) "should be demanded of all institutions
and organizations." "Capital and corporal punishment should
be banned by national and international law because violence
is wrong and should not be supported by the state." "Automatic state support should be provided by the state for any
children whom people choose to bear or adopt." "Adults
should have equal rights to adopt or care for children irrespective of marital status or sexual orientation."

Those are expressions of popular political opinion at this
time in our society. Some can be related to an idea of the absolute, but necessarily carry other implications with which their
supporters do not necessarily agree. Others are easily disproved and they all at least require careful definition. There is
no suggestion that the above beliefs are trivial, immoral, or
wrong-headed (although some are), but taken as absolutes
(expressed in laws, judicial judgments, or charters of rights)
they all at some point imply conflict with religious values and
traditional freedom, as well as conflicting relativist values.
They depend on moral and ethical judgments to which both

empirical knowledge and conflicting value-bases and traditions should be applied in the modern, democratic state.

The collapse of a belief in an absolute moral code is one
reason why modern times have seen the rapid growth of alleged
inalienable human rights. Many of these rights actually stem
from a traditional interpretation of the good; some stem from
traditional common law; but others stem from what MacIntyre
calls "emotivism," an enthusiastic devotion to a moral cause
that has no clear base in a developed and sustained moral code
(see his book *After Virtue*). In the West, human rights have
come to replace, for many people, a traditional moral code
based on a belief in the good; the vacuum created by the weakness of the Judaeo-Christian tradition is quickly filled. The new
moral order becomes a god; the West is busy trying to impose
its cult of human rights on the rest of the world, most notably
on the Muslim world. There are many problems with this impe-
rialist endeavour, just as there were with the imposition of the
Roman empire two thousand years ago, and of Christianity
during the age of Christian expansion.

The belief in universal human rights (as distinct from a sense
of what is right) is perhaps the most widely defended enthusiasm
of the current age. It is essentially an eclectic, individualist creed
and does little for the sustenance of country, society, or community, strong versions of those collective entities being incompatible with the human rights faith. Strong, individualist believers in
human rights logically identify their enemy as any collective
entity, most obviously a powerful religion or a nation-state (or a
would-be nation-state such as Quebec) It is by no means evident
that the new religion will or should overcome the various ethnic,
national, and religious communities that survive, even today.

One problem is that the large communities most able to fend
off individualism are likely to be those least imbued with a
coherent absolute interpreted in a manner compatible with the

fundamental virtues. Thus, the generally reasonable and tolerant Christian societies of, say, the Netherlands and New Zealand of 1960, have been significantly eroded by rights-based emotivism, while the extremist Islam of Taliban (in Afghanistan), the Algerian terrorist opposition, and Sudan may withstand it. One of the enormous strengths of the Western tradition is that its absolutism (itself an amalgam of Greco-Roman and Judaeo-Christian ideas) has been tempered, first by the Reformation and then by the science, philosophy, rationalism, and individualism of the last three centuries. Most absolutes—however good their basic formulation—require some moderation. They attract fanatical enthusiasts just as much as secular beliefs in socialism, capitalism, patriotism, or universal human rights.

One might infer that the thesis being developed here implies that people hold religious views ultimately only because they have individually determined that there is an absolute good. Such an assumption would be obviously false. People are Roman Catholics, Jews, or Seventh Day Adventists for many reasons and motives. Many "inherit" their religion through the family and community. Today, people join denominations and sects because they meet God or Jesus Christ, often at a time of crisis in their lives; some recall the moment they were "saved." People's reasons for joining, or not joining, are many and complex.

I believe that there is good and evil and that it is sensed by most people, only a minority of whom have worked through their understanding in a logical procedure, and those mostly after the fact; most people sensibly intuit their existence. Many educated people deny their relativism (at the same time as they deny an absolute) because they recognize or sense the nihilism to which acknowledged relativism leads. It is likely that most people in the world would find it difficult to articulate their notion of an absolute good in intellectual terms, but they do know right from wrong. The distinction that I am making between good and evil is an intellectual convenience, one which many consider unnecessary. After all, some people without a clear faith in the good or God (non-believers) have a stronger sense of right and wrong than others with faith. That undeniable fact does not negate the truth of right and wrong. To the contrary, the assertion of a truth is strengthened when many people, of entirely different backgrounds and cultures, believe it even without accepting a theological or rational dogma.

Rationally, there either is or is not some absolute good, irrespective of how many or how few have thought deeply about that divide. I go further; it is inherent in humankind to believe in good and evil. Those who deny their existence are still quick to praise or condemn their fellows on moral grounds, usually on the basis of the degree of similarity to their own values and actions. One beauty of a religious tradition is that the moral eye should not simply be a reflection of oneself; a moral weakness in oneself is not to be praised in others. If values were really free-floating matters of taste, it is hard to see why people should be so critical of those of others and care so much about the propagation of their own.

I have made the implicit assumption that it would be irrational for Christians, Jews, and Muslims to deny that God is the source of good; if God were not good it would be impossible to make any overall sense of the Bible or the Koran. At the same time, I realize that some mainline Christians, particularly highly secularized liberal intellectuals, are unwilling to label themselves as believing in a moral absolute. I am not arrogantly dismissing them from the ranks of Christians. Non-Christians are quick to seize on some evidence of inconsistency among Christians to dismiss Christianity as a whole. Extreme nihilists may claim total consistency among their adherents perhaps, but even their claim is more one of rhetoric than practice. There are many holes in the tent from which one may view, or deny, the elephant. None can be totally accurate and complete.

There are scientists who keep their science in one pocket, their religion in another, remaining strong believers. Some people may even cling to literal biblical interpretation, but others, like me, see truth in myth. There are also those who look to physics for the final interpretation of a living god, one who will unify the meaning of the creation of the universe and an all-powerful god. Probably most are atheists; if they have any vestigial religious feeling at all, it is vague nostalgia kept for baptism and funerals.

Of particular interest in the context of a scientific search for good and God is the renowned biologist Edward O. Wilson. He asserts first that one can distinguish two beliefs: *either* I believe in the independence of moral values (what I call a moral absolute), whether from God or not; *or* I believe that moral values come from human beings alone, whether or not God exists ("The biological basis of morality," *The Atlantic Monthly,* April 1998). He is not unsympathetic to supporters of the traditional belief that there is a fundamental moral code, (significantly represented for Jews and most Christians in the Ten Commandments as well as, for Christians, in the teaching of Jesus), agreeing that it is very difficult to maintain communities that have no allegiance to those fundamental values. Wilson then departs sharply from traditional teaching, arguing that morality is genetically encoded. He uses the term "consilience" to describe his fundamental thesis that eventually we shall discover a single overarching truth bringing together spirituality, biology, and physics. He also concludes that his explanation is fundamentally inconsistent with the traditional one that morality is of divine origin, so-called natural law.

His genetic thesis, despite his rejection of religious tradition, is in fact less inconsistent with Christianity than it is with the newer secular tradition that we all manufacture our own values, that the aim of raising children is moral autonomy, and that children should be given open sets of moral choices from which they should freely choose. The immediate *consequences* of his thesis (but not its ultimate truth and practice) are not dissimilar from those of traditional Judaeo-Christian teaching, as he recognizes. If societies that do not promote certain traditional values are unlikely to survive, then it seems logical to promote those qualities in our children, as distinct from such fashionable values as high self-concept, self-fulfillment, and moral autonomy. If the valuable qualities are genetically encoded, it makes more sense to support the genetic tradition than fight it, unless it can be shown to be particularly harmful to contemporary society.

So the conflict between his biological explanation and the traditional religious explanation lies, according to Wilson, in the nature of its origin; the rational consequences of the positions are not necessarily incompatible (although they may be—one may choose to subordinate genetic inclination as being unsuitable to modern times). Even if we assume that he is correct in hypothesizing a genetic base for certain aspects of morality, we are still no further forward, however, in determining the point of origin of morality. Chemical changes in the body may *reflect* changes in thought and personality, as distinct from *causing* them. If certain genetic characteristics are shown in the future to be related to certain kinds of conduct, we shall still not be in a position to assert a uni-causal explanation of the studied behaviour. It is generally accepted, by believer and non-believer alike, that behaviour is greatly influenced by social context and human will.

Even if we go further and provisionally accept the possibility of truth in the core of Wilson's hypothesis (i.e., some forms of behaviour are genetically encoded and caused), it is interesting to juxtapose it with Budziszewski's brilliant exposition of the traditional idea of natural law (in *After Liberalism*, 1998), that universal values are imprinted on the hearts of every human being (the idea that Wilson thinks he will refute). It is tempting to see the two as being mutually exclusive (as Wilson claims), but a hundred years from now it is possible that their differences will be seen more attributable to different definitions and explanations than to differences in fact; the unity Wilson hopes for may not be what he expects. It is possible that genetic encoding took place precisely because natural law was "written in their hearts." If the genetic discoveries are used negatively to downplay or erase personal responsibility and independence, the concept of virtue, and the self-direction of the human spirit, then they are harmfully false; but they can be helpful to the extent that they promote understanding and knowledge of the human condition, and the importance of fundamental values and civic behaviour.

Genetics does not address the crucial questions: Do human beings have genuine freedom of choice between good and evil? Is there such a thing as independent human will? Even if there are inherited propensities towards some socially useful attributes, the discovery will be not be substantially different from that of other genetically-influenced qualities with which we are more familiar—intelligence, introversion, aggression, sexual desire, and distinctiveness based on sex. Debates rage as to the genetic contribution to those traits; it is politically correct in a time of the politicization of science to attribute homosexuality to a gene, but behavioural and value differences between male and female to socialization. A more likely proposition is that the genetic contribution to both those and other measured behavioral traits varies according to the strength and character of the social context and the individual's will.

If one rejects the existence of human freedom, one can either choose personal predestination (which may or may not be in the hands of God) or an extreme genetic and environmentalist science that explains human behaviour solely in terms of inheritance and culture. There is no point in repeating the arguments for the existence of human freedom. Just as there is no final proof of objective existence, there can be no final proof of human choice. But the fact is that virtually no one really denies it; and even those who deny it in some circumstances (by, for example, attributing unpleasant occurrences to spirits, God's anger, or the social and physical environment) usually take actions to avoid nasty events (by jumping out of the way of an oncoming car or calling in the fire department when their house catches fire).

So, if there is good and evil, and if human beings have the freedom to choose between them in some circumstances, then the discovery of the effects of our genetic and cultural inheritance, while they may help explain some of our behaviour and habits, do not remove from us the central human characteristic: the union, unique to human beings, of consciousness, free choice, and a knowledge of right and wrong. The conditional "if" is crucial; some readers will have already departed, rejecting the idea of right and wrong. Unfortunately, most of those who do reject the idea of right and wrong refuse to face the consequences of their decision; without good, important values are fundamentally subjective. Many of them inconsistently still talk grandly of universal values or universal human rights, as if they were the absolute they have denied.

Another related human quality is the idea of the *daemon*; the idea that human beings (all or some) have a sense of direction, a sense of destiny which is neither simply a matter of conscious choice nor something environmentally determined. There is considerable anecdotal, biographical evidence of this phenomenon. The argument is well articulated by James Hillman in *The Soul's Code*, and by Canadian novelist Robertson Davies in his trilogy beginning with *Fifth Business*. Edward Wilson would explain the *daemon* genetically, but there is no evidence yet to that effect. Some (but not Hillman) see it as an expression of God's will. It is not mentioned here to bolster the idea of God, but rather to illustrate the complexity of the human condition, and the danger of jumping to overarching, tendentious, pseudo-scientific explanations. As a skeptic, I am not prepared to attribute the entire ragbag of things I do not understand to the Christian God; no more am I willing to attribute it to the god of science, costumed in either genetics or physics. Some people do appear to develop a strong sense of mission, purpose or direction early in life from which satisfactory diversion proves impossible. There are things that do seem meant for us, at least for some people.

The problem of an absolute good can be examined from a different perspective. Returning to Bishop Berkeley's train, which may or may not exist outside the station when it leaves our sight, we may ask, by analogy, if an absolute good would still exist if all human beings were to be destroyed in a galactic catastrophe; is the good essentially external and infinite, or is it internal and co-existent with the human being? The easy (and not stupid) way out is to observe that if there is no human being remaining, it matters not a tittle if good remains or not. But it does matter intellectually. Suppose we imagine that a small colony of human beings, primitive people with little education and no sophisticated science or religion, somehow survives the destruction. Will the spirit of good (God) be accessible to them? The modern non-believer will answer that they will manufacture their own narratives to explain their condition, survival, and hardships. Wilson will argue that they will re-create fundamental values from their genetic inheritance, and Budziszewski that God has imprinted the good on their hearts, which they have freedom to choose or reject.

Is the good simply something that resides inside the human being or is it external and independent? Rationalists will argue that if it resides only within the human being, it cannot be absolute; after all, the universe certainly existed before the human race began, and may exist after its demise. That argument defines an interior sense of good as being subjective, a product of our individual or collective imagination, partly genetic, partly learned. But Budziszewski would respond that the God that implants the good exists with or without human existence.

A.N. Wilson (not to be confused with Edward Wilson) develops the dilemma with exceptional clarity in a discussion of Kant's philosophy found in his fascinating book, *God's Funeral*. He uses the example of the robin's red breast. Is the breast actually red, or is it only perceived as red by the optics of the human eye? For example, dogs do not identify red. The most reasonable answer is "both"; there has to be a quality of redness because it is seen equally by nearly all human beings, but the eye has to be capable of recognizing it (and some eyes cannot). The analogy with the good is not perfect; we can establish empirically, to most people's satisfaction, the existence of the robin and its redness (like Berkeley's train), but we cannot establish empirically, with absolute certainty, the objective existence of good. But most human beings do believe in the objective existence of matters other than material objects. I have argued that even those who seem most relativist also defend non-material matters in the form of values or beliefs (e.g. human rights, capitalism, or socialism) with argument that implicitly claims objective truth. I believe that of all the non-material concepts, the most widely assumed objective truth is good; it is believed because it is true and because it is indispensable. While one must admit the fallacy in any direct analogy between material and non-material concepts, one must at the same time accept the reality that neither material nor non-material concepts can be finally proven to the unbeliever; empiricism is unconvincing to the person who rejects the reality of the material world.

There are three intellectually respectable positions vis à vis objective existence. One can believe that everything is subjective (i.e. believe in nihilism); one can believe in the empirical reality of material objects, but believe all else is simply a product of human subjectivity; or one can believe that there is truth in both material and non-material concepts. The last position is the most widely held, if one observes simply what people say and do in daily life, but the origin and substance of the "true" non-material concepts are not matters on which consensus is ever likely.

Most non-believers (members of the second category above) have no problem in accepting the concept of, as just one example, society; other examples include reciprocity and tyranny. If society existed before human beings conceptualized those ideas (and it did), is it not also reasonable to believe that the most fundamental non-material concept of all, good, existed, ready to be expressed, before human beings developed the consciousness to interpret it? Extra-terrestrial beings may investigate human society after it ceases to exist. In that sense too, good may have meaning outside the individual human mind.

In practice, it is of little interest to us whether good existed before the human being developed and will continue to exist after the last human being disappears from the planet. Such a belief, however, is not inherently unreasonable.

It is possible that in time we shall have a better intellectual sense of the unity within the meaning of life, and that the question of the internal or external character of the good will seem as irrelevant as is the counting of angels on the head of a needle today. The most reasonable provisional answer is that the good is external as well as internal to the human being; the human being has to have receptors able to comprehend it, but it exists ready to be apprehended. It is not a constituent of the conscience (although conscience may be used to gain access to it and to store it). It is not simply a part of our genetic base, although aspects of appropriate behaviour may be found to be genetically transmitted.

I have used the inexact analogy between our knowledge of the objective reality of our world and universe (even though such reality cannot be finally proven) and our knowledge of the good. Even though there is no final proof of objective, material reality, almost everyone accepts it and, more important, almost everyone describes that objective reality in the same way. In contrast, not only do many people deny the existence of an objective (absolute) good, there are differences among different descriptions of the good, even among those who believe in it. People's perceptions are not, however, as opposed as is frequently claimed, as Edward Wilson and Budziszewski inadvertently illustrate. Although it must be admitted that there is more variation in spiritual observations filtered through the mind than there is among observations filtered only through the eyes, we should not forget how often our eyes mislead us, for the simple reason that what we see and understand is itself a product of the mind. Just as our mind often draws wrong conclusions from what we see (in magic shows, for example), consider the many occasions when highly intelligent and trained scientists draw totally different conclusions from the same data, the more so when they study politically contentious issues. My wife and I are as likely to agree on the character and motives of someone whom we know as we are on the physical description of an unusual bird of which we have caught a fleeting glimpse.

Most will agree that there can be no final, agreed determination of the origin of life. Any advance, any grand conclusion, in biology and physics is open to the question: "But what is the force that gave rise to the initial impulse? What was the source of the dynamic that led to life being formed from heat, water, and minerals? And what is their origin?" Similarly, there can be no final evidence of the origin of good and evil.

There are at least three hypothetical expositions of the absolute good (if one leaves aside disbelief). The first is that there is a spirit of good (which we may call God) that has objective (but not material) existence. It does not exist in time or space. It has no end and no beginning. It is towards that good that the emerging human mind has striven to move; it is available, but not everyone has the ability (there may be a physical or a mental incapacity) or the will to endorse it. That is the explanation preferred and emphasized here. God is therefore infinite in the sense that one cannot conceive either a beginning or an end.

The most rational, the most scientific, is that the good simply emerged with human consciousness. Human beings have become conscious of their choices, are aware of their freedom to actively choose one behaviour over another. Good is a part of that consciousness; it is still an absolute, a naturally occurring part of the framework of human consciousness, as real as pain or thought.

The third version of the origin of the good may be seen as approximating one version of contemporary, liberal, progressive Christianity, and earlier expressions of pantheism. By this account, God is the name for the spirit of all life; life is God's breath and what distinguishes animal (and, perhaps, vegetable) matter from inert mineral. God is therefore a part of all living things, and the human capacity for conscious, abstract thought and virtue is simply the highest form of

God's spirit; in a sense the human being is made in the image of God, being a higher level of God's expression than the amoeba, bacterium, hyena, and dolphin.

The problem with the second (scientific) account is that its apparent logic is somewhat superficial. It explains a psychological need for a good (or god) as much as it explains its objective existence. The absolute could then be interpreted as being essentially individualistic; everyone has a sense of good, but people's senses differ. Put simply, the more rational one is in trying to describe the good's origin, the more one is likely to conclude that it does not exist, that it is a chimera. But, in a circle, we ask, "But why is there so much common urge—against self-interest?"

The problem with the third account is that it leads to a de-emphasis of the good and the substitution of a nebulous faith, where nature becomes a kind of intrinsic good. If God is a part of all life on earth, the good, as known by human beings, could well be an unimportant appendix. Indeed, there is little reason to join a Christian church (the Christian tradition becoming then no more than a mystical tale, hanging, if it remains at all, by the thread of belief in essentially irrelevant literal New Testament facts, one that can be and usually is discarded). The only ethical consequence of being a believer would be some vague expression of environmentalism, where one has to draw a line between killing a bacterium and a koala bear, poison ivy and a potato. If one were to take this view seriously, the difference between being truthful and just with one's fellows and attempting to save a rat or flesh-eating bacterium from destruction would be, at most, one of degree. Followers of this interpretation are unlikely to be convinced by much of the following chapters. The basic nature of pantheist ethics is relativist. The reader should not conclude that I am rejecting any sense of responsibility for the earth, the environment. In later chapters I shall illustrate how the good is not limited to interpersonal behaviour. The earth is our canvas, but we share it with others. That implies that we should ask ourselves, as one example, "What is due to an animal that we have domesticated for our use?" My objection to pantheism is that it marginalizes the fact of the human being as the only creature with the knowledge of good and evil—the centre of religious belief.

As for the more literal, biblical interpretations of God, their problems are well known and there is no need for me to dwell on them in depth. If God made the universe and our world and made mankind in his own image, why did he wait so long to put people on the earth? If he is all-powerful and all-knowing, why does he allow terrible catastrophes to happen to good people? If he is all-powerful in the conventional sense, what happens to freedom of choice? Is not belief in pre-destination the logical conclusion from an all-seeing, all-powerful, and all-knowing God? If all is pre-destined, we are all absolved of personal responsibility—it is not the devil but God that made me do it. I shall not dwell on these well-rehearsed problems for three reasons. First, skeptical readers will already have dismissed fundamentalism; it is likely to be among the reasons why they are skeptics. Second, my purpose is not to destroy people's faith in God, but to make it credible and reasonable. Third, one of the main themes of this book is that there are many views of and pathways to the truth and the good. Mine is just one, and not necessarily the most valuable or helpful to every reader. A central axiom of the book is that religious faith is a hinge for action. It would be arrogant in the extreme if I were to suggest that my version of Christianity is the only or best activator for that hinge.

The existence of good is evidenced by our capacity to choose it over evil; it cannot exist without personal freedom. As Alasdair MacIntyre points out, we all make choices every day; the very fact that we sometimes dither and change our minds illustrates the freedom we have, even when it is only a matter of choosing what clothes to wear. There is often a good to choose and that decision is not simply based arbitrarily on personal advantage, convention, and indoctrination. We may reject the good or change it to fit our own condition (indeed we cannot help but change it as we interpret it through our own experience). One may live a life while entirely rejecting the good, but few go so far. Much more often we re-arrange our notion of the good to serve our current purposes; this is made easier if we deny its absolute character. It is that danger that makes recognition and understanding of the good so important in a secular and relativist age. There is a danger that clever people, although able to recognize clearly the wrong behaviour of others, will find explanations and excuses for their own, because good is so complicated—and relative.

There are two conclusions to my argument up to this point. It is reasonable to believe in an objective good; indeed, nihilism is the only other completely rational account of the human condition. Beyond that, reasonable and desirable consequences stem from a belief in the good. I believe in the good because it makes more sense to believe than not to; and I believe because the consequences of disbelief are, probably in the short term, inevitably in the long term, destructive.

We nearly all believe that other people exist in the same way that we do ourselves, that they do not only exist in our imagination; life is not a dream. We believe that much human action is freely chosen. We believe that we have individual consciousness, which allows us to learn, perceive, and choose. We also spontaneously believe, sometimes despite ourselves, that some things are good, others bad—when parents put the interests of their children before their own; when strangers help us when there is no possibility of personal gain

95

or public recognition; when a researcher stands up for truth, even when condemned, even fired, by superiors; when a woman cunningly murders in calculated and violent ways; when a man beats and steals from those who are weakest and least able to defend themselves. Even those who deny the existence of moral action (arguing that all superficially good works are motivated by individual selfishness, by the wish to seem good to others), are ready to condemn action which they decide is wrong. There can be no good without bad, no bad without good.

It is fashionable in the developed West to explain everything or almost everything by reason and empirical science. Even some educated mainline Christians try to defend their faith empirically, falling prey to the irrational emotivism that so often characterizes the non-religious moralist. Some liberal Christians disparage those who interpret Old Testament myths as literal truth, but still cling irrationally to their own worship of a virgin birth and physical ascension, as though a religion of the spirit must be supported by their carefully selected set of alleged historical and miraculous facts (while the miraculous facts believed by others are based on ignorant foolishness). Quickly discarding the good as, unlike the infant Jesus, a human confection, they soon follow the secular line and define good in fundamentally meaningless secular terms.

But if we look deeply into our hearts, we know that we are capable of good and evil, unless that knowledge is obscured by a set of emotivist ideologies, or a passionate worship of 'me' and 'more.' The first rationale for belief in the good is reason; we experience a sense of the good, which is exterior at least in the sense that it is outside our normal conscious experiences. But reason could take us equally well in a different direction, to belief in nothing or to belief in an individualist good. The belief in absolute good must be supported by faith, because the trials, disappointments, and sadness of life will surely test any belief there can be any overarching good. Why believe in good when all around you there is misfortune and when so many seem to have little interest in the good life? Alternatively, why believe in good if all goes well, and one is in control of one's life, busy accumulating more? And why believe in good, if, when one finally musters up the courage to do the right thing, one receives only condemnation (as a religious bigot, perhaps)?

While the good is the crucial starting point for a reasonable belief in God, it does not encompass the entire meaning of God. Further, there are additional reasons for believing in God, but they are justifications after the fact, to which I shall turn in later chapters. The consequences of belief in God strongly favour belief over disbelief, both for the individual and for community and society. While that proposition supports the Christian life, it cannot convince the skeptic of the very existence of God. If there are no personal consequences from one's belief in God, one's faith is betrayed and worthless; instead of being a spur to right action and a scold of wrong, it becomes a focus of false pride and comfort. But if belief depends only on desirable consequences, it lacks truth and substance.

In an interesting essay on Christianity entitled, "Can we be good without God?" (published in *The Atlantic Monthly,* December 1989), Glenn Tinder argues that the Christian belief that everyone is persistently sinful and that everyone can be exalted (by finding God) is the only firm ground for belief in the equality and dignity of the human being. He concludes by quoting from a prayer written by Dietrich Bonhoeffer after he was imprisoned by the Gestapo: "Give me the hope that will deliver me from fear and faintheartedness." Tinder asks, "If we turn away from transcendence, from God, what will deliver us from a politically fatal fear and faintheartedness?"

FROM GOOD TO GOD

My basic starting point is that there is good and evil. Most people behave as though they exist; and most people also say they believe in God, even if they belong to no form of religious community. Some of that belief is certainly a cultural residue, a feeling that one should not declare oneself an atheist. It is safe to predict that the proportion of genuine believers in North America will decline, as it has in Europe. The point is that even in the most irreligious times and places there remains a widely sensed feeling that there is good, and that there is a God. Those who deny God usually quickly construct some facsimile.

We should remember that even in Christianity's first millennium, including its first and crucial two hundred years, the social environment was not peaceful, harmonious, and devout; Christianity did not survive comfortably. The next millennium's nineteenth century progressive belief that one could manage very well without the prop of an imaginary god was neither true nor novel. In England, rationalism had strong roots in the eighteenth century and, before that, the European Reformation had led to a multitude of dissenting sects and denominations. We in the West may congratulate ourselves that we are the first to manage without God, but we are neither the first nor have we managed very well. The stain of Stalinist Russia (and its imitators in China and Cambodia) and Hitler's Germany will not be quickly erased.

Important questions arise from a conception of God as good. **What is the nature of this absolute good? How do you know? Is that all there is to God—a vague sense of an absolute good somewhere out there? Why should I let the good, even if there is one, interfere with my busy life?**

Strong Christians may ask: **You have it back to front. Is good the source of God, rather than God the source of good,** and everything else in this world? And where does Jesus fit in? How can you found Christianity without Christ?

Those questions are not addressed in seven orderly paragraphs, but they do indicate much of what the rest of this book is about. This book could reasonably begin with morality and the good life, or God, or Jesus Christ. The three are ultimately conjoint. The skeptic's first three questions are particularly relevant at this point.

Good is the most important defining quality of the human being; consciousness, reason, and abstract thought are marvellous tools, but they are ultimately unimportant without some idea of human purpose. Perhaps the favourite mantra of our secular times is "progress." But who defines progress? Its core meaning in practice appears to be more, expressed, in terms of more material goods and individual freedom. Neither of those goals is closely associated with God, virtue, or Christianity.

The good is not some free standing object somewhere out there that we can accept or reject. Virtue is good in action. In chapter five, virtue and moral behaviour is examined in detail. Here, it is sufficient to carry forward the idea that the good is important in itself because of its gift to humankind, but is becomes crucial when transformed into virtuous behaviour.

The following excerpt from early Christian times serves several purposes. It provides a concrete (and Christian) example of the good life and illustrates also (in response to the second set of questions) why it is not heretical to found a version of Christianity in the moral life. Aristides was a Greek Christian living in the first and second centuries A.D. He wrote that:

> Christians are the ones who have found the truth. For they know the God who is creator and maker of everything and they worship no other God but him...They do not commit adultery, they do not engage in illicit

sex, they do not give false testimony, they do not covet other people's goods, they honor father and mother and love their neighbors, they give just decisions. Whatever they do not want to happen to them, they do not do to another. They appeal to those who treat them unjustly and try to make them their friends; they do good to their enemies. Their women are chaste and are virgins and do not engage in prostitution. Their men abstain from all unlawful intercourse and impurity, and all the more the women likewise abstain, for they look forward to a great hope that is to come. Moreover, if they have male or female slaves or children, they urge them to become Christians so that they can hold them in affection, and when they do become such, they call them brothers without distinction. They do not honor strange gods. They are humble and gentle and modest and honest, and they love one another. They do not overlook widows, and they save orphans; a Christian with possessions shares generously with anyone without. If they see a stranger, they bring him into their homes and greet him like a real brother—for they call one another "brothers" not by physical connection but by the soul (Taken from Wayne A. Meeks, *The Origins of Christian Morality*, 1993).

The nature of the Christian moral life at the end of the twentieth century is developed later, but it is important for readers, as they approach my conception of God, to determine their reaction to that passage. It is presented as a generally sound, if imperfect, account of the virtuous life. One does not have to believe either that this is an accurate account of how most Christians lived in early Christian times, or that it is the definitive and final expression of virtue and Christian morality. Those, however, who dismiss it as an example of the obsolete tradition that is killing religion today, or as the kind of self-righteous hypocrisy that has led so many Christians to abandon their faith, are unlikely to be convinced by this book, or, in my view, to accept Christian truth. Accepting God does not mean accepting some vague thing out there, ready to help us in time of need, but never interfering with our own plans and desires. Rejecting the goodness of God denies the entire Judaeo-Christian tradition. A clever rationalist would uncover paradoxes and contradictions; Aristides' account does not precisely reflect my own expression of the good Christian life. But it does present a reasonably coherent historical expression of virtue, based on truth, courage, and justice, that most observers would see as being admirable in its historical Christian context. No one can perfectly express the goodness of God, and expressions will inevitably differ according to the social context. But the truth of God is immutable; it is only our understanding and interpretation that change; most Christians will feel some affinity with Aristides, almost two thousand years later.

While an account of Christianity may begin in many places, a denial of a central place for Christian morality strikes at the heart of Christianity. To state that God is good is not to take a blind step of faith, or to develop a hypothesis; it is a simple statement of truth. God is not good in the sense that "Richard is nice"; it is not a *characteristic* of God. God is good loosely in the sense that bread is food, but beyond that; he is the only spiritual food. The good is God and God is good. But those statements are incomplete, because they might imply that God is only good, narrowly defined in terms of virtuous behaviour, that he has no other qualities. So it is important to develop an idea of the meaning of God, beyond the necessary foundation for his existence.

God is referred to as "he" throughout the book as a common convention. It will become apparent that God is not human in any normal sense and certainly not male. The use of "she" would, by its unfamiliarity, emphasize the human quality I wish to dispel and "it" would be confusing and disrespectful.

THE DIMENSIONS OF GOD

To define God's dimensions is to tread dangerous ground. Believers of all stripes agree there is a mystery attached to God's nature. All I can do is to make a sketch of what I see. The attempted sketch can be seen as a sign of arrogance (how can one know the ineffable?); but to limit God to the concept of good, however central and reasonable, would be unhelpful.

Truth is the first word, after good, that comes to mind when one tries to examine the meaning of God, and of our existence. The human being is often seen as a truth-seeker; the power of abstract thought is used to probe, propose, explain, describe, imagine, and discover. The first statement of the early Christian quoted above describing the qualities of Christians is that they have found the truth. One could claim for truth a pre-eminence that would not be justifiable for any other quality beyond the good, including love. After all, a desire for truth underlies my claim for the good. If what I am writing is a pack of lies, if I am to write something entirely different tomorrow, then my argument has no value. The reader, to appreciate the book, must believe that at least I am trying honestly and sincerely to discover truth. The earlier part of this chapter is an attempt to convince the reader that good is truth.

Truth, like most terms applied to the absolute, has a number of meanings. Many people, at least in academic argument, limit truth to scientifically determined facts. The only truths, by this account, are those that are established by careful scientific, empirical investigation. Facts have little to do with the idea of truth intended here. In practice, almost everyone has an idea of truth that goes well beyond the facts. (And we should bear in mind that many acclaimed so-called scientific facts turn out not to be facts at all. This is particularly so in an age of politicized junk science, when allegedly scientific statements are made with respect to, as examples, climatic change and genetically-modified foods, based on the flimsiest, selective, and politicized data).

I have argued that it is unreasonable to deny the existence of an absolute good. Truth for most religious people quite reasonably encompasses values as well as facts. When we say someone is "nice" or "unpleasant" we usually have evidence in mind, although it may not meet the highest standards of empirical science; even when the evidence seems to be factual (e.g., it consists of empirical evidence of behaviour with which all present concur), its classification in terms of motive (the quality of niceness implies motive as well as behaviour) is usually based on subjective interpretation and judgment. Does that contradict my account of an absolute objective good? The existence of an objective good does not entail that any or all human beings have a perfectly reliable interpretation of the good and evil expressed by others. (Indeed, the Christian knowledge of our essential sinfulness contradicts such reliability). When honest, reasonable people, speaking without unfair prejudice, describe someone as "unpleasant," they are referring to a selection of characteristics that would generally be associated with that word, e.g., aggression, dishonesty, and malice. The statement may be true, provided one accepts its limitations; it does not imply that the person is irredeemably evil, that he always exhibits those characteristics, or that he is lacking in positive attributes.

Truth to many people consists of personal honesty and integrity. Human discourse, including scientific investigation, cannot exist without this form of truth. Ironically, the discovery and publication of facts depends on a transcendental form of truth. When transcendental truth becomes less central in public life, there is a corresponding tendency for purveyors of alleged truth to distort, conceal, or falsify. I refer here not only to the inevitable human tendency to select facts to fit the hypothesis, but to the active fraudulence of falsely claiming that research supports politically attractive opinions, for example that even minor exposure to secondhand tobacco smoke is a danger to health in any public place. In that particular case, large scale research was designed in the United States to support pre-determined convictions.

Truth lies at the heart of human conduct. Animals cannot lie although they may deceive and dissemble. Lying does not simply mean misstating a fact. We all make false statements because we exaggerate, tease, joke, tell imaginative stories, forget, are ignorant, or have unwittingly deceived ourselves. That is rarely lying (although such contexts may be used as a cover for lies). It is the intentional , but not necessarily planned, statement of a falsehood in a serious attempt to mislead, whether directly or indirectly, that betrays God.

God's truth lies in the apprehension of transcendental understanding. The truth of God can reasonably be interpreted as permitting the expression of the highest forms of human experience, most crucially, the search for the good. Far from being potentially inconsistent with the good, truth is inseparable from good. Those who think they know truth without claiming any knowledge of the good miss truth's most important element. And those who believe they can be good without truth thereby betray their claim. Those who think that being factually honest constitutes truthfulness will soon find they are mistaken. An unnecessarily malicious expression of fact is not being true to one's neighbour.

Personal dishonesty is the most direct way to defect on God. Little lies do indeed turn to big ones; being untrue to others is frequently accompanied by dishonesty with oneself. It is like the poison ivy I see on my land; one little sprig indicates a larger spread that is concealed in the bush. Those who claim they tell "only" white lies purely for the benefit of others usually end up with some personal advantage from them.

Power is also a universal referent of God, and perhaps the one that leads to the most confusion. The Christian God is referred to as being all-powerful, almighty. Coupled with other human attributes, that statement often leads to the mystification of both believers and non-believers. A muddled and easily refuted belief in an almighty God is probably the most frequent cause of the failure of faith.

If God is all-powerful and all-knowing in the conventional sense, one of two propositions follows. Either life is pre-ordained, human freedom an illusion; or, if he decides not to protect good people, he is the author of evil and catastrophe. Both those propositions are improbable and unreasonable. Just as no one (other than small children and the insane) really believes that the world outside themselves is simply a product of their own minds, almost no one acts according to the proposition that everything in life is already pre-ordained by God. We take time to choose our clothes, our entertainment, and our behaviour toward others. We all in our hearts believe that we make choices; we know that we change our minds. We sometimes choose to do the right thing when we would rather not, and we sometimes knowingly choose the wrong path. More often we make daily choices that are neither moral nor immoral, or that are only recognizably such after the event. We try to escape danger and disease, behaviour which makes no sense if our fate is already decided.

The second (and complementary) idea, that God chooses to have people raped and tortured, is equally implausible in the same way. At one time, many Christians believed that harm was done to us as a punishment for our sins. The idea is found equally in the Old and New Testaments. While I accept that acts against nature or the good usually entail (i.e., usually contain the seed of) some form of retribution or punishment, that is entirely different from saying that all hurt stems from human sin. The punishment for wrongful acts (sins), whether inflicted by others or oneself, stems from one's separation from the good; it is part and parcel of having the responsibility of accepting or rejecting God's goodness.

Many contemporary Christians are inconsistent in terms of the proposition that God permits or chooses evil and catastrophe. While they do not usually claim that a volcanic eruption, a violent hurricane and a car accident are God's decisions, they do see God's hand in something nice happening to them, such as the recovery from illness, and, in the case of one minister I knew, finding a parking place. I reject the categorization of God as being a kind of all-knowing superman, choosing who will get cancer, and who the prize. It is also important to distinguish between the evil that we do and natural catastrophe. The reader should not be too quick to castigate me for an unChristian argument. A central proposition of the Gospels and Pauline letters is that individuals must choose the right way; if we can make choices, God is not all-powerful in the sense that he plans and approves all activity.

Nevertheless, God can be seen as being almighty in one way. Consider the analogy with the game of chess, in terms of both correspondence and non-correspondence. Is the king almighty? The black king can take any opposing white piece on the board in the appropriate circumstance. But he does not determine everything that takes place on the board. If one were to identify our god with the black king, that king's movements do not determine all the action of Satan's pieces. In the end, checkmated by white, the king may be defeated.

Before that defeat, any white piece may check (attack and threaten to terminate) the black king.

The correspondence with God is far from perfect. As discussed earlier, there is no Satan directly equivalent to God, as the two equal kings oppose each other in chess. There is no general acceptance among Christians that God and Satan are equivalent in power, and even the metaphor of Satan has outlived its usefulness. Evil lies in the absence, the rejection, of God more than in the presence of an equal evil spirit. A person unable, as a result of mental disability, to perceive good is incapable of evil. To be evil, one must know and reject good. That is a concept long-recognized by our courts; in contrast, some African societies (e.g., the Masai) believe that harm, without consideration of motive, is sufficient evidence to be used in the determination of retribution. In practice, we in the West may have become overly obsessed with motive, but the Masai are surely too little. God, like his counterpart in chess, does not control everything, but the human world of good and evil is asymmetric.

The king in chess, although he does not have total control of the board, is still a powerful piece, together with the queen, who could be compared to God's agent, Jesus Christ. The crucial differentiation is this. While black is, in the end, as likely to be defeated as white, God, the good, is never defeated, never removed from the game; evil can never annihilate good (although evil may have a long run in the game of life). In that sense, God is not just powerful but almighty. There can be no checkmate for God. God is almighty in the sense that he cannot be defeated. The good can always overcome. In the most terrible circumstances, Bonhoeffer's sacrifice of his life in defiance of Hitler, Anne Frank's courageous life refusing her categorization as inferior being, God can win, even in apparent loss. Death, where is thy sting? Victory depends on God's almighty goodness and the human courage to announce it; the enemy is as much faintheartedness (lack of courage) as Satan. Evil happens when good people do nothing. God is not responsible; rather is evil the manifestation of our separation from God.

Perhaps the most frequent identification with God in contemporary times is that of *love*. This is one of the most confusing and puzzling of usages. Love comes in many shapes and forms. There are two important dangers in discussing love—the first is in seeing it as a generic term with many forms of expression, all emanating from God. The assertion that "God is love" is far more problematic than the ones that "God is good," "God is truth," and even "God is all-powerful." The second danger is in seeing love as taking totally distinct forms, only one of which can be seen as being a part of God. Hence the confusion.

The most common usage of love today (excluding statements such as, "I love tomato ketchup") is the combined expression of emotional (erotic) and physical (sexual) love. That example can usually be distinguished from God's love; today's casual sex is little different from that among, for example, cats. Yet at the same time marriage is seen as a holy commitment, and sexual congress is an integral component of marriage. There is nothing definitively good about sexual desire; it is a part of life, like eating, play, and work. Even so, it can also be part of an expression of God in the right circumstances. The beauty of good children and grandchildren emerging from a happy marriage can be accurately described through the metaphor of "gifts from God." The multiple expressions of a good marriage based on commitment are a genuine and significant expression of the truth and goodness of life. Being true to one's spouse includes sexual fidelity, but love in marriage goes well beyond that instance. It will be recalled that MacIntyre denies the existence of virtue in solitude; its expression requires community, and the traditional family is the foundation of true Christian community.

Different from erotic love is the enduring, non-sexual love between two human beings, for example, between mother and child, between spouses, and perhaps between close friends. (I exclude for the moment Aristotelian friendship based on loyalty and shared commitments, although the two overlap.) Like erotic love, there is nothing necessarily good about those relationships, but they may be an expression of the good, just as erotic love may be. Parents love their children instinctively, as cats may be said to love their kittens, but that instinct is not the distinctive love that is accessible to human beings as a part of the truth of God. Parents' love of their children may be different in kind as well as duration from that of the cat; it may transcend events and continue long after children leave home and live independent lives. It is of course strengthened when children honour their parents. Similarly, love between siblings, where it exists, is increasingly, in the modern age, one of a less deeply-rooted affection, but may still be true love when continuing to adolescence and beyond. Affection is a positive quality, but it is closer to the good feelings and manners one attempts to display to all one's fellows than to deep and enduring love. Love does not come and go according to circumstance. I hold many people in affection, but truly love only a few.

The love within friendship, in MacIntyre's and Aristotle's sense, is an important virtue (and hence a part of the good), but it is important to recognize their narrow definition of the term. Friends must be partners in a worthy cause. They must have bonds of loyalty forged by overcoming difficulties. In my own modern and mobile life, I have seen little sign of this kind of friendship, in myself or others.

Aristotelian friendship always and mutual affection some-times exclude two important forms of what we term friendship today. Important people, and some not so important people, talk of their many friends (numbering in the hundreds perhaps). Most of the people described as friends of this kind—neigh-bours, people we meet in work and leisure activities, people we invite for a meal or even to share a holiday—are not Aristotelian friends. Often the feelings are barely positive; the relationship is built on need, loneliness, convenience, or even ostentation (if one's frequently mentioned friends include important or influ-ential people). Closely-knit gangs and small communities whose activities and purposes are harmful or at best unhelpful, or where there is no real commitment or difficulty involved, are also excluded from any true conception of love and virtue.

Modern life makes Aristotelian friendship difficult, putting more weight on the nuclear family for bonds of love, common purpose, friendship, support, and affiliation. It is likely also that modern life makes God's love more difficult to reach, not only in that way, but amid its rush and confusion.

The links of acquaintance are not, however, trivial. Commu-nity is based on such relationships. A Christian community is usually necessary for a continuing relationship with God. But the positive feelings we have for most members of our community, mainly people like us, should not be confused with the love that is part of the God as truth (although they should benefit from its universal expression). I return later to the confusing expression, "the love of one's neighbour," which has almost nothing to do with love in the sense I am using it here. It is confusing both because "neighbour" here means everyone (not merely acquain-tances towards whom one has positive feelings) and because the behaviour implied stems from attitude and faith more than from strong, enduring interpersonal emotion; it may derive from God, but it would be foolish and totally dishonest for me to claim that

I love the Bishop of York, let alone Jorge Estancias of Quito, in the way that I do my children. Similarly, one should not confuse the daily civility of life in work and leisure, important as it is, with the powerful force of God as love.

There is in addition an increasingly common and unhelpful usage of the term love in modern life, self-love. Advocated by Rousseau as the central goal of child raising, self-love (often known as high self-concept) is the antithesis of Christian love. This theme will be developed more later when I turn to the expression of virtue in the Christian life. At this point, it is sufficient to note that self-love is the denial of others as equal in the sight of God. It requires the worship of self and is a direct contradiction of Christian humility.

A distinction should be drawn between self-love and self-knowledge. The latter is a human quality that is necessary for living a full life, and is entirely compatible with humility, but is unrelated to spiritual love, which is always directed outside self. Self-knowledge requires the acknowledgment of our individuality, our dignity, and worth before God. It requires understanding of our strengths and weaknesses, in the same way that we should recognize the strengths and weaknesses of others, in those we love and those we do not. Self-love means that one should take pleasure and pride in one's own importance. Of course if you believe that love of self is good for you, it follows that it is good for others, providing that their attitudes do not detract from your own sense of worth. Truth has by then long since flown out of the window, and true love obscured.

When Christians talk of loving others as one loves oneself, the emotion is not one that has much in common with love. If one loves God, then indeed you should respect your neighbours, and treat them as you would like to be treated. But loving them could easily lead to problems, such as coveting your neighbour's wife.

Love of God is transcendent, being the source of all our true human love. Love in that sense is an inseparable and incomparable aspect of the good. MacIntyre accepts this by showing that the good can only flourish in the company of others; the person who lives an entirely solitary life cannot express the good. This is not to say that having lots of "friends" (in today's terms) is better than living a quieter life. If one looks at the bustle of "friends" on popular television programs (such as the eponymous "Friends," titled with disingenuous irony), one quickly sees that there is no relationship between time with friends and the pursuit of a good life. Clearly there are good people who thrive on company, and others who do not; extremes are cause for concern. One's care for others is selfless. One does not think first of what value they can be to oneself; nor should one collect people (friends) to escape from self-knowledge, duty, and responsibilities. The virtue of justice is to see and treat all others as one would want them to see and treat oneself; to treat them in a disinterested manner, that is to say, in a way that is not contingent on their potential advantage to oneself. It is an essential component of the good, and an entry point to the virtues. I shall show later how doing good things in order to build up a high score card with God is not the way of a good life. There is overlap between love and virtue; one cannot use true love to behave in a way inconsistent with truth, justice, and courage, although it is obvious that any form of love can lead to questionable behaviour. It requires judgment to determine when love cease to be true love, i.e. love compatible with virtue.

What I have tried to do here is to disentangle the strains of a word that is one of the vaguest in the English language. God and good are one. True love is an expression of the good that characterizes us as human; it goes beyond instinct, beyond the rational, but it can never be entirely separated from our rational and animal natures, even though it supersedes them. The human character, mind, and motive are so complex and so compounded that it would be the height of foolishness to imagine that one could classify human action simply within categories. It would be equally unwise to conclude that there is no true love, no truth, and no ultimate good.

To assert that God is love is both true and false. The word is used in so many and inconsistent ways that it is better to look at the different expressions of "love" than to talk generically, perhaps implying that sexual appetite among adolescents is God-given, or that one should care for one's neighbour's children and parents, as much as, and in the same way, as for one's own.

There remain two other properties that are frequently associated with God, but which cannot be reasonably seen as a crucial part of the absolute. Service of God, Christians claim, is perfect *freedom*. Freedom is not an unusual property in animal life. We often see household pets changing their minds just as we do. Our cat asks to go out, then changes its mind when we open the door and it sees the snow or feels the cold. Wild animals are even used as exemplars of freedom.

What is distinctive about human freedom is the ability to consciously postulate various actions and their consequences, and above all to make choices on the basis of good and evil (not simply by judging the consequences). Freedom is a necessary but insufficient requirement for good. What Christians mean by "perfect freedom" is the conscious choice to do the right thing, fundamentally to love God. The contemporary worship of a libertarian freedom as a good in itself is as much opposed to "perfect freedom" as self-love is to love of God. Christian love is perfect because it is selfless; Christians talk of emptying themselves before God; they do not refer to loving God as a result of their being exceptionally fine specimens of the human species.

It is a mistake to see oneself as following "God's will" when one takes a correct action, if that action is made without choice (because one can conceive no alternative) or if it is made for ignoble motives. My mother gave me some rare praise when I was fourteen. She congratulated me on my patience in playing table tennis for hours on end with a French girl staying with us on an exchange visit. She was not a good player. I felt guilty because I knew that my behaviour had nothing to do with patience and generosity and everything to do with the good view of her breasts when she bent down to pick up the ping-pong ball at her end of the table. Following God, means being right with God, not doing that which gains the approval of others who are important to us.

Freedom is no more intrinsically good than is food (or a vaguely defined love). Food is required for life. If a person's survival is at stake, it is not surprising if he is less aware of right behaviour. Freedom is necessary, by definition, to lead a good life. It is impossible to live fully without a sufficiency of both, but they are not part of God. It is possible, and people do, exercise freedom in separation from or defiance of God. Evil acts, I have said, can only be made freely.

Beauty can be seen as a property of God. The appreciation of music, art, and drama is sometimes a way to see the good, either because the good is expressed or realized in art or because the development of aesthetic sensibility makes us more sensitive to the meaning and presence of God. It may, however, be safer to interpret beauty, like freedom, as a means rather than an end. The term "beauty," like love, is used in very different contexts. We may talk of Mother Teresa being a beautiful person. When we do that we are thinking of internal beauty. Princess Diana, who died to much more fanfare at about the same time, possessed far more external and superficial beauty, but was she a beautiful person? We may know people, usually sincere believers in religious faith, whose internal faith and serenity is expressed in an external beauty in their demeanour. I have met several people in that category, none of whom would be classified as notably handsome, pretty, or sexually attractive. It is a far cry from such people to Hollywood's "beautiful people," whose beauty is usually entirely external. Although there may well be such a thing as objective beauty (research on different cultures' apprehensions of the beautiful suggests there is), it would be dangerous to associate those objects, animate or inanimate, with God. Physical attractiveness, aesthetic or sexual, is by no means commensurate with virtue. Charm, for example, may be a moral disadvantage, because it so readily manipulated for selfish purposes.

Thus, while there are situations when it makes sense to refer to freedom and beauty as being aspects of God's goodness, a generalized association is better avoided. The next chapter includes commentary on the problematic overlap between aestheticism and spiritual faith.

In this chapter, I have provided an idea of how God is manifested in our lives. It is also important to understand some of the facets that I exclude. I have already expressed some limitations of God. His power is not expressed in predestination. He does not have the power to cause or halt an earthquake or bring back to life a person killed in a road accident. Simply, God is not a souped-up human being able to accomplish the things we might like to do if we were Superman.

Christians often speak somewhat mysteriously of a personal God. I reject the notion of God as an image of man or the human being as an image of God. That idea recalls a picture of a god being a white male sitting up in space in a splendid gown. God is personal in the sense that every individual has equal access to him, can draw from him, can learn from him—as an individual, not simply through the intermediary of a priest (although such mediation often helps). Because of the ambiguity, I avoid the term "personal God." In the next chapter, I consider further the nature of communication with God.

It may seem that my God is simply a set of abstract qualities. If one looks at his attributes carefully, it will become evident that the qualities are inextricable from our life on this planet, alone in our consciousness and our responsibility, but alone among others. The concept of God is difficult to separate from a virtuous life, because there is no point in worshiping a god whose essence has no application to your life. It is no coincidence that the last hundred or so years have witnessed both the alleged death of God and the erasure of the concept of virtue from civil discourse.

What I mean by asserting that God is not a souped-up human being is really quite straightforward. It is inevitable that, as we look through our hole in the tent, we try to explain what we see, what we want to see, in terms of ourselves. This book's view is through my particular hole. That does not mean that there is no actual god, but only our own subjectivity, nor that if we can just find the right hole we shall see the entire truth. Plato's metaphor of the cave is appealing; we are like slaves toiling away looking at the shadows in the back of the cave, trapped in our material and emotional transient wants and fears. Our task is to turn to the light. In the Christian expression of George Herbert:

> I got me flowers to strew Thy way;
> I got me boughs off many a tree;
> But Thou wast up by break of day,
> And brought'st Thy sweets along with Thee.
>
> The Sun arising in the East,
> Though he give light, and the East perfume;
> If they should offer to contest
> With Thy arising, they presume.

Can there be any day but this,
Though many suns to shine endeavour?
We count three hundred, but we miss:
There is but one, and that one ever.

The aesthetic effect is enormously enhanced when the words are put to music in a song by Ralph Vaughan Williams. We are incapable of grasping the full magnitude of that sun— but *there is but one, and that one ever.*

Recently, my wife and I took Bible study classes and studied the story of David in the Old Testament. The Jews of his time took a fatalistic and personal view of God and saw God's hand in every victory and defeat. There was considerable discussion in the study group of God's decisions and choices, some of which were callous and cruel. My God does not choose or decide; he is not sitting somewhere, physically or spiritually, thinking about what he will do with me next. God does not "do things" in a human or animal way; God is, but we see no beginning and no end; there is none.

A more effective metaphor for God than an old man with a beard in a white robe, in turn, kindly generous and furiously vengeful, or even that of a sun, is that of an ever-flowing river. We can always reach out to it; we have instant access. We can ignore or deny it. We can live our whole lives and refuse to venture close; but it is there. My God does not decide, choose, intervene, think, talk, destroy, resent, favour, love, punish, or think; instead, he is.

When I was quite young, I remember my mother quoting the adage, "How odd that God should choose the Jews." Despite the anti-Semitic flavour of that saying, it would indeed have been peculiar if God had chosen the Jews, or the Christians or any other ethnic group, or if God were today on the side of the democracies, helping them spread "universal" human rights among modern non-believers. It is much less odd to think that the Jews were among the first to begin to recognize and delineate the truth of God, to choose God. Just as Jesus advised his followers to give to Rome that which belongs to Rome, and to give to God what belongs to God, so we should accept our human qualities (of choice, decision, and action) and look to God for those transcendent qualities which lie outside human beings, but to which we have access.

It is easy to jump to wrong conclusions from this preliminary account. Later chapters will fill out the meaning of the Christian God and of Jesus Christ. At this point, Christians will be apt to exclaim that my account is not of God, but merely a vague spirit. How can this God have mercy, grant forgiveness? Where is God's grace? What is the meaning of prayer if God cannot decide how to answer? Non-Christians may wonder why they should bother to learn about Christianity if its God is such a shriveled and impersonal thing. Those are important issues that remain to be addressed. It would be a mistake for critics on either side to jump to dismissive conclusions about how those issues will be resolved in my account. The issues derive significantly from the problem of communication with God. Non-believers claim there can be no communication, except in human imagination. Strong believers see communication in the same sense that human beings communicate with one another, as a conversation. My view is that communication is possible without conversation; that we may have a sense of God, the ever-flowing river, without having to imagine that he speaks English to me and Arabic or Swahili to others; naturally we understand him in our own language and culture, but they are our property, not his. God is there; we can disclaim him, but he remains. The nature of our relationship with God is a central part of the next chapter.

CHAPTER 3

THE BIBLE AND THE ESTABLISHMENT OF CHRISTIANITY

In Chapter 2, I offered a definition of God and sketched a picture of the dimensions of God. A comparable picture could have been derived from other theist religious traditions. God is clearly not the property of any one group of people. A non-believer may reasonably ask, "Even if I assume that there is some truth in your account of the truth of God, so what? Why should I worship him? Why should I be a Christian and go to church? If I live a moral life, why do I need God? If he does not have human characteristics, how can I talk to him?" This chapter begins the answer to those questions.

In this next section (and in the book overall), I am indebted to the writing of Christopher Lasch, in particular to his book, *The True and only Heaven* (1991).

Lasch suggests there are three ways that one can believe in the Christian religion. The first is to believe in the factual accuracy of the Bible. There are innumerable variants within that tradition. Almost no one believes every word, but fundamentalist Christian denominations accept most of the Judaeo-

119

Christian narrative as inerrant truth, with particular emphasis on the factual accuracy of the Gospels. Many mainline Christians, including evangelical members of the Anglican church, while rejecting the factual accuracy of much of the Old Testament, believe at least in the literal truth of the core statements of the life of Jesus—that he was born of the Virgin Mary, the physical and unique son of God; that he had miraculous powers; and that he was crucified and physically resurrected. For the skeptic, fundamentalism is out of the question. The account of the origin of the world is clearly legendary. God's actions as recounted in the Bible, particularly but not only in the Old Testament, are not, by the broadest stretch of the imagination, compatible with the account of the good I described in Chapter 2. On the other hand, once one begins to retreat from fundamentalism, then the slippery slope begins: How far can you go? Fundamentalists point out, accurately enough, that versions of liberal Christianity know few limits, and almost any interpretation and consequent behaviour become acceptable. Fundamentalists and skeptics alike wonder why some mainline Christians accept that the Bible as a whole is a mixture of history, myth, legend, and fiction, while at the same time maintaining that the no more credible core narratives of the Gospels are factual.

The second basis for Christian belief is that the Bible is true, not in the sense that it is factually and scientifically accurate, but that it is an expression of spiritual and moral truth. Judaeo-Christianity thereby becomes a myth in the sense that it is a traditional narrative built around truth. The skeptic cannot be expected to swallow this version whole without argument and careful thought. Even in terms of moral doctrine, in terms of how we should live, there is considerable contradiction and ambiguity within the Bible. Which part of the story should we choose, and why? This book is plainly anchored on this second approach, as the previous chapter on the nature and dimensions of God illustrates. Its purpose is to show that the broad Christian tradition does represent a reasonable and defensible expression of religious truth.

Lastly, Christian belief has, particularly since the middle of the nineteenth century, been based on aesthetic appreciation. For followers of this tradition, its truth lies in the beauty of the story and its expression. Aestheticism has been a dilemma for Christianity since the earliest days. Should churches be beautifully adorned with fine objects and moving impressions of the life and death of Jesus? Or should there be an ascetic spiritualism, without props from sentiment? Today, the conflict continues, as much within denominations as among them. In some churches, beautiful forms of worship, music, and ritual risk becoming substitutes for spiritual understanding; in others, leaders' and participants' involvement is so captivating that the service may be a barrier rather than a bridge to communication with God; emotional self-expression replaces a more sober assessment. Some may find comfort in a beautiful service; others are enraptured by a charismatic climate. But many are repelled when emotion, irrespective of its source, replaces truth.

It is important to clarify why I cannot ground my faith in the first or third approaches. At the same time, I must emphasize that the Christian life is more important than the doctrinal differences among those who follow it. Lasch quotes Henry James, "Better risk loss of truth than chance of error—that is your faith-vetoers' exact position." It was a position that could never serve as a guide to religious life, or to an intelligent understanding of the good. The "agnostic rules for truth-seeking" laid down by "scientific absolutists" betrayed a "suspension of judgment that ignored the whole field of religious experience and its testimony to the power of faith" (289).

It would be both ludicrous and arrogant for me to claim that because I think that my version of truth is *better* (i.e., more valid) than fundamentalist or aesthetic versions, I am therefore a *better* Christian. It is for that reason that the critiques of the other two positions are brief; my purpose is not to go to war against other Christians, but to trace a way for non-believers to embrace a particular version of the faith. Obviously, I believe, like most people, that my own account is the most sensible. Equally, I believe that no person can fully understand the truth of God, and certainly not one whose life has not been concentrated on his being. Henry James's brother William, a founder of philosophical pragmatism, saw truth in the multiplicity of forms of worship; if people worship, there must be something to worship. My own position is different, based primarily on a perception of transcendent and absolute good rather than on human practice, but I share the James brothers' plea for tolerance of different routes to God. Nevertheless, I cannot myself base spiritual faith either on accounts of alleged miraculous happenings or on sentiment unsupported by reason. Aesthetic appreciation may well be one pathway to the truth, but it does not constitute the truth.

Thomas Reeves (1996) gives a convincing account of the decline (in membership, importance, and influence) of the mainline Christian churches in the United States, principally over the last fifty years. A parallel decline has taken place in Canada; in England both the significance and the attendance of the established Church of England have plummeted. Reeves describes a steady slide down the slippery slope as more and more Christian doctrine is sacrificed to secular trends and ideology. He notes that the fundamentalist and evangelical churches have held their own against the secular tide. It is paradoxical that I am largely sympathetic to his account, although it concludes with a defence of an essential, factual basis for

Christian belief that I do not accept. While Reeves makes many sensible suggestions for Christian renewal his starting-point remains the factual accuracy of the gospels with respect to the Virgin birth, the miracles, and the physical resurrection. The need for a return to the Christian life comes second, but it hangs on a belief that most people will quite reasonably no longer accept. The reason he gives to persuade those in doubt is precisely what led them to disbelief in the first place.

It is ironic that so many Christians, while justifiably critical of scientists' reliance on empirical facts, should themselves cling to a set of supposedly scientific facts as a platform for their faith. They see the abandonment of reliance on those central stories as the way to total disbelief; I see it as the beginning of a revelation of Christian truth, which has nothing to do with miraculous happenings and everything to do with the source of ultimate truth, religious teaching and doctrine, and the good life. The reason why, in the past, loss of belief in the alleged facts has led to abandonment of Christianity is precisely because children were (and still are) told that they cannot be Christian if they do not accept those facts. If there is a forced choice between belief in the factual truth of the (contradictory) gospels and exclusion from Christian ranks, most sensible young people will and do choose the latter. They soon refuse to believe in miracles and virgin birth, and leave the church, just as they come to disbelieve in Santa and the tooth fairy. Thousands of adolescents and adults reach the not unreasonable conclusion that there is no good reason to believe in those facts, so throw out the baby of Christian truth with the bath water of miracle. Reeves assumes that a lack of belief in the factual Christian core prevents people from leading a Christian life; conversely my assumption is that many people are looking for some approximation of the Christian life, some code and meaning of life, but cannot accept the supposed facts on which it is said to be based.

It does not follow at all that Christian liturgy must be edited in keeping with modern times. (I prefer Cranmer's traditional Book of Common Prayer to modernized Anglican versions). My hope is that there will continue to be broad acceptance of the different ways in which people interpret Christian myth. I, for example, accept that the metaphors of Jesus born as the son of God and resurrected after his crucifixion are central to the Christian tradition, and find them aesthetically and spiritually helpful and true.

Generally, tying spiritual truths to historical facts is unwise. Religious truth can be neither proved nor disproved by scientific or historical fact; in the previous chapter I argued that the good cannot be proven, but that it makes more sense than the alternatives. Two thousand years ago, it doubtless made sense to base a change in traditional belief and practice on alleged events; it was the custom. No one would believe in a leader or god who lacked access to magical powers. Jesus pronounced that God was not the sole preserve of the Jews, but was universal. Whereas today such teaching would be heavily buttressed by philosophical and ideological argument, in those times the author of the revelation also required some empirical evidence, based on physical happenings and personal experience. Recent discoveries about the history of the times of Jesus can neither establish nor discredit the truth of Christ's teaching; Christian doctrine does not depend on whether ten or ninety per cent of the sayings of Jesus recorded in the gospels are authentic. It is sad that so many Christians have abandoned their religion because they have lost faith in the factual accuracy of the gospels. For the secular world so well represented in the media, Christianity can be and is dismissed by offhand references to superstitious belief in a virgin birth and miracles. Clinging to a few allegedly essential facts among the biblical wreckage and providing emotional appeal to the less educated and most gullible form a serious barrier to the faith of increasing proportions of educated and skeptical non-believers. It is no coincidence that Christianity is in decline in the once-Christian developed world, and on the ascendant in the less developed nations, where more primitive beliefs have been undermined by Western civilization.

I do not hold fundamentalists (or mainline Christian believers in literal truth) in contempt, and am irritated by the sometimes supercilious and dismissive attitudes of liberal Christians towards those with a larger set of claims to historical fact than theirs. It ill becomes those who believe in a miraculous birth and death to condescend to those who also believe in additional miraculous, but no more extravagant, happenings recorded in the Bible. There are different ways to truth, and the means to the end are less important than the end, the acceptance of God and his goodness. I do not deny that I find the beliefs of many Christians to be strange and unreasonable.

Even so, the more I talk with secularists (and I have spent most of my life in the company of secularists possessing little or no religious belief), the more truth I see in G.K. Chesterton's claim that when people cease to believe in God, they do not then believe in nothing, but in anything. The most highly intelligent, highly educated people I know defend angrily and emotionally a variety of unsupported beliefs. Examples include the dogmas that no one ever chooses to live on welfare, that divorce is not in the least harmful to the children, and that capitalism is the problem, socialism the solution (or vice versa). David Frum records the recent social history of the United States (*How We Got Here From There*, 1999). The seventies were perhaps the first significantly secular decade in that country—secularism had become established in parts of Europe earlier. The widely accepted beliefs stemming from that era are hard to comprehend—fewer than thirty years later. One of the most appalling narratives concerns enforced busing to rid the country of school "segregation"; the policies persisted long after their resulting violence, widespread opposition, and miseducation had become apparent, enforced by politicians, judges, and officials whose own children were carefully shielded from their regulations. If one judges people by the way they live rather than by what they profess, Mennonites, Jehovah's Witnesses, Mormons, and Seventh Day Adventists come out better than the elites who hold them in contempt.

One may wonder why so many mainline Christians oppose fundamentalism so strongly. By attacking others as religious bigots, they distance themselves from something close to their own tradition while ingratiating themselves with their educated secular and liberal friends; they show that they are tolerant, the supreme liberal virtue. The motive is readily understandable; we live in liberal, secular times. It is human nature to attempt to identify oneself with the dominant élite by joining in attacks on non-members of low status; it is one of our unpleasant and enduring human characteristics to connect ourselves to those who are in the fashion, and to denigrate those beyond the pale.

Despite my sympathy with the many good people of strong traditional faith, I am obviously not one of them. My rejection of an aesthetic base is less self evident. Indeed, I have acknowledged a role for aestheticism in Christian faith and would not myself join a church with unattractive rituals. Aestheticism, by definition, places reliance on beauty, on feeling, as being at the heart of one's faith. In Chapter 2, beauty was identified as a somewhat ambiguous quality of God. Evil is not always antithetical to superficial beauty; it may pass undetected more easily in that guise. Sadism and masochism lead to a form of aesthetic experience, satisfying to some. Aesthetics can be and is used to aid virtually any purpose, good, banal, or bad. Nevertheless, aestheticism, in the form of beautiful places of worship, fine language, and emotionally expressive music, can be an important contributor to Christian belief. It would be a grave error to assume that rational cognition is the only valid path to true faith; we learn from teaching, example, experience, emotion, instinct, and intuition, as well as rational induction and deduction. Religion's relationship with aesthetics is analogous to its relationship with reason. Reason and aesthetics (the religious spirit is inseparable from the emotions) are necessary for a true apprehension of God, but both can lead us astray. Reason is not the summit of man's wisdom, and neither is aesthetics. Both have intrinsic value, in the advancement of knowledge and the provision of desirable pleasure; both may lead either towards or away from good. Neither is the end, the goal, which is the truth of God.

So, while I am more of an aesthete than I am a fundamentalist, I am as sympathetic to the fundamentalist version of Christianity as to the aesthetic; while the fundamentalist, however wrong-headed I may consider her factual claims, places knowledge of God first, the aesthetic Christian places the aesthetic experience before truth; the aesthete is often a relativist. The aesthetic Christian may well be the more likely of the two to be tolerant, acknowledging the disparity in human experience, but tolerance is not a basic Christian virtue. (It is a common mistake to mistake Christian forgiveness for tolerance). If the Christian places faith in good, truth, integrity, courage, justice, and the love of one's fellow human beings, then lies, corruption, cowardice, injustice, and hatred cannot be readily tolerated. The fundamentalist is the more likely to keep in place the essentials of being right with God and with one's fellow human beings. If the fundamentalist is susceptible to excessive intolerance, the aesthete is equally so to extremes of tolerance.

As with any classification system, one must be careful not to place faith in the exactitude of watertight divisions. People are far too complex to be neatly placed in one of three, or a hundred, categories. Lasch's three categories are only helpful to the extent that they help to illustrate important differences in religious faith. They are not particularly useful to differentiate among religious sects and denominations. Not only do individuals lie between the categories, but within a single mainline denomination (e.g., the Roman Catholic or Anglican) one will find representatives of all three of them.

My account of Christianity and interpretation of the Bible are based on Christian teaching as essential truth. The narrative of the Bible is interesting, not as factual history, but as a crucial part of the development of spiritual and moral truth.

BIBLICAL CHRISTIANITY

It may seem to the devout Christian believer that Jesus is peripheral to my account of Christianity. If one does not believe in the miracles attending his life, what is so special about him? Why *Christian*? The answer should be obvious. If it were not for Jesus and his teaching, there would be no Christian tradition, no Christianity. Although the initiation and growth of Christianity probably owe much to stories of miracle and mystery, the continuing attribution of miracles to Jesus results from the truth of his teaching, rather than truth arising from miracle. If Christian truth depended only on miracle, it would have been abandoned long ago.

The intensity of study of and belief in Christian teaching is difficult to account for in miraculous terms; so is the widespread acceptance of Christian teaching, both among people who have scarcely heard of Jesus and among those who formally reject Christianity. One should also remember that Jesus was not the only person of his times to whom miracles were attributed (as we see throughout the Old Testament and in the Dead Sea Scrolls), but he is the only one to have given birth to a splendid religious tradition. On the other hand, it must be admitted that there remain millions of Christians for whom the miracles form a foundation for their faith, a base that helps to convince them of the truth of Christian teaching. All Christians can agree that the miraculous and legendary accounts of Christ's birth, life, and death are an integral part of the Christian myth.

There is no unanimity among Christians about the relative status of God, Jesus Christ and the Holy Spirit. Among Anglicans, traditionalists are said to give priority to God, evangelicals to Jesus, and charismatics to the Holy Spirit. My sense is that the mainline churches lean more to Jesus than they used to, perhaps because the picture of Jesus emerging from the Bible is more forgiving and loving than that of God, supporting the intellectually bankrupt notion of good without evil. Clearly, my account centres Christ's significance in his expression of God's truth; the Holy Spirit is a metaphorical expression of God's accessibility to everyone, Christian or not.

Christianity is broadly based on the entire Bible, not simply on the New Testament. Jesus was a Jew and based his teaching on Jewish tradition. It is not a matter of importance to my argument exactly how much of his religious perspective is derived from the competing Jewish traditions of the time. The God I have described is founded in the Judaeo-Christian tradition.

The Old Testament: Sin and the Ten Commandments

Two vital fundamental truths in the Old Testament merit particular attention. The first is the legend of the fall, the story of Adam and Eve. The central message of this tale is that we err, or sin, by choice. Sin is part of what it means to be human. Other animals cannot sin because they do not have knowledge of good and evil. Those assertions do not necessarily imply that one must accept the traditional interpretation of original sin, that sin is born in the child. It does mean, however, that sin comes to human beings naturally, not simply as a result of bad, or inappropriate, family and environmental conditioning.

I reject the popular notion that children are entirely innocent, until they are corrupted by an evil society, their parents, and schools. My rationale is not derived only from religious teaching, but from reason and common sense. One only has to observe young children closely to see how quick they are to manipulate their loving parents (the more unconditionally adoring the parents, the more patent the manipulation), to feign hurt, and to attack siblings if they feel they are receiving more attention than they deserve. It was once claimed by psychologists that babies are incapable of complex emotions. Now they acknowledge that even before they are a year old, children experience and express jealousy. The fact that different children behave differently in similar circumstances is not consistent with the cause being environmental; it is entirely consistent with the belief that children inherit aspects of character and make choices themselves influenced by both their inherited qualities and their experiences.

It may be argued that animals do bad things and exhibit jealousy, that both animals and children have to be trained. Just as one cannot prove the existence of good and evil to the determined unbeliever, so one cannot prove that human beings are more than simply highly trained and genetically developed animals. The reality is that virtually all of us believe that we have freedom of choice and agree that we knowingly choose the wrong way. So when we see young children begin to choose wrongful action deliberately, it is not because they have been corrupted or trained, in any normal sense of the word. It is simply that they have gained knowledge, like Adam and Eve, of good and evil.

Drawing very fine, and final, lines between original sin and a natural tendency to sin, and between nature and nurture, makes little sense. Two things are clear: We are all sinners, and our misbehaviour is not simply attributable to our treatment by our parents and assorted others. It is all too fashionable to blame parents, schools, and society for all our faults. It is not a question of either genetics or environment, or even of two independent sources of influence; there is a complex interaction between our cognitive and emotional natures and our experiences, both heavily influenced by our personal choices.

For those who object to my continued use of the word "sin," I emphasize that it simply refers to conscious behaviour inconsistent with the good. Later in the book, Christian upbringing and education are discussed; that discussion follows from the point here that nurture and nature are not alternatives; one cannot reasonably choose between them, or ignore the interaction of personal responsibility. It makes no sense to assume that children are born pure, in the sense that babies are good or virtuous. One can argue that they are born both good and bad perhaps, but it is more plausible to say that they are born with the propensity for good and bad choices and actions. No hard line can be made between conscious and unconscious, deliberated or undeliberated, choices. Some undeliberated actions are clearly instinctive, but spontaneous action may stem from character, a character which is partly molded by choices made in the face of experience. While it is unwise to think of very young children sinning—sin requires a conscience and a level of self-knowledge—it is naïve to insist that young children cannot choose to do bad things.

Still, two powerful questions remain. What is the value of a legendary account of the beginning of mankind that anchors human behaviour in sin rather than in goodness, and that paints the female as the evil temptress? How can a tiny, innocent child reasonably be described as a potential repository of sin?

The truth of the biblical account of Adam and Eve does not anchor human behaviour in sin. Quite the reverse, it describes sin as an aberration, albeit one that we cannot avoid. The acceptance of evil and sin stands in important contrast to two prevalent views in today's secular world. The first, popular among the educated classes, is that there is no such thing as sin; inappropriate behaviour simply results from inappropriate upbringing. The effect of this belief is to condone first, bad behaviour, and later what I define as sin. The result is that what is socially permissible (in the furtherance of tolerance) becomes broader, to the point where almost everything (why not everything?) is understandable and tolerable, once we understand the individual's genetic and experiential background. Ironically, those who adopt that line of argument are fiercely critical of those who oppose them (particularly those with religious faith); logically, they have no reason to judge anybody or any behaviour or belief.

The story of Adam and Eve tells us nothing about the physical origin of the world or of the human being, but it does tell us the essential truth about our unique human nature, our capacity for good and evil. It matters not a tittle who tempted whom in the story; in ancient times, woman was seen as the temptress, just as God was given male attributes, and just as a man had the opportunity to proclaim the word of God. The sex of God, Adam, Jesus Christ, and the apostles is irrelevant to our belief.

It would indeed be callous and cynical to look at small children and talk of their sinful nature. As I have said, even young children are capable of bad, antisocial behaviour. However, we should not excoriate their "sins" any more than we would convict an insane or mentally incompetent person who has committed a criminal offence. Clearly, while small children are capable of pleasing and displeasing behaviour (and wise parents quickly accustom them to the categories of good and bad), they are not sinners. No reasonable church, or parent, would expect a five-year-old to confess a "sin." By the time most children are ten, however, they are capable of sin; their mental capacity is almost fully developed. Between that age and late adolescence, young Christians are typically confirmed (in some denominations baptized); they are of an age to know and understand good and evil.

I am arguing that the abolition of sin, in the context of the death of a meaningful God (he may remain as a kindly old Santa Claus), makes sinful acts more acceptable and more commonplace. But what about goodness? In the absence of sin, has it any real sense? If all behaviour were to be classified as good (providing one understands the motives and circumstances underlying it) the term good loses all meaning; there can be no virtue. Without evil, there is no good. So it is simple and logical that God and evil should together be condemned as rubbish by many educated elites.

Rationalists go to extreme lengths to deny good. Many traditional Christians were upset that Princess Diana, whose behaviour right up to her death exhibited an extreme narcissism, and with it, a disregard for what is often scorned as bourgeois morality, should be glorified in death. In contrast, little media attention was paid to the contemporaneous death of Mother Teresa, who had lived, for the most part, a saintly Christian life in the service of the poor. There was defensive commentary at the time suggesting that there was nothing noble in Mother Teresa's life because she acted in the interests of her own spiritual glory.

Without belief in good and evil, any apparently good behaviour can be cynically deconstructed as being motivated by glorification of self; even spontaneous and silent acts committed in private anonymity can be cynically misinterpreted. As I have said, that line of thought is quite consistent; if there is no evil, there is no good. If there is no meaning in life, no absolute good, no God, then no behaviour is better than any other, except in terms of one's own self. One may decide to appear good to others, or to imagine a fanciful god, but activities in pursuit of those purposes are no more worthy (within a state of nihilism, where nothing is worthy) than lying, bullying, assaulting, and cheating to gratify oneself and one's friends. But those who speak from the facile but definitively empty ground of nihilism, should not then expect others to take interest in what they go on to approve or disapprove.

The second fundamental truth of the Old Testament lies in the Ten Commandments. Moses first discerned the ten vital rules for the conduct of life. Those rules, in slightly differing order and form, remain an important part of both Judaism and Christianity. They will be familiar to many, but they are summarized here for those, like me, who have never memorized them.

There is only one God. He alone should be worshipped. God's name must never be abused. Time must be kept clear every week to worship God, free of the ongoing demands of worldly activities. Honour one's mother and father. Do not murder. Do not commit adultery. Do not steal. Do not speak falsely or maliciously of others. Do not envy the families, the way of life, or the material possessions of others.

Unfortunately, the Decalogue is rarely recited in mainline Protestant churches today; at most, a short summary of the first two commandments is read, conveniently avoiding the specifics that members of the congregation are most likely to transgress.

There are perhaps two reasons for the Decalogue's decline, given that there is rarely an open attack on those traditional rules within the Christian church. The first is that the rules are essentially negative; they are prohibitions. Jesus preached a more positive code of conduct, of the golden rule and forgiveness. That is much the preferred approach today, with more emphasis on the good of God and Jesus, less on evil and sin. A problem with that approach is that talk of our essential goodness leads directly to the assumption that we have no sin in the first place; even if we all do things we ought not to do, we should not feel too depressed about it. God forgives us, so why should not everyone else? God loves us so we are worthy people. We really should feel pretty good about ourselves; high self-concept and self-esteem replace self-knowledge and self-respect. Overemphasis of Jesus' mercy towards sinners ignores the bottom line, "Go, and sin no more."

Another reason for the decline of the Commandments is that some are clearly discomforting in the secular world. Adultery is so openly accepted today that many ministers appear to be wary of condemning it from the pulpit, probably because they are well aware of the church members who continue to take Communion even though they have left their spouses to live in a sexual relationship with a friend, perhaps but not necessarily a future partner.

My wife, Nora, used to discuss the Decalogue with her grade six classes in an upper-middle-class public school. Some of the students never attended church and most were totally ignorant of the Commandments. They expressed particular surprise at the prohibition of adultery; from television, they had come to assume that if a man and a woman, on good terms, were together in private, sex would surely follow. Almost in the same category is stealing. Apologists for the poor frequently condone stealing on their part, rationalizing that it is no worse than what financiers do every day. Some will even argue that governments have "stolen" their rights from them. Many people, young and old, Christian or not, assume that cheating on one's income tax is normal and acceptable if there is little or no chance of being caught. Carefully composed newspaper articles describe, without conditions or judgment, the confidentiality of overseas placement of investments. It is unusual today for a minister in a mainline church to translate the traditional rules into terms recognizable by members of the congregation, more common to inveigh against the immorality of government and business, of them rather than us.

But what of the Old Testament as a whole? What does it mean for the contemporary Christian skeptic? The Old Testament is an inescapable part of the Judaeo-Christian tradition. I emphasize the key concepts of the fall and the Decalogue, but truth, as distinct from historical fact, can be found in many parts. Isaiah has particular appeal to Christians because the prophet is seen to be predicting Christ's birth and life. Jews and others may argue that there is nothing particularly novel in Christ's teaching, other than his illegitimate claims to divinity. Isaiah (56.6–8) asserts that foreigners who "love the name of the Lord" and "hold fast to my covenant" will be "accepted on my altar; for my house shall be called a house of prayer for all peoples," thereby anticipating Christ's most crucial contradiction of traditional Jewish law. In practice, it is of little importance whether Isaiah foresaw a revolutionary Jesus or if Jesus drew from his teaching; either way, there is continuity.

Christians are also apt to lay claim to David, a central figure in Jewish tradition, and the reputed author of some of the most beautiful psalms, partly because Jesus is said to be his descendant. But central to the story of David is his love for Bathsheba and his "contract" murder of her husband, Uriah. The prophet Nathan confronts David with an allegory based on David's own behaviour. Not recognizing himself as the evil protagonist, David demands to know the identity of the evildoer; "You are that man," is the famous reply. David is in some ways an improbable Christian hero, although the combination of violent greed and conspicuous generosity makes the story of his life plausible as well as interesting. As David M. Gunn in the *Oxford Companion to the Bible* tartly comments,

> The account of his (David's) incarceration ('until the day of their death') of the ten concubines whom he abandoned to be raped on the roof of the house he fled hardly conjures a character of courage or responsibility (1993, 154).

The story of David, if he is seen as a leader of his times in whom evil and good adhered rather than simply as a hero in the tradition, is graphic and compelling. His involvement with Bathsheba illustrates how readily we rationalize our own wrongful acts, and fail to see ourselves as others see us.

A continuing theme of my book is that believing in God and claiming Christianity as our religion are of little worth if those two acts have no influence on the way the way we live. In the Old Testament, I have emphasized the importance of the notions of good and evil and the guidance provided by the Ten Commandments. In Chapter 2, I quoted from Aristides' early Christian guide to the good life. Christian belief is a hinge to action; if it breaks, the belief is also torn asunder.

Unpopular today in mainline churches are important sections of the Old Testament where the practical conduct of one's life is discussed. The Book of Proverbs, as an important example, is not simply a laundry list of occasionally contradictory instructions. It should be seen rather as a discussion of the problems of daily life, with ideas that the reader is invited to consider. Once again, there are keys to future Christian teaching; "When pride comes, then comes disgrace; but wisdom is with the humble" (11.2); "Those who trust in their riches will wither, but the righteous will flourish like green leaves" (11.28); "Whoever walks with the wise becomes wise, but the companion of fools suffers harm" (12.20); "Do not say, 'I will do to others as they have done to me; I will pay them back for what they have done" (25.29). This important book contributes to "one purpose—the formation of a whole person by leading a student on paths of uprightness, intelligence, and conviction to human fulfillment" (Cox 1993 626, in the *Oxford Companion*). For the Christian, the Old Testament is a necessary prelude to the New. The now accepted Apocryphal and Deutero-canonical books reinforce the continuing theme.

> All wisdom is from the Lord, and with him it remains for ever. The sands of the sea, the drops of rain, and the days of eternity—who can count them? The height of heaven, the breadth of the earth, the abyss, and wisdom—who can search them out? Wisdom was created before all other things, and prudent understanding from eternity. The root of wisdom—to whom has it been revealed? Her subtleties—who knows them?
> —Sirach (1.1–6)

The New Testament and Jesus Christ: The Establishment of the Christian Religion

The status of historical facts about Jesus and his life is clearly not fundamental to my version of Christian faith. What matters is the truth of Jesus within his tradition. I do assume that Jesus was a living person, a fact denied by only the most zealous opponents of Christianity. In this section, as in this chapter generally, I rely heavily on *The Oxford Companion*. Strong believers will find this chapter too summary and simple to be helpful, but the book is addressed to the doubtful. The intent is to develop an interpretation of Christianity that is reasonable in the eyes of thoughtful people not already committed, either to Christianity or to an alternative.

One crucial fact is that the Jesus of the Bible was a Jew and spoke from the Jewish tradition. I pointed out earlier that the prophet Isaiah anticipated many of the teachings of Jesus. Some Christians believe that God spoke through Isaiah to predict the coming of his son, Jesus Christ, and his teachings. A more reasonable interpretation, I suggested, is that,

> Jesus was influenced by the prophecies of Isaiah, where the coming of the reign of God is a central theme.... Jesus' teaching is shot through with allusions to Isaiah (Fuller, 1993, 357).

There is no discontinuity.

The biblical narrative of Jesus is sometimes divided into three parts: Stage 1 materials meet some of the following criteria: multiple attestation; not derived from Judaism; consistency with other materials; and likely origin in the Aramaic language and a Palestinian setting. Stage 2 materials were shaped and transmitted in the oral tradition. Stage 3 materials consist of interpretations by the evangelists. Obviously, there will never be agreement on exactly what fits into which category, and from my perspective the classification of various items is not of great importance; that thirty per cent of members of the revisionist Jesus Seminar vote that certain words were actually spoken by Jesus is only of passing interest.

Although there is some value in a reconstructed sketch of the authentic Jesus, one that mainly serves to describe the limited claims that are probably based on a factual history, it is important to bear in mind that Christianity's truths draw from a range of sources and narratives; Christians are inevitably selective in what they choose to develop their portrait of Jesus.

Fuller observes that Jesus emphasizes that, "God demands not just outward conformity to the law but the whole person, and not just love of neighbour but love of enemy.... The rich young man must not only keep the commandments but sell all he has and follow Jesus" (357). Central to his teaching is his doctrine of love, repentance, and forgiveness. The coming of God's rule makes it possible to love God and one's neighbour, to repent one's mistreatment of neighbours, and give and receive forgiveness. The Commandments require the love of God and consideration of one's neighbour; Jesus' teaching requires the expression of that love in contrition, and the acceptance of God's grace.

The death of Jesus on the cross may reasonably be related to the propitiation of sin. His acceptance of his fate reflected his ultimate and absolute love of God , and showed the way for our own "justification" (a term to which I return in the next chapter). Justification does not pronounce us innocent but helps to bring us into a right relationship with God (364). Most centrally, Fuller concludes, "Christ has ransomed believers 'from every tribe and language and people and nation and... made them to be a kingdom and priests serving our God' Revelations 5.9–10" (366).

Before turning to the Sermon on the Mount, Jesus' most famous teaching, I must re-emphasize the importance of humility. It may be argued that it is more Stage 3 than Stage 1, and that it is also a virtue in the Jewish tradition. It is nonetheless quintessentially Christian; humility is one of the hallmarks of the Christian tradition. Love of God, the golden rule, courage, and justice were already well developed, either within the Jewish tradition or within the broader Greco-Roman tradition, to which the Judaeo-Christian ethic is closely related. St Thomas Aquinas and other Christian leaders have combined Aristotelian and Christian truth, humility being an essential component drawn from the latter.

It may be claimed that Jesus himself lacked humility in arrogantly seeing himself as the son of God, but it is far from clear that he ever made that claim on his own behalf. His reference to God as Father is not proprietary, as the opening words of the Lord's Prayer ("*Our* Father") indicate. It is generally thought that he referred to himself as the "son of man" on many occasions, but that is a deferential term. His acceptance of social outcasts and occasional disinterest in the more powerful are also an indicator of a humble spirit, as is his reputed washing of the disciples' feet. To Jane Austen, the foremost Christian novelist (or perhaps more aptly, novelist who is a Christian) in the English language, humility is a core virtue, evidenced most famously in the character of Fanny in *Mansfield Park*. Fanny is not an appealing character today, and *Mansfield Park* is not, partly for that reason, one of her most popular books. True Christian teaching itself is not obviously appealing; it does not bring instant gratification and happiness. Austen's Christianity, with her aversion to self-glorifying puffery, is the more compelling because it is an intrinsic characteristic, not an expression of pride or piety.

The traditional prayer book of the Church of England (*The Book of Common Prayer*), notably in the Prayer of Humble Access, where members of the congregation are likened to crumbs under God's table, also places humility at the centre of Christian piety. Even in contemporary services, humility, if much less graphically expressed, remains inescapable.

Jesus is the origin and central spirit of the Christian church, not a nominal first president whose significance is shrouded in time. At the same time, the Christian tradition, which includes the four Gospels and Paul's teaching (which may antedate the Gospels), historical writing both within and outside the Bible, as well as nearly two thousand years of interpretation, discussion, and debate, has a life and meaning beyond what most scholars accept as the factual words of the historic Jesus.

The Sermon on the Mount may be seen as having a status intermediate between Stages 1 and 2. According to Guelich (1993, 685–9), the Sermon, while not a paraphrase of a single sermon given to Jesus' disciples at a precise moment in time, does appear to be an accurate reflection of what is known of his teaching. Many Christians see that sermon as the central testament of the Christian faith.

The beginning of the sermon (Matthew 5:2–7:28) reflects Isaiah's prophecy; the people of the Kingdom are those who:

> stand before God empty-handed, vulnerable, seeking a right relationship with him and others, open to receive and express his mercy and forgiveness with integrity, ready to experience and establish peace (Guelich, 688).

The first set of demands made of Christian followers (5.21–48) is troubling to many devout as well as more liberal believers. It is here that Jesus re-interprets the Commandments. It is not enough to avoid murder and adultery; it is sinful simply to bear anger or "look at a woman with lust." Jesus asks that his followers love their enemies—"loving those who love you" is grossly insufficient. In short, "Be perfect, therefore, as your heavenly Father is perfect."

Readers may remember the famous occasion when President Jimmy Carter, an unusually committed Christian to become leader of a major Western power, admitted to having lusted in his heart—to considerable public derision. Jesus' more extreme demands in the Sermon on the Mount can readily be seen as being unreasonable, to the point of being impossibly utopian or even ridiculous, in any age, among any people.

The second set of demands (6:1–7:11) deals with Christians' relationship with God. "So whenever you give alms, do not sound a trumpet before you... When you are praying, do not heap up empty phrases..." but, "Pray then in this way."

There follows the Lord's Prayer. It is followed by some explanations of what has gone before and examples of piety. Notable are the stricture to "not store up for yourselves treasures on earth, where moths and rust consume and where thieves break in and steal; but store up for yourselves treasures in heaven;" and the profound advice to the skeptic,

> Ask and it will be given you; search and you will find; knock, and the door will be opened for you. For everyone who asks will receive, and everyone who searches finds, and for everyone who knocks the door will be opened. Is there anyone among you who, if your child asks for bread, will give a stone? Or, if the child asks for a fish, will give a snake? If you then who are evil, know how to give good gifts to your children, how much more will your Father in heaven give good things to those who ask him! (Matthew 7:7–11.)

It is easy for non-believers to react cynically to all this, "Well then, what are we supposed to do, get ourselves sterilized and then inhabit a cell in a monastery out of the way of temptation, groveling for food?" Even solid Christians are likely to find it a bit much to be accused of sinning for simply allowing a single sexually inappropriate or angry thought to enter their head. It is important then to decide what this famous sermon means to us. By that, I do not intend that we should determine precisely what Jesus was thinking when he gave his original sermons, or exactly what Matthew thought he meant. It is impossible to put ourselves in someone else's mind, even within our own culture. It is more reasonable to attempt to determine a core meaning within the Christian tradition. But that too is far from easy, because there are variations within the tradition.

One point does seem clear. The sermon is a wonderful expression of twin themes within the Judaeo-Christian tradition. Speaking to the head and the heart, it tells us: As members of the faith, we must attempt to make ourselves right with God and we must deal fairly and justly with our fellow human beings. Those traditional truths, not announced for the first time by Jesus or Matthew, are central to the heritage. The sermon goes beyond those two widely accepted truths, however.

In contrasting the traditional Jewish Commandments with this sermon, we should remember its context. A printed version of an oral sermon is not a learned discourse in a book of philosophy. It is a rhetorical, persuasive address, not an elaboration of moral reasoning. Indeed, it is not at all a comprehensive code of conduct. The demands and prohibitions are simply examples; listeners were supposed to be sufficiently knowledgeable about biblical prescriptions not to need them all listed.

What the sermon does say substantively, beyond the two key, traditional truths listed above, is that it is not enough for us simply to obey the letter of the moral code (the Decalogue); we must live by its spirit. It is insufficient not to murder, not to steal, and not to have sex outside marriage. We are wrong before the point of action, when we allow ourselves to hate someone so much that their death might come as a relief, to take more than our share, or to flirt with another person to arouse our own and the other person's latent sexuality.

Does the sermon exaggerate in order to make those important points? Of course. Has there ever been a moving and persuasive speech that has not been touched with hyperbole? Indeed, if public speakers have to qualify and limit every assertion and implication every time they seek to persuade or educate, they are likely to succeed in neither; the listeners will be either bored to death or convinced the speakers have nothing of value to say. Discussions, arguments, speeches, sermons, and addresses are not the same as scientific reports, philosophical papers, and tomes of law.

Imagine a labour leader convincing an audience of union members by quietly suggesting that one or two corporate leaders have on occasion put rather too much emphasis on company profits and not quite enough on employee satisfaction; or a conservative politician stating that our courts in a few cases may have tended to put the interests of the accused slightly ahead of those of society and the victims of crime. More likely the labour leader will claim that the only driving motive of fascist corporate leaders is to satisfy their own personal greed and ambition by laying off loyal, long-term workers who have given their lives to the company; and the politician will proclaim that unelected judges seek ever more personal power to make decisions against the will of parliament, making life easier for the most vicious criminals, without consideration for the peace-loving citizens who are the backbone of our country. In turn, the evangelical Christian leader may say that the moment we allow the slightest evil thought to enter our heads we are on the path to hell and everlasting perdition.

The skeptical reader may react along these lines. "You have gone well beyond explaining the Sermon on the Mount in terms of the tradition; you have reduced stern demands to gentle admonitions. Simply, you seem to think the sermon says what you think it ought to say." The criticism is not entirely unfair. In this case, as in many others in the book, my argument will not be acceptable either to strict, mainline Christians (let alone those of a more fundamentalist persuasion) or to secularists. I have acknowledged that there is no virtue in being opposed from both sides; being in the middle is proof of nothing more than not being on the ends. My thesis here recurs throughout the book. There is important and beautiful truth in the Sermon on the Mount; it should not be simply discarded on the grounds that, taken literally, it becomes impossible, inhuman, even as a goal. There are many points between the two extremes of blind belief and ridicule. There is no reason to believe that Jesus refrained from rhetoric or that those who reconstructed his teaching were reluctant to mold his teaching in their own perspective.

Even though the sermon is both beautiful and truthful, I do not consider that it advances an intelligible or novel interpretation of the tradition very far. Quite the reverse, it draws attention to enduring Christian schisms, between asceticism and full involvement in daily life, between spiritual withdrawal and political action, between simple faith and aesthetic exploration.

Reference has been made to the problem of the place of aesthetics within the Christian religion. To what extent do music, artifacts, and buildings promote faith and to what extent do they become substitutes for it? The argument broadens beyond aesthetics. To what extent should Christians live in the world, and to what extent outside? The reference to a retreat to the monastery earlier was not entirely facetious. Even today, there is a tendency for many Christian denominations and sects to separate themselves from the world; reference is less to the dwindling Roman Catholic monasteries, abbeys, and convents, than to Seventh Day Adventists, Jehovah's Witnesses, and the Amish. Among Jews, there is a marked difference between the Orthodox, who live significantly within their own communities, and the Reform, who, like liberal Christians, participate fully in the external world, to the point where many become inseparable from it. Inside Islam, both Sunni and Shiite, there is differentiation between those who are willing to accept the modern world in part, and those who wish to reject it totally, exemplified by secular Turkey and Taliban Afghanistan respectively.

In early Christian times, as now, most Christians lived slightly ambiguous lives, attempting to balance their Christian faith with involvement in the larger community. The incongruence between living a Christian life and participating fully in the world has existed from the beginning.

Christ's teaching, as reported in the Gospels, is inconsistent, even contradictory. At times, as in the Sermon on the Mount, he appears to be ascetic to an extreme. That which is of the world is the enemy of human kind. The canonical Gospels report the virtue of giving up one's worldly goods, even to the extent of disowning one's parents; nothing must come between the individual and God.

At the same time, there are incidents where Jesus is far from unworldly. He attends a wedding in what appears to be a well-to-do family and turns water into wine—nothing ascetic about that. Asked who owns a Roman coin, he advises that we give to Caesar that which is his, and to God that which is his, indicating a separation between our material and spiritual lives.

Perhaps most telling is the parable of the talents, reported by both Matthew (25.14–30) and Luke (19.12–27), but not by the more ascetic John. A man, going on a journey, gives his three slaves five, two, and one talent respectively. When he returns, the first two have doubled their share, while the third has hidden his single talent for safe keeping and still has just the one. None has given any of his share to those worse off than he. Jesus would have us take the one talent from the third and give it to the slave with ten talents, saying , according to Matthew, "...to all those who have, more will be given... from those who have nothing, even what they have will be taken away... throw (this worthless slave) into the outer darkness." The parable is sometimes awkwardly interpreted as a metaphor that we should use our personal qualities to the advantage of those around us, wishful thinking on the part of clerics, the more obvious moral being that we should make the most of our advantages, that we should be open to life. (Individualists will see it as an early plug for capitalism!) The parable certainly does not suggest that our duty is to ignore our human qualities and retreat to a life of prayer without consideration for our own or others' material needs.

It is impossible to be sure whether Jesus himself is better represented in the ascetic or the worldly tradition; what we do know is that both directions are important parts of Christian tradition from the time of Jesus until today.

Meeks provides a vivid picture of the conflict in early Christian times in a chapter entitled *Loving and Hating the World* (1993, 52–65). The early schism between the Gnostics and the victorious mainstream is well characterized by the Gospel of Thomas, later to be excluded from the writings selected to form the New Testament. Thomas takes Jesus even further in the ascetic direction than John: God will not admit merchants and traders to heaven; those who retain ties with their parents are like the offspring of a prostitute (because God is their only true father); it is the solitaries who will enter the bridal chamber (heaven); we should be passersby. Divesting oneself of one's worldly goods has nothing to do with helping the poor, rather is it a step towards the repudiation of the world—death and admission to heaven are the destiny and goal of life.

A more orthodox interpretation of Jesus' separation from the world is that we are enjoined to put aside previous allegiance (both pagan traditions and an overly rule-bound version of Judaism) in order to follow Jesus and his disciples. Even so, that overall Christian vision remains essentially within the Jewish traditions of the time. Jesus is not a Karl Marx overturning Adam Smith, but a Thomas Jefferson redefining democracy.

Although most readers today will favour the orthodox interpretation over Thomas' asceticism, we should remain aware of the problems and errors to which the accepted view, like any orthodoxy, may lead. For example, medieval Roman Catholicism became an authoritarian church that essentially denied the individual's right (and duty) to choose

the right way, a central tenet of Christian teaching. Dosto-
evsky (in his great work, *The Brothers Karamazov*) famously
imagines Jesus returning to life at the time of the Spanish
inquisition. The Grand Inquisitor decides that Jesus' teaching, that every individual must knowingly choose the truth
and the light, is heretical, a threat to the church, which
depends on miracle, mystery, and authority; Jesus must be
sacrificed a second time. The constricting authority of the
monopolist church was a major cause of the revolution represented by Protestant Christianity.

The Gospel of Barnabas, to which I refer more directly in
the next chapter, takes a route quite opposed to that of
Thomas. Barnabas, i.e., the writer of the Gospel bearing his
name, sees Jesus as angrily separating from the Jewish tradition, at the same time making it clear that Jesus disclaimed any
special relation with God, which conflicts with Paul and traditional interpretations of the Trinity. The unitarianism of Barnabas' version of Jesus was readily embraced later by Islam (for
which Jesus is a prophet). Barnabas, like Thomas, is not part
of the Christian canon.

We appear to have reached an impasse. We have only limited knowledge of what Jesus actually taught. If we look to
the canonical versions of his teaching, we find important
inconsistencies. If we look outside the canonical books of the
New Testament to writing from the early decades and centuries of the Common (Christian) Era, we find major variations in the basic Christian message, one being unworldly, the
other very much of the world.

I have insisted that we must look to tradition as much as
to what is assuredly attributable to Jesus. The traditions consist of the canonical writing, notably the four Gospels and
Paul's letters, early Christian life and writing, and the numerous continuing Christian ideas, lived and written, up to the

present day. In a way, the banished deviants of the past, on both sides, are helpful in pluralist modern times. If one were to relate a single, clear, unambiguous, central picture of God and truth from Jesus' teaching , no skeptic would ever be convinced. The side branches help us see the richness and variation of the entire tree, whose powerful central trunk helps explain the survival of Christianity over two millennia.

It remains striking that so many people over so many centuries have struggled so brilliantly to define Christian truth. We should be cautious about re-interpreting tradition. At the same time, the Christian (and Judaic) tradition is not a single line, but a montage, sometimes not clearly decipherable, sometimes internally contradictory, which still somehow manages to reflect glorious truth.

Christian dogma, which dates from relatively early times, is discussed in the next chapter. Before turning to the early Christian tradition, the flesh on the bones of Jesus' teaching, I shall summarize what Jesus established, in the context of the Judaic tradition.

There is one God who represents all that is good, including the presence of abiding love. The two essential demands of us are that we live in right relation with God and with our fellows. The Ten Commandments lay down the basic rules of moral life. That code is insufficient, however, because our transgressions begin in our hearts not with our outward behaviour. The first rule in our relations with others is to act towards them as we would have them act towards us. To address that challenge, it is necessary for us to love God before all else, and let his essence rule our relations with others. God is a universal God, accessible to all who approach him in good faith. Sin, our separation from the good of God, is a central part of the human tradition, but our improper acts may be propitiated if we truly follow the example of Jesus and determine to lead a righteous life in the future. I infer that both Thomas and Barnabas, as well as the authors of the Gospels, would agree with that summary, with the understanding that each would insist on adding much to it.

THE EARLY CHRISTIAN TRADITION: DEVELOPING THE MESSAGE

The entire Christian tradition is inseparable from any discussion of Jesus, because of the unreliability and confusion found in Paul's letters and the four Gospels. There are important conflicts both within the Bible and without. "Turning the other cheek" is perhaps the single prescription that is most identified with Jesus and his life, yet his reported behaviour toward the money-lenders is a contrary instance; God himself is not portrayed as possessing unrelieved mercy and kindness in either the Old or the New Testament. Beyond that, the Bible is highly selective in its inclusions. The determination of what Jesus said has value, but more necessary for my purpose is the behaviour (at least the approved behaviour) of his followers.

Paul is usually seen as the principal founder of the Christian church. Paul, a Jew, saw Jesus as renewing the Jewish tradition, rather than breaking from it. Above all, Paul believed that Jesus was the son of God; the relationship of Jesus to God is dealt with in the next chapter, in the context of a discussion of Christian doctrine. For Paul, Jesus was the incarnation of Jewish prophesies. Although the age to come was not fully revealed, the resurrection of Jesus and the coming of the Holy Spirit signaled the rescuing of believers, Jewish or not, and their placement in the kingdom of God's son (Drane in the *Canadian Oxford*, 1993, 578). Paul was not simply concerned with transcendental belief in Jesus and the Holy Spirit. He was dwelt on the implications for the structure of human relationships and for the growth of God's people to "the measure of the full stature of Christ" (Ephesians 4.14).

151

Paul's letters to the Romans, the Corinthians, and the Galatians provide an excellent summary of the early Christian tradition. They were probably written, for the most part, by Paul himself and they remain of central importance to contemporary Christianity. That said, there would be few Christians who would accept every word of Paul's beliefs; the skeptical Christian will undoubtedly believe less than the devout believer, but the debate is not essentially between believers and dissidents, but about selection of the pieces one wants to follow.

To the skeptical Christian, Paul's importance lies in his understanding of the relationship between the human condition and God's truth. To the devout, Paul's truth lies primarily in his interpretation of the death of Jesus, his relationship to God, and an understanding of God's grace. The next chapter examines Christian doctrine more closely. Here, I am turning to the meaning of Christianity for the conduct of our lives, as a basis for the more extended discussion in Chapters 5 and 6. What follows is an attempt to interpret in a summary way the relevance of some of Paul's teaching to contemporary Christianity.

Paul examines two important aspects of Christian belief in his letter to the Romans. A question that insistently haunts adherents of any religion concerns the place of outsiders, not only those who deliberately renounce the believers' god, but also those who never have the opportunity to make a knowledgeable choice. Did all those who lived before Christ go to everlasting hell? What about good-living, highly moral Japanese or Muslims today? Paul asserts that "[W]hat the law requires is written on their hearts"; they instinctively follow the law, and God will judge "the secret thoughts of all" (2.14–16). If the personification of God is removed, Paul's argument is consistent with my earlier argument that access to the good is universally accessible.

From that answer springs the question, "Well, then, why bother joining a religion if, in the end, it does not make any difference, if God is equally accessible to all" That practical question is a focus of Chapter 7. At this point, I shall place Paul's answer to the question in the context of my argument. Believers "are now justified by (God's) grace as a gift" by means of Christ's redemption. Jesus has shown us the right way by his own example and teaching. His willing acceptance of death challenges us as believers to choose the right way, not trusting in ourselves but in the acceptance of God's truth and goodness, which is always there and available. So, non-believers are not *ipso facto* bad people; many are better people, more in tune with the good, than are many Christians. On the other hand, believers can, obviously and literally, access God by means of Jesus' life and death, in a way that non-believers by definition cannot. The Christian route to God and truth is not identical to alternative routes; Christians see their route as the true way, the right choice.

For that reason, non-believers see Christians as arrogating to themselves a special relation with God, effectively asserting their status as superior beings. Clothed in that negative language Christian belief sounds like objectionable arrogance. But then any philosopher or religious leader, anyone who has a coherent world view, is making the same claim to superior knowledge and wisdom—but there is one exception. The nihilist states there is no truth, no good, only human subjectivity. Even nihilists are apt to enjoy tearing down what they see as the primitive (i.e., inferior) beliefs of others. Although nihilist assumptions are prevalent in the journalism and art of the late twentieth century, even those who use nihilist argument (either directly or in its postmodern or existentialist guises) as a club to beat believers, typically hold their own equally dogmatic, ungrounded beliefs as evidence that they are not really nihilists. They are like the dancer with the seven veils. None of the veils has much substance, but without them, the point of the dance is lost. That is why so many use nihilist argument to destroy the faith of others, at the same time refusing to acknowledge that their argument equally destroys the worth of any moral or ethical proposition.

The difference between nihilists and believers (in a religious absolute) is that the superficial dogmas of the day, based in an unjustifiable faith in individual autonomy, are poorly grounded in superficial emotivism. Christianity's claim of access to God, while recognizing the possibility of other routes, is no more arrogant than the world views of contemporary philosophers and scientists; indeed, Christian humility (a quality not widely valued in an individualist society) should make it less so.

Love has an important role in Christianity. Love of God is demanded in the first commandment, but Paul extends that demand. In the previous chapter, I painted love as a somewhat enigmatic characteristic, frequently unrelated to religious truth. Not only does it have many definitions and aspects, it is not, if defined broadly, a co-extensive property of God. The problem is partly a semantic one; the English word is used so loosely that any clear meaning is soon lost.

Love is sometimes seen as the first quality desired in a Christian. It is one thing to recognize truth, good, and God, but if there is no will to love, then the recognition is without value. At the same time, I have argued, one must avoid seeing every alleged manifestation of love, in every day parlance, as a sign of God's presence. To Paul,

> ...love is patient; love is kind; love is not envious or boastful or arrogant or rude. It does not insist on its own way; it is not irritable or resentful; it does not rejoice in wrongdoing, but rejoices in the truth. It bears all things, believes all things, hopes all things,

endures all things. Love never ends....And now faith, hope, and love abide, ...and the greatest of these is love (1 Corinthians 13:4–8,13).

Paul describes love in the context of a caring love of truth readily extended. Hope also becomes an important part of Christian faith, a part that is often overlooked in an age when presentism, belief in progress, and a preference for meaningless optimism prevail.

Paul writes vividly, if not always consistently, of life after death, a difficult concept for thoughtful mainline Christians. He chides his listeners for wondering where the body goes, distinguishing between "heavenly" and "earthly" bodies, between the physical and the spiritual:

Death has been swallowed up in victory. Where, O death, is your victory. Where, O death, is your sting? The sting of death is sin, and the power of sin is the law (1 Corinthians 15:54–56).

Victory comes from Jesus who has set us the example of the perfect life, ending in victorious death; we should all excel in the work of God, because in him work is not in vain (1 Corinthians 15:35–58). Death is not a defeat, not an end, for the person who has followed the way of Jesus.

An atheist may say of a woman nearing the end of her life, "The impending death is no tragedy. She has led a good life and is loved by her children." Christian belief goes beyond that, because the Christian God is totally different from the atheist's idiosyncratic sense of the "good life." The good that lives after us as believers is much more than friends' and relatives' unrooted memories of happiness and good times; the good lives on in and for others, as well as in the continuity of recognition of God. The spiritual good that is left is not memory of enjoyable times, but the love of what is right.

What I have tried to do here is draw out in simple terms the essence of the Christian faith as it emerged in the first hundred or so years after Jesus' death. My central interest lies in how Christian faith should direct our conduct, but conduct emerges from faith; the ten rules are necessary but insufficient. I am developing the idea that truth lies in the heart of Christian faith, and that it is a wholly reasonable truth.

This is an important juncture in my argument. I have attempted a sketch of early Christian belief. I have made only slight effort to distinguish what comes from Jesus and what comes from the various interpretations of his predecessors and followers for three reasons; there is no consensus on a dividing line; there is some ambivalence, even inconsistency, within Jesus' own teaching and practice according to the Gospels; and what is of most practical importance today is the truth within (and beyond) the Christian tradition.

A number of issues have emerged from discussion of the early Christian faith. Many early Christians saw Jesus as the greatest in a line of prophets, speaking the word of God. Some of those would, more radically, see any affirmation of Jesus as the physical son of God as sacrilegious; if God is spiritual, how can he take a material form? Conversely, the conventional Christian belief that Jesus was of divine origin, born of a virgin, was well established in the early years after his death.

Heaven and hell are usually viewed today as conditions of the spirit, quite removed from the time and place of the material world. Thus heaven is a state of being with God, hell being separated from him. In contrast, millions of Christians still believe in heaven and hell as two distinct alternatives, as final and everlasting destinations following death.

A unity was sometimes seen between spirit and flesh, but they were also seen as being two conceptually different elements. There is a conceptual distinction made throughout this book between the spirit and the body, even though I admit that we may at some time find convincing evidence of an underlying unity. But the claim that unity means that genetics and environment have total explanatory power is and will remain unconvincing—we all know in our hearts that we make our own decisions, and change our minds. I do assume that we have freedom of choice, at the same time accepting that there are important influences from our genes, our upbringing, and our social circumstances that make us far from randomly predictable. But if we were entirely unpredictable, our choices made by chance, then we would not be making free choices either. Free human choice involves a basis, a set of criteria, on which decisions are made; choices made in a vacuum would indeed be without meaning. There are many influences on us, and some are more tamed than others, but we all choose when and if to follow our conditioning.

The Christian life was seen by some groups as an ascetic one, separated from the temptations of the material world, a life (as a passerby in secular terms) devoted solely to the worship of God. Other groups were more ambivalent, with the Christian way as being in the world, but not altogether of it. The patterns of life stemming from the two perspectives diverge to extremes. That duality of interpretation is of central importance in this book, concerned as it is with the implications of Christian belief for the conduct of life. There is a crucial and practical question: In a secular world, how can we and to what extent should we separate ourselves within a secure enclave?

Christians should separate themselves psychologically from the material world, even though they mingle with it, if they are to live Christian lives; if they do not we shall be immersed in it. As Meeks, writing on John's Gospel, puts it, "...the 'work of God' is 'to believe', and the one commandment of Jesus is 'to love one another.' Both faith and love, in the Johanine vision of life, separate from the world and bind one to the other believers. It is an intensely corporate, sectarian vision" (p.60). According to the Johanine tradition, "If one loves the world, the love of the Father is not in that person" (1 John 2:15). What is "in the world" is "the desire of the flesh and the desire of the eyes and the ostentation of life" (v.16). Meeks continues,

> Any high-minded Greco-Roman moralist might have said the same thing and also agreed that 'the world passes, and so do its desires' (v.17). What is novel about the Johanine vision is that what is set over against this superficial worldliness is not rational high-mindedness, but rather a passionate, practical love that binds members of the group exclusively to one another and to the God they believe in (p.61).

Although the Johanine writings are more ascetic than the other gospels and Paul's letters, even they show that the choice is not simply between being in the world and retreating hermit-like from it. The message foreshadows the development of a continuing church which provides a haven for believers, who still live their daily working within the larger society. That, I suspect, is the answer for those skeptics who sincerely want to live their religion, as distinct from becoming nominal members. Simply, if one lives only with secular unbelievers, it is almost impossible to be absorbed in the Christian spirit.

There is one central perception that underlies anything that is written about Christianity. In the next chapter, some of the details of dogma are interpreted, but we should be careful not to lose sight of our own God. The argument advanced in Chapter 2 is that God represents the good; it is knowledge of God (whatever terminology is used) that makes the human being distinctive. Belief in God and belief about good conduct are inextricably linked.

Avoiding both the niceties of biblical fact and falsehood and the details of God's being, many nominal Christians, adopting a vaguely Christian-like or Unitarian philosophy or religion, decide, "There is a basic truth to the Judaeo-Christian tradition. I believe in the golden rule. I try to lead a balanced life, making my way in the world and trying to do the right thing. Whether I call myself a Christian or not, or whether others see me as one, and whether or not I go to church are not important as long as I live a good life." There is nothing intrinsically wrong with that outlook on life, and undoubtedly many such people live better lives than do many practising Christians. In later chapters, I examine some of the problems that face us in the complexities of contemporary secular society. It is not easy to find the right way alone. Unfortunately, it is all too easy to make a proclamation like the one above, another thing entirely to stand by undefined and poorly developed principles, when there is no public statement, no public accountability, and minimal private confession. Living a good life alone in a materialist world is much harder than when one lives at least partly within a supportive spiritual community. None of us is impervious to influence from the immediate social environment.

For that reason, Christian dogma, the subject of the next chapter, has value. If one joins a church, if one formally becomes or reinstates oneself as a Christian, one should come to terms with its dogma (which is not the same as accepting one interpretation as final truth). It is easy for skeptical Christians to become hypocrites, mouthing words they do not believe. It is a short step from making dishonest professions of faith to disregarding the rules of Christian conduct, on the grounds that, "No one believes all that stuff. All those old-fashioned rules are out-of-date in the third millennium." The next chapter is an attempt to make Christian dogma accessible and meaningful to the skeptical Christian.

CHAPTER 4

CHRISTIAN DOGMA
AND THE SKEPTIC

There are many Christian denominations, and as many interpretations of dogma. The dogma referenced in this chapter is an Anglican version, simply because I am an Anglican and it is the dogma with which I am familiar. There is no implication that Anglican Christianity is closest to truth; I came to Christianity late in life and, had circumstances been different, I could as readily have become a Roman Catholic or a Presbyterian; there is much that I admire in each of those traditions. My personal attachment to the Anglican denomination is based, apart from my background, on the beauty of its language and music and its centrist, eclectic, and traditionally tolerant position among the Christian churches.

Dogma is helpful in helping make sense of one's day-to-day spiritual life. More conventional Christians may react to my interpretations with anger or scorn, in the belief that I first decided to become a Christian and then proceeded to twist Christian dogma to fit my pre-conceived world view. I have not attempted to turn Christianity into Unitarianism, but I may well have travelled along that route. The label is less important than its truth and utility, and the latter quality is particularly important in this chapter.

In Chapter 1, I described how I began attending a church to support my daughter, who was to be married in an Anglican church. Almost certainly, I was also seeking meaning and spirituality in my life. What attached me to the church was the teaching of Tom Rooke, an evangelical and traditional Christian; simply I listened to him and heard truth. Sometimes he used language I did not fully understand and accept, but I reached for and found truth. I also received excellent teaching from John Webster, now teaching at Oxford University, and Jim Packer, at that time of Regent College, Vancouver. My entry to the church was not so much based on reasoned deduction as on an inductive apprehension of truth. In a sense, this chapter replays what I learned. I see some expression of truth in most Christian dogma and it is that truth that I want to explain to those skeptics, who, like me, are struggling to make sense of a mysterious spirituality. At the same time, the interpretation that follows is obviously based, like the rest of the book, on one window on the elephant.

In the last chapter, it was suggested that there is no clear evidence that Jesus himself believed he was the physical son of God, that half his genes originated in the spiritual world. *The Oxford Companion* suggests that Jesus considered himself to be one in a line of prophets. Discussing his "self-understanding," Fuller writes that his common reference to himself as "the son of man" means the human one, "best understood as a self-effacing reference" (1993, 360). He does continue, however, "that there was a final quality about his message and work that entitles us to conclude that he thought of himself as God's final, definitive emissary to Israel" (360). The use of the terms *Rabbi* and *my Lord* did not denote majesty, but were titles of respect accorded a charismatic person, he continues. He concludes that there is "only limited evidence for an explicit Christology in Jesus' self-understanding, and such evidence as there is critically suspect" (360–361). To the skeptic, the probability that Jesus did not consider himself to be the physical son of God increases rather than decreases his overall credibility; he was a teacher and servant of others, not primarily concerned with his own importance. It is precisely his humility that makes his message engaging and convincing. Although some of his followers quickly claimed him to be the flesh of God, many others did not.

The different traditions in early Christianity were also discussed in Chapter 3. The Gospel attributed to Barnabas quotes Jesus thus—

> God is a good without which there is naught good; God is a being without which there is naught that is; God is a life without which there is naught that liveth; so great that he filleth all and is everywhere. He alone hath no equal. He hath had no beginning, nor will he ever have an end, but to everything hath he given a beginning, and to everything shall he give an end. He hath no father nor mother; he hath no sons, nor brethren, nor companions. And because God has no body, therefore he eateth not, sleepest not, dieth not, walketh not, moveth not, but abideth eternally without human similitude, for that he is incorporeal, uncompounded, immaterial, of the most simple substance (from Ragg and Ragg's translation, 1973, 17–18).

Many conventional Christians would readily accept that quotation were it not for the explicit reference to God's lack of sons. It is from that fine rhetoric and from my account, in Chapter 3, of what the early Christian tradition has taught that I now proceed.

The Nicene Creed is a good place to begin because it has underlain the dogma of the mainline Christian churches for over seventeen centuries. Written almost three hundred years after Christ's death, it cannot be asserted that it directly or simply reflects his teaching. Indeed, the reason for its writing was precisely to suppress widespread dispute and dissent and impose an official version.

There are always problems in determining exactly what religious figures meant in their letters and sermons, even when accuracy is authenticated or assumed. Rhetoric and metaphor are not devices discovered in the twentieth century, although one might think so when one listens to many Christian interpretations of the Bible or its parts. Nevertheless, there is no doubt that the Nicene Creed was deliberately intended to establish a basis for Christian belief, including the central and literal belief in Jesus as the physical son of God. After the first Nicene conference, a process led to the subsequent selection of the canonical books of the New Testament. Large numbers of mainline Christians still accept literal interpretations of the miraculous elements of Jesus' life, and skeptics are often viewed as being close to or in fact being heretical.

Despite that, some will be surprised by the assertion that it would be difficult to find many educated Christians, including ordained ministers of mainline churches, who accept the entire Nicene Creed as literal truth. Typically, conventional believers extract core elements as being necessary bases for Christian belief today, quietly laying some portions aside. I may go further than most others, but my concept is not without precedent.

Below is a traditional version of the Creed, from the Anglican *Book of Common Prayer*, interspersed with my translation for the skeptic.

I believe in one God the Father Almighty,
Maker of heaven and earth,

And of all things visible and invisible:

I believe in God,
whose goodness is universal and invincible,
who alone gives authentic meaning to our world.

And in one Lord Jesus Christ,
the only-begotten Son of God,
Begotten of the Father before all worlds;
God of God; Light, of Light; Very God of Very God;
Begotten, not made;
Being of one substance with the Father;
Through whom all things were made;
Who for us men and for our salvation
came down from heaven,

I believe in the teaching of Jesus Christ,
God's messenger on earth,
who truly reflected God's eternal goodness.
I believe Jesus lived to serve God
and to redeem all people from sin.

And was incarnate by the Holy Ghost
of the Virgin Mary,
And was made man, and was crucified also for us
under Pontius Pilate.

I believe that Jesus lived and died for us,
a willing sacrifice for the mitigation of our sins.

He suffered and was buried,
And the third day he rose again
according to the Scriptures,
And ascended into heaven,
And sitteth at the right hand of the Father.
And he shall come again with glory
to judge both the quick and the dead:

Whose kingdom shall have no end.

His teaching did not die with him, but remains as
God's and his judgment on us,
both as we live and when we die, for all time.

And I believe in the Holy Ghost, The Lord,
The Giver of Life,
Who proceedeth from the Father and the Son,
Who with the Father and the Son
together is worshipped and glorified,
Who spake by the prophets.

I believe that God's spirit is accessible to everyone,
in the form of good and truth, interpreted by Jesus
Christ, permitting us to
live full and open lives in the light of God.

And I believe One, Holy, Catholic,
and Apostolic Church.
I acknowledge one Baptism for the remission of sins.
And I look for Resurrection of the dead,
and the Life of the world to come.

I believe in one universal church
based on the acknowledgment of the God
of everlasting truth and goodness.
I acknowledge baptism
into membership of the church
as a means of access to God's grace
and look to the goodness in our lives to continue
after us.

I am not, I hasten to say, suggesting that my or any revised
version should replace the traditional one. My point is that the
traditional creeds are beautiful myth, myth that contains essential truth. Even skeptics will not all rush to endorse my exact

translation, which illustrates precisely why we are better off with the original. How many decades and how many angry exchanges and divisions would it take to agree on a new one? In 325, the Nicene Creed was approved by a massive majority of a highly selective group. In 2000, it is impossible that any conceivable revised version would receive consensual support from those who call themselves Christians, or from their leaders.

Critics, religious and non-religious alike, may see my tacit acceptance of the traditional form of the creed as hypocritical. But that can hardly be the case if one publicly explains what one sees as its truth. I do not jump up in my church in an attempt to impose my version on everyone else, but neither do I dishonestly claim to believe that the Christian myth is primarily based on an elaborate set of magical historical facts.

Before strong Christian readers too hastily brand me as a heretic, they should recall the comments of the official Commission on Doctrine in the Church of England (published in 1938 as *Doctrine in the Church of England*).

> Statements affirming particular facts may be found to have value as pictorial expressions of spiritual truths, even though the supposed facts themselves did not actually happen...It is not therefore of necessity illegitimate to accept and affirm particular clauses of the creeds while understanding them in their symbolic sense.

Even a superficial study of the creed raises questions as to why the factual truth of the virgin birth (with its requirement of spiritual genes) and the physical resurrection should be considered crucial to Christian belief in this age, understandable as it may have been in 325. After all, few mainline Christians believe that Jesus Christ factually came down from heaven and today "sits at the right hand of God." No more do they believe that Jesus "ascended into heaven," in either corporeal or spiritual form, for the simple reason that they know that in the universe there is no up or down—the world of 2001, unlike that of 325, is not flat. They do not believe in heaven as a physical destination, for Jesus or for human beings. Our disagreement is not a choice between all fact and all legend, but about what is the essential truth of the creed.

Conventional Christians are also indeterminate about what they understand by Jesus "coming again." Christian leaders are sensibly vague about the "second coming" of Jesus, with perhaps the most common interpretation being the metaphorical one that we are judged in some way at our death, that our lives are then examined in the light of God's goodness and the life and teachings of Jesus. Another interpretation (and one does not have to choose between them) is that our daily lives and actions should be seen in the context set by God and Jesus. It is not Christian to calculate that one can live one's life selfishly, perhaps with an occasional confession to free one's conscience, as long as one is prepared for a deathbed "repentance"—an act which is unlikely to be sincere in those circumstances, and, sincere or not, insufficient to offset a discreditable life overall.

Similarly, the "resurrection of the dead" is interpreted in mainline churches in a variety of ways, with most ministers and priests understandably unwilling to accept a literal division of human souls into those bound for heaven and those bound for hell, with or without a half-way station in limbo, either material or spiritual. Our spirit, our soul, whatever that may be, does survive us; since becoming a Christian, I think more about the lives of my maternal grandmother and her sister, the two examples of Christians I knew and admired when I was a boy (at the same time as I inconsistently rejected their religion, which in an important way made them what they were).

If the creed's "Apostolic" is taken to imply an episcopal church (governed by bishops who succeed the apostles), millions of the strongest and most sincere Protestant Christians will dissent. Yet it is reasonable to assume that that is what the conference intended, given that those attending were bishops. I see no religious or spiritual demand for an apostolic church; popes and Church of England bishops through the ages have not always been models of Christian devotion. There are material advantages to the apostolic tradition, in that a good, strong pope maintains some coherence within the Roman Catholic church; the archbishops of Canterbury, with less authority, have been less successful in the Anglican church. But coherence comes at a price. Belief in male priests and rejection of all forms of birth control, irrespective of the circumstances, are both far from obvious Christian truths and difficult to decree on the basis of a reasonable interpretation of the broad Christian tradition.

One may try to guess what was in the minds of those who wrote the creed, but, again, few thoughtful Christians believe that any specific writer or collectivity in Christian tradition is infallible anyway. Even if we were able to determine which parts of the creeds were and were not considered factual when they were written, in the minds of most of those present, there is no need for us today to follow blindly, ignoring all we know about the writing of the Bible and the larger Christian tradition excluded from the conference.

Some skeptics will be wary of joining a church where many members, perhaps most, believe to be factual a number of statements that they themselves consider improbable or even ridiculous. That feeling is understandable, and I would not be a church member if I thought I were the only one not to take all dogma literally. That would indeed be hypocritical. I might have joined a Christian church in 1972, when I became a Unitarian, had the Christian churches at that time appeared to be more open to dissent. But today, there are few if any members of mainline congregations, including the ministers and priests, who take every word of the creeds literally.

More important to me is whether the key ideas and values behind the church are true, in the broad sense of that word. It is not of great religious or spiritual significance that some people have different beliefs about factual truth from others. One supports political parties without signing on for every plank in their platform and every act taken by the government one voted for. Indeed, it is sensible to doubt the wisdom and courage of those who always agree with the position of their party and its leaders. Support and love of family persist without unquestioning belief in the infallible virtue and unlimited wisdom of all its members; overly protective parents who deny any failing in their offspring are objects of pity or amusement.

I frequently oppose the public policy positions taken by leaders of the Anglican church in Canada. I could never see, for example, why it should be morally preferable to choose to take a vacation holiday in Cuba under a totalitarian regime, as advised by my diocese, rather than one in Florida, part of a democratic country which has welcomed thousands of refugees from Cuban totalitarianism. It is commonplace for judges to disagree on the interpretation of carefully enacted laws; why should one expect everyone to agree to a single interpretation of a set of beliefs originally composed centuries ago?

If we expect our church, or any document written by human beings, to be infallible, we shall surely be disappointed. God is by definition infallible, but he can only be interpreted by fallible people. In the unlikely event that Jesus was infallible, such infallibility must contend with the ambiguities and inconsistencies within the biblical records of his words and actions.

I turn now to components of Christian dogma, explaining them in traditional terms together with my own commentary. My view of the nature of God and Jesus should be reasonably clear by now. In most religions, God is understandably given human properties; even I refer to "him" not it. It is difficult (and unhelpful) to avoid metaphor in the discussion of spiritual truth. I do not see God as being superhuman, a superior version of me. Nor do I see Jesus as being physically of "one substance" with God, for the good reason that God does not have material substance, but I do see him as being the exemplary founder of the greatest spiritual and moral tradition the world has known, based on an exceptional access to the spirit of God. My purpose here is to develop the essential truth and value of important aspects of traditional dogma.

The 1952 revision of Griffith Thomas's book *The Catholic Faith*, first published in 1904, is my primary source for the traditional explanation of dogma. The title refers to the Anglican Catholic, not the Roman Catholic, faith, but the differences between them have little bearing on my interpretation. In the following chapters, my concern is with Christian behaviour, morality, and duty. In this chapter, I am interested with what the Christian believes, in terms of a personal faith.

Atonement is a difficult idea for many Christians, and a barrier for non-Christians. It is, however, significant. In my translation of the Nicene Creed, I referred to Jesus sacrificing himself "for the mitigation of our sins." Griffith Thomas states that Christ has suffered for our sins, the just for the unjust, in order to bring us to God. The church has declared that Jesus "redeemed me and all mankind" because Jesus suffered and was crucified to reconcile God to us, and to be a sacrifice, not only for original guilt, but also for the actual sins of all human beings (52).

One does not have to believe in a divine plan or in any particular factual version of the events surrounding the death of Jesus to recognize the importance of the separation between God and the sins we commit on earth. Jesus was certainly not the first to attack sin, but he was exemplary in the strength of his confrontation; the recognition of sin as a universal attribute is a crucial contribution of Judaism. But Jesus was not simply addressing Jews, insiders, or any chosen people. He was neither the first nor the last martyr to choose death, but the symbolism of his death is unique. Put simply, the atonement means that Jesus chose to die to demonstrate to us, to all human beings, the importance of right behaviour, and paradoxically, to show us that there is life after sin; we can be forgiven. One can personify the forgiver as God or Jesus, but the reality is that we can be forgiven as we forgive others, not just by ourselves and those whom we have harmed, but in that great river of life, of goodness. Nonbelievers are particularly derisive of forgiveness, particularly in its Roman Catholic form of interpersonal confession and absolution. They claim that forgiveness is a formal licence to go out and sin again, and return again for another absolution. To me, genuine regret, penitence, combined with genuine desire for good, helps to wash away the stain of our bad behaviour in that eternal river. Sin and confession can be and are trivialized; Jesus did not tell his followers to sin and then confess, but to confess and sin no more. The continuing life of Jesus within the tradition is testament to the importance of his message. The direct confession of sin, to the person who has been hurt or to a priest, is likely to have more effect on us than a private sense of misgiving, whether it is soon to be rationalized and put aside or left to gnaw at our conscience.

Forgiveness lies between wrongdoing and the healthy continuation of one's life. Lives consumed with jealousy, envy, greed, corruption, hunger for power, and love of self are apt to be consumed by bitterness and corrosion. That is not to say that non-Christians are inevitably affected by those qualities; but they are evident in many public and private lives in the secular world. The contrast between the Christian life and the corrosion of day-to-day secular life is most affectingly described in a novel by Georges Bernanos, *The Diary of a Country Priest*, originally published before the Second World War. It shows the effects of a lack of contrition, of unrecognized sin, of denial. On the other hand, a life consumed by unassuaged guilt (deep regret not mitigated by confession), while a lesser evil, is also likely to be constricted. In the same way, a failure to forgive others who, correctly or not, one believes have brought one harm can also embitter one's life; Christian contemplation helps to rid one of grudges, however justifiable they may seem at the moment.

Narrow Christian asceticism, found in the original Gospel of Thomas (not to be confused with Griffith Thomas) and the monasterial tradition, and, to a lesser extreme, in the writings including the Gospel attributed to John, makes it easier to avoid the temptation and sin of the world, but may also thereby miss the joys of the world, most obviously those of children and family. While the ascetic path is one path to God, and one that may be appropriate for many at times of their lives, living a Christian life does not require that choice. Moreover, as with all choices, there are dangers in asceticism; there may be too much contemplation of self and one's right relation with God, to the exclusion of others whose lives one might enrich, as well as a too narrow life that misses much of the glory and beauty in truth. In short, complete absorption in the world is likely to result in lack of genuine contrition, unassuaged guilt, failure to forgive others, and spiritual corruption, but almost total separation from temptation is not an authentic answer for most people—it is also a separation from much of life.

Forgiveness for our own misdoing is difficult for the Christian skeptic, because it may be imagined as coming from an unbelievable man-god, or a living Jesus, who can, personally and directly, assure him that all is forgiven. But the skeptic too needs access to forgiveness, and can find it in that river of goodness, that flows interminably, and in which waters the skeptic too may bathe, and live again in the light. In the traditional terms of the *Book of Common Prayer*, God "desireth not the death of a sinner, but rather that he may turn from his wickedness, and live"; I interpret the comma after "wickedness" to suggest that "live" means more than "stay alive." When feasible, forgiveness by the others with whom one lives is a key part of recovery. Reasonable forgiveness both of oneself and of others makes for a harmonious and full life. Constant dwelling on the past, the wrongs given and received, shrivels and dulls one's spiritual progress. One makes amends as best one can (often impossible for mistakes only half-buried in the past), and goes on to *live* in harmony with God and one's neighbour.

Atonement lies at the heart of the meaning of Easter, the most important Christian time of celebration. The meaning of Easter draws too on pre-Christian times, delight in the renewal of life in the northern hemisphere spring. Jesus died and was indeed born again, in the sense that he is alive in the Christian faith. Easter is both a time of sadness, if one thinks of our never-ending inhumanity, (do we not read of "crucifixion" every day?) and a time of joy, when we determine to overcome our nasty habits and begin anew.

Christian use of the term "atonement" is thus different from Jewish interpretation. For Jews, the Day of Atonement is the day on which God judges their behaviour; it is part of their most important celebration, Yom Kippur. Obviously, early Christians, many themselves Jewish, drew from the Jewish tradition; equally obviously, Jews do not see value in the story of Jesus' death.

Christians talk about living in the *grace* of God. Grace, according to Thomas, consists of all of God's gifts to our spiritual life; they have two major components. First is God's favourable attitude towards us, his presence in Jesus; second is his giving us the power and blessing to act in his name, the gift of the will and determination (87).

The importance of grace is that it is accessible to all; the power of God's goodness is such that anyone with faith can reach it and use it. It is not a question of special people being given grace by an almighty power, while others are left out; that idea would certainly seem ridiculous to the skeptic. But there is nothing unreasonable in believing that the good is always there for everyone; all that is needed is for us to accept and embrace it. If our belief is strong enough, we can both reach out to it, believe it, and then act on it. It is worth quoting again the beautiful words from Matthew 7:7–8:

> Ask, and it will be given you; search and you will find; knock and the door will be opened for you. For everyone who asks receives, and everyone who searches finds, and for everyone who knocks, the door will be opened.

Sanctification is the state of admission of the spirit of God, the acceptance of grace. Some Christians put special emphasis on being saved and will tell you the day and time when that event took place. Other Christians, not only skeptics, reject the idea that, for them, there is or can be a time and place, an event rather than a development or turning; for many, becoming a Christian is both spontaneous and, paradoxically, gradual. It is spontaneous because neither the cause nor the decision is immediately identifiable; but the conversion takes place over time. It may not be helpful to try too hard to find Jesus or God behind every crossing, behind every piece of fortune. One does not find God's river by means of a map or formula, but by living in the right and recognizing his power and grace.

The word "saint" is usually used to refer to all members of the church, in good faith, to all those who have accepted God's grace and have tried to welcome the spirit of God. This does not of course mean that saints are all exceptionally well-behaved. But saints can be distinguished from non-church members, not because God has chosen them, but because they have freely chosen God. Both Christians and non-Christians sometimes see the claim to a distinction between saints, those sanctified, and outsiders as a denial of God's universality, as a claim to elite status no different from the Jewish claim to have come from a chosen people.

I see it simply as a matter of definition, lacking any specious assumption of superiority. It is invidious for an American to describe herself as a Democrat if she has never joined the party and never votes in an election. It is offensive to call oneself a liberal if one does not support, for example, individual freedom and freedom of speech. Clearly, Christian access to God means acceptance of God's grace (in whatever terms one chooses to use) and the will to be a Christian in good faith, to be sanctified. There is no necessary implication that others can have no access to God, but simply that they cannot honestly call their access Christian.

Without jumping to the extreme of claiming that any person can reach God by whatever means makes her feel good, one would be arrogant to claim that Christians can determine precisely which other routes are legitimate and which unacceptable. Skeptical as well as most other mainline Christians recognize that God is universally accessible, which is not the same thing at all the same as asserting that any route to God is as good as any other.

The Christian God is ultimate truth. Are there other reasonable ways to describe and reach the true God? Undoubtedly. Are all religions and sects of equal truth and value? Certainly not. I have little doubt that some Muslims, and members of many sects and religious faiths, find God's truth as effectively as or better than many Christians, but there are clearly others, in all parts of the world, who deny the good and live inharmonious or evil lives.

By recent tradition, a Christian is baptized soon after birth, one of the two holy sacraments (the other being the Lord's Supper, Communion). Baptism is a sign of membership in the church but is always "conditional," having no spiritual power of its own, according to Thomas (103). In some Christian churches, baptism is delayed until adolescence, when individuals will understand and determine their own choices. Later, I discuss the religious education of children; suffice it to say here that the young adolescent is not necessarily in much better shape to truly choose the right way than is the newborn baby. As I have said, there may be no single moment when one sees the light; and adulthood, increasingly in the current age, is a time for moving both in and out of faith. Confirmation, not a sacrament, but an important and deliberate act within the individual's life, is used in many denominations to secure sanctification, to confirm genuine membership in the Christian church.

There are arguments for both early and late baptism; I see nothing wrong, no denial of freedom, in marking young people as children of Christ and raising them within a set of beliefs. The most determined atheists teach their children some widely shared values as truth (such as not being nasty to their brothers and sisters), as well as, all too often, some peculiar pieces of groundless ideology (perhaps that all people are the same, that poverty is the fault of government, and that everything is relative). It would be perverse for Christians not to raise their children as Christians; talk of human autonomy is empty—yes, of course, they should and will make up their own minds as adults, but in the meantime it makes sense to try and

make them good and decent people. If one's first goal is autonomy, freedom, then one contradicts Christian thought, but
freedom is necessary to become a Christian.

Justification is the process by which the individual deliberately moves towards God. It might be seen as starting naturally
during one's preparation for confirmation (or adult baptism
and confirmation) and continuing afterwards, but that is not
necessarily the case. The adult convert may be moving towards
God long before preparation for baptism or confirmation
begins; some converts choose never to go through the formal
rituals. The word "justification" is known to computer users
as the means by which they align the text with the left- and
right-hand margins of the page. That is a good metaphor for
Christian justification; we smooth out our rough edges.

According to Thomas, "Atonement is the Divine side, Justification the human side of redemption." It is connected "with
the one question which, beyond all others, has been exercising
the mind and conscience in all ages: How shall man be just with
God?" It is concerned "with our spiritual relation to God, not
with our spiritual condition of soul in the sight of God." "Sin is
self-assertion, disobedience, rebellion" and justification is the
means by which we restore the "true relation with God" (55).

Prayer lies at the core of Christian belief, but it is also at
odds with modern life. Many people, both Christian and non-
Christian, mistakenly identify prayer with wants (often mistakenly described as needs). Modern life is increasingly material, and, as we become richer, our wants become more diverse
and ever more costly. One might hope that as one's basic needs
are satisfied, there will be greater emphasis on the spiritual life,
but that appears not to be the case. More material possessions
sometimes feed a competitive frenzy for more. Even in the
mainline churches in countries like Canada, where death from
hunger or lack of shelter is almost unknown, one would think

that the greatest emphasis would be on Christian spirituality and conduct; in fact, some churches seem obsessed not only with poverty, but with the relative distribution of material goods, in a word, with government, the state. Prayer to God is in practice replaced by demands of the state.

According to Thomas, prayer is a sense of need, an expression of desire, and an attitude of consecration (89). "Prayer is the means of expressing and maintaining our right relation to God." It leads to the "constant realization of the presence of God." By prayer "the will of God is made known to us." "Who does not realize constantly the 'plague of his own heart'? Who is not ever confronted with the terrible fact and awful possibilities of 'indwelling sin'? Yet who does not also know that 'prayer is power,' because it brings power? The heart becomes garrisoned, the conscience is made more sensitive, the will is strengthened, and the soul protected on every side." We "perceive and know what things we ought to do." God's service is "perfect freedom" when prayer "lubricates" life (90).

In short, the purpose of prayer has little or nothing to do with our daily wants, everything to do with our spiritual needs, needs we may not fully understand until we pray. It is true that the church language of prayer all too often defines prayer apparently or factually in the language of wants. Church members are asked to pray for a good harvest and for the recovery of a person suffering from disease or accident. There are even rotating prayers, where various churches, ministers, bishops, criminals, and troubled countries are prayed for in turn.

A friend of mine liked to say that God always listens to our prayers, but sometimes he says no; but the language of wants is unhelpful, even when it recognizes that the most reasonable and desirable wants, such as the recovery of a young mother from a dreadful illness, may be rejected. Thomas helpfully identifies prayer with our right relation with God. Prayer may be seen as a way station during the process of justification; it gives us time to review our failures and think of better choices tomorrow. Our spiritual needs have nothing to do with better housing or a new car, or even for the *miraculous* recovery of a dying loved one.

The essence of prayer is communication with God. But, the skeptic will quickly ask, "Communication is two way; how can your non-human God talk back to you?" That question is as simplistic as it is pertinent; it assumes that communication can only take place between two living human beings using the same language. That is not so. Human beings, particularly in the day of the triumph of what we mistakenly call communications— telephones, e-mail, public relations, and advertising—are addicted to talk. But even our pets frequently communicate their feelings and wishes to us; books and pictures communicate ideas; we see signs all around us, such as trees turning red and orange as summer wanes, that tell us what is happening in the natural world around us. We sense as much from those whom we love as much as they tell us. So why should it be difficult for our apprehension of God, whose rules may be "written on our hearts," to help us understand where we have gone astray, and help us find a better route? But pets, books, trees, and loved ones are concrete, God is abstract, it will be said. But everything concrete has to be processed through our minds; our understanding of the good speaks to us as eloquently as our memories of admonitions from our parents; God is likely to be more accurate and more powerful to a practising Christian because his message is reinforced and attended regularly.

It is sometimes thought that prayerful communication is between mind and conscience; believers may think that their conscience is effectively expressing the word of God. That may or may not be the case, depending on the person and the circumstance. One's conscience is built up significantly by means of life experiences. It is perfectly possible to feel guilty for having done what one knows to be the right thing, if the social context and peers support, teach, and expect ignoble and unjust behaviour, or if there is a conflict between friendship of and loyalty to an individual who we know has already done or is going to do something wrong. But a properly constructed conscience is one way in which the good may be communicated, and the evil reproved. God can only communicate through our conscience if we allow it. Contemplation, reason, the example of others, and the reading of formal prayers are all contexts in which God can communicate; but it is easy enough to shut off God, and most of us do.

Making ourselves right with God is the prime purpose of prayer, but it is not the only one. Prayer for our neighbours, unhelpful if it assumes that God is going to annul the ravages of cancer or hand them a winning lottery ticket, is helpful if we can genuinely reflect on their needs, their problems, and our right relations with them. Prayer then serves a dual purpose; we make ourselves right with God partly by making ourselves right with our neighbours. Our neighbours are not the people next door, or friends and acquaintances. Our neighbours include those whom we dislike. As we pray for them, not out of condescension or self-righteousness, but in humble spirit, recognizing our own shortcomings, and looking at our own behaviour through their eyes, the dislike may diminish or dissipate.

It is difficult, in a secular world, to separate prayer from the wants and "rights" of consumers. It is quite wrong to see God as an obedient magic servant who will do our bidding if we are righteous people; that is the consumer's god. It is equally wrong to think that God is keeping a score of our good and bad actions (even if we think in metaphorical terms). It is simply our job to plough ahead, looking for the right way, with God's help.

One of the greatest errors is to assume that God will give us what we deserve, and that God will intervene to help good people when they are in trouble, or save them from an automobile accident. We all know that bad or nasty things happen to good people, that volcanoes do not simply explode on the wicked, that criminals and liars sometimes profit, and that fear, horror, and death are not neatly distributed along lines of religious faith. Indeed, it is offensive to imagine that a humanized God could save people from disease and danger, because that capacity would mean that God either wills the untimely death of good people or stands indifferently aside when they face destruction.

Does that mean it is wrong or ignorant to pray for others in need? It all depends on what we mean when we pray. It is not wrong to pray for another's recovery (expressing one's sympathy), but it is inappropriate, if by praying we are making God directly responsible for the outcome. However, if prayer is seen to express empathy with others and if we think about what we are able to do to help some of the afflicted whom we claim to feel for, then it is of great value in our Christian life. We may sensibly well pray not only that we are ourselves are in a right relationship with those in need, but that they too accept their fate with courage and dignity, and come to terms with those around them.

That is not all. There are two other reasons why prayer is important in terms of our relations with others. Hope is a vitally important attitude and feeling in the Judaeo-Christian tradition, notably in the epistles of the New Testament. Prayer is entirely commendable and appropriate when it dwells on hope. If a close friend or relative is dying from an irremediable disease, we should think of the good she has contributed in her life, be grateful for what she has given others and ourselves, and hope that what is left of her life will be peaceful, accepting, and filled with a sense of completeness. She may die fighting her disease, but we should not hope that she goes raging against God and fate into that dark night; her own good will continue, as will her God, who has no responsibility for her pain and death.

But of course, hopeful prayer is not solely for the dying and afflicted, and not at all for the dead. Rather surprisingly, the Anglican church's contemporary Book of Alternative Services includes prayers for the dead. It is equally irrational for the fundamentalist believer and the skeptical Christian to ask God to intervene on behalf of those already dead. If there is an aware afterlife of heaven or hell, that choice is made at death; and if there is not, (and I do not believe we shall meet our family and friends after death) there is nothing at that stage to pray for. We should of course remember the dead, an act that is closer to the Anglican and Protestant tradition.

Prayer for those we know, who are not in any immediate trouble or danger, is also highly desirable in the sense that we can hope for them, and be grateful for what they give. In that sense, I frequently pray, in the context of meditation, for my wife, children, and grandchildren; that prayer is often a form of gratitude.

There is one other sense in which prayer may be helpful, one that is particularly difficult for the skeptic. Only the most determined rationalist insists that events, such as the course of accident and disease, are simply explicable in terms of current scientific knowledge of the body's physics and chemistry, that there is and can be no connection between mind and emotion on the one hand and physical events on the other. No one fully understands those complex relationships, but that does not mean they do not exist. It is clearly possible that the knowledge or sense of support and sympathy from others will improve one's chances of recovery from a disease. We know, for example, that the mind and emotions affect such problems as hypertension, strokes, and heart attacks. Even accidents are not simply a matter of bad luck; some are more predisposed than others. Indeed, non-believers are apt to put as much faith in luck as fundamentalists place in God's direct intervention. The causes of human behaviour are many and complex. Both chance and faith in God play their parts.

The admission that prayer may possibly affect the course of various physical problems may be seen as contradicting the earlier assertion that God does not choose to save some from death and not others. There is no contradiction. One cannot at this time fully understand the ways different people react to the support of those around them, known or unknown, but one need not therefore jump to the unreasonable conclusions that any surprising recovery must be attributed to personal intervention by God, and, as a necessary corollary, that God has decided to kill another good person off in the prime of life, by willing a surprise fatal heart attack or horrifying road accident. Indeed, such a leap of illogic is, I believe, preposterous. One may reasonably pray for others without blaming or praising God for whatever ensues. At the same time, one should draw and rely on God's goodness to make one's prayers authentic. A half-hearted or insincere prayer is corrosive.

Although there is a considerable gap between a literal understanding of the Nicene creed and my metaphorical interpretation, there is often an easier leap for the skeptic in traditional prayers and psalms, some centuries older (and less political in origin) than the Nicene creed. Once one makes allowance for some unavoidable humanization of God, many are as true and valid today as they ever were. Spontaneous prayer is valuable in private, and our lives are unlikely to be improved by simply mouthing familiar, formal prayers in church if our minds have strayed to the world of what we have to do after church. But spontaneous prayer can also be readily corrupted into self-pity, as we dwell on our own afflictions, and even more so if we ask God's intervention to help ourselves in material ways, or if our prayer for others is based substantially on possible inconvenience to ourselves. Moreover, a personal, spontaneous, and genuine prayer in church made publicly by one person may be meaningless and even disconcerting to others; it is not a sign of humility to assume that our own problems, and those besetting our own family, take precedence over those of others. The best approach is a combination of private communion with God, in our own way, our own time, and alone, together with the regular recitation of traditional prayers in a church setting, where many of like mind join together. The two do not mix well. The recitation of formal prayers alone may easily become formulaic; the imposition of one's own concerns on unsuspecting others can be self-seeking.

As in many other aspects of life, spiritual growth benefits from both regular routine and spontaneous authenticity. If we constantly search for the new and the stimulating, we may lose our centre, constantly searching for some new titillation. If we rely solely on the tried and true, we may become dulled and restricted. There is no perfect combination that suits everyone.

In short, prayer requires a number of conditions to be effective. One must first have faith in God, a firm belief that a good exists that one must love. That faith should be accompanied by knowledge of one's own imperfections, but not by a morbid sense of worthlessness. The knowledge of good and evil is a precious human quality; it can be a burden (in the form of persisting guilt and a lack of self-respect), but it is also potentially liberating. The skeptic has no expectation that God is a human answering machine waiting to address his wishes, even if they would be expedient for him. God will provide neither Nintendo for the child nor sight to the blind, but will give access to the strength to manage without them. Although God does not speak, one should listen and learn as well as talk.

Is the dogma described in this chapter really necessary? If one believes in God and lives a good life, is that not sufficient? Some of those who have drifted away from their childhood religion find dogma particularly repellent. It is difficult to lay down the prerequisites for becoming a skeptical Christian, which is a good reason why more orthodox and fundamentalist Christians find skeptical and liberal interpretations so abhorrent. There is a slippery slope; when one starts down the slippery slope, where should one stop and why?

I cannot prove to the skeptical Christian that she must accept the dogma described in this chapter, but some form of dogma is the framework that makes sense of being a Christian. The dogma that has a life of centuries still makes sense today if it is translated into our ways of knowing. Once that is accomplished, it could well be superfluous or divisive to try to change the language of the church. Most people find a framework helpful; the lack of it easily makes one's religion self-serving.

Although current liturgy used by traditional churches has stood the test of time,, there is no essential reason why it should not be changed to make it more intelligible—it has already survived translation into hundreds of languages and forms of worship, provided that the change is consensual rather than divisive. The many existing paths to Christian truth, represented in denominations and sects, as well as in divisions within those sections, should not be seen either as desirable diversity or as regrettable discord, but simply as the inevitable outcome of different perspectives as people of different origin and experience seek the elephant through holes in the tent, or, to change the metaphor, turn blinded towards the searing light of God. There is no cause for distress because the Anglican church, as one prominent example, is divided within itself—some churches high, with services and doctrine similar to traditional Roman Catholicism, others evangelical, charismatic, and traditional Protestant, some liberal and secularized in terms of human conduct, others conservative. If there are different paths to truth, it is unreasonable to expect Christians all to choose the same one; if the Nicene creed cannot bind (and it has not since the Reformation), what else can?

There are two other important elements in Christian life as well as fundamental truth and its associated dogmas. Christian conduct and church membership are the subject of the remaining chapters. The former is the more crucial, just as the truth of God is infinitely more important than its dogmas. Religious faith and its development into a code of expression are of minimal value if they are represented neither in the pattern of life that members believe they ought to follow or in their actual behaviour. As for church membership, it is simply a means to help realize the other three elements: knowledge and love of God, understanding of their expression, and Christian conduct.

There are two core aspects to my religious faith. One is the idea of an absolute God who represents an objective truth; the other is the idea that belief in God must make a difference to how I live my life. If the truth of God makes no difference to one's life, then why should one care about one's own or others' beliefs? If it makes no difference, then it really does make sense to confine Christianity to Sunday morning—the expectation of the non-religious secular public, one all too often fulfilled by secular Christians. In that case, it is difficult to distinguish a choice of church from a choice of a concert, a game of bridge, or a movie. It is rational to conceal, from oneself and others, what is of no enduring importance to anyone.

The next chapters are significant in a way that this chapter is not. A framework may help, but when the understanding of right is internalized, it becomes almost superfluous. In contrast, conduct speaks more about character than does any professed dogma. When we die, we shall not be remembered because we attended church, knew the rites, and prayed a lot. We shall be remembered for what we were in the sight of family, friends, and neighbours, for our character, for what we returned to God's ever-flowing river of life.

In Chapter 3, reference was made to three versions of Christianity, a factual and fundamentalist version, which saw the Bible as relating, in its essentials, factual truths about God and Jesus Christ; an aesthetic version, which interpreted Christian writing in terms of a narrative, the spirit of which stems from its beauty; and my mythical version, which interprets Christian writing as providing a compelling version of the truth about God and the human condition—the narrative being a mixture of historical fact and figurative embellishment. My commentary on dogma in this chapter is based on that third interpretation; in developing spiritual truth, the precise division between historical fact and metaphor is irrelevant. The interpretation will be unaffected if future research shows that either more or fewer of the biblical narratives are historically accurate than is currently assumed by most historians.

None of this is to assert that the other two interpretations are simply wrong-headed and harmful, any more than the choice of Christianity implies that, everywhere where it differs from Islam or Buddhism, it, not the alternative, is correct in some finally, objective way. Certainly, fundamentalism sometimes leads to or is captured by a terrible evil, evidenced throughout Western history. Equally surely, a faith based only on aesthetics can easily leave its adherents free to live a loose and immoral life, which many do. The third way, of myth, is as open to abuse as the others; once one interprets truth broadly outside a narrow tradition one is prey to any passing enthusiasm. If everyone were to agree on what a truly Christian life is and then live that life, the world would be a different place, but neither of those events is imaginable. People would no longer be human, with a knowledge of good and evil. All human projects are snagged by evil. The quality of reason, which permits us to choose between good and evil, guarantees there can be no final agreement and no finally perfect world. So the next chapters are not paths to Utopia, but a painstaking attempt to put Christian truth into contemporary action in the democratic West.

CHAPTER 5

VIRTUE AND CHRISTIAN CHARACTER

I have attempted to establish a basis for the Christian faith on a reasonable interpretation of the Christian tradition. That faith may be seen as being revealed in the sense that the individual has to be able and willing to perceive what others claim does not exist. There remains an air of mystery, of uncertainty, about the nature of God, notably concerning origin and communication with human beings, but not one of internal contradiction or blind faith. Even if readers embrace most of the argument up to this point, however, their religion is meaningless if it is not translated into behaviour. To believe in the good and at the same time ignore it belies the initial affirmation. That statement does not imply that one's Christianity consists of building up gold points with God, only that genuine love of God requires an attempt to act on that love. Chapters 5 and 6 examine Christian faith in action. What follows from an acceptance of the various aspects of God that I have presented? I first establish a Christian code, drawn from the tradition and then, in the following chapter, place it in the context of contemporary life.

P.J. O'Rourke, a light-hearted American commentator on the human condition, has observed that, "Everyone wants to save the world; no one wants to help Mom do the dishes." I do not know whether O'Rourke is a Christian or tries to live a Christian life, but his comment does capture an essential Christian truth. We first improve the human condition by putting ourselves right with God and our neighbours, not by delegating our responsibility to government and its agencies. Promoting socialism, capitalism, or universal human rights, as the solution to the human problem, however sincere and unselfish one's rationale, does not absolve one from helping one's neighbour in a direct fashion; indeed, involving oneself with secular causes (for the greater good of mankind) easily provides a cover for not doing more for others directly.

There are traps for the Christian in today's secular world. The fundamentalist Christian may dwell so much on sin, particularly the sins of others, that loving God is lost in a flurry of denunciations of the ungodly; she may believe so strongly that she will try to pass laws to force others to act on her convictions. There is also the danger of withdrawing from the world in a renunciation of all secular concerns. The liberal Christian, in contrast, may become so involved with the secular world that his religious vocabulary becomes indistinguishable from that of secular ideology, typically in some form of left-wing politics. Governmental actions recommended by mainline Christian leaders often appear unconnected in any direct way to Christianity, but closely identifiable with fashionable secular causes. Canada's United Church is referred to as the New Democratic Party at prayer because of its leaders' tendency to preach left-wing solutions. Ideologues on the left have abandoned Christianity as much as their counterparts on the libertarian, capitalist right, and those still hanging on to their Christian faith frequently express it most vocally in terms of demands for more money for health care and welfare. Meanwhile, the Christian aesthete may separate herself from the daily concerns of others in a search for beauty in music or art.

The problem for the skeptical Christian living in a secular democracy is to find a way that remains connected to life around us, but which also assures an attempt to make Christian rather than politically ideological choices. At this point, the relevant questions raised by Hans Küng are: **What deserves forthright contempt and what love? What is the point of loyalty and friendship? What really matters for man? What may we hope?** To which I add a summary question: **How do we make Christian choices within a complex industrial society in which there are many questions to which there are no simple right and wrong answers?**

It is important to note that every decision we make is not either an expression of Christianity or its betrayal. That point seems too obvious to state—after all, taking a bath is not more Christian than having a shower, eating carrots not more worthy than eating squash. Nevertheless, the danger of defining our every political choice as being the Christian way is a real one. Thoughtful Christians, living in a secular, pluralist, and divided society, are apt to couch their own decisions in terms of right and wrong, Christian or unChristian, without thinking through why other Christians may legitimately disagree. That is one of the traps into which these two chapters may fall. But those who disagree with my conclusions should also think carefully about the moral and Christian, not simply the secular and ideological, base for their dissent. For example, the decision to describe my views as "intolerant" (an all-purpose criticism used in modern times to describe religious disapproval of any statement or behaviour) should only follow the determination of exactly where and why a line should be drawn between what is and is not to be tolerated. None of my readers will tolerate everything. It is insufficient to announce that in effect, "I am more tolerant and therefore a better Christian (or citizen)"—only the sincere nihilist tolerates everything.

The difficult decision is no more automatically in the Christian domain than the choice between carrots and squash. For example, some parents choose to treat their different children in ways varying with their individual interests and capacities. One child may benefit from expensive musical training, another less expensive support in soccer. Equally, parents may choose to treat each child the same, on the grounds that their children should receive exactly the same opportunities and level of financial effort. Should parents' bequests vary inversely with the wealth of different adult children and directly with the numbers of their dependants? If yes, does that hold even when the least advantaged has been profligate, lazy, and fecund? It would be hard to argue convincingly that there is a simple Christian answer to such questions. In the next chapter, I argue that there are many important moral areas of modern life where there is no single, clear Christian way, although there are nearly always some non-Christian choices.

INDIVIDUALISM AND COMMUNITY

A basic problem of modern times concerns the tension and conflict between these two important ideas. Liberal Christians argue that Jesus was, in contemporary terms, an egalitarian, or, to put it bluntly, a socialist before his time. That form of egalitarianism is often expressed as a kind of left-wing communitarianism, despite the difficulty involved in conceptualizing any of today's pluralist nations (Britain, the United States, or, least of all, Canada) as consisting of a community. There is an important liberation theology at the heart, or, depending on the country, on the margins, of the Roman Catholic church. Mainline Protestant leaders, I have suggested, as well as prominent Roman Catholic bishops, are sometimes indistinguishable in their public comments from left-wing politicians.

On the other hand, early Christians and evangelical Protestants since the Reformation have emphasized the individualistic character of Christianity, whereby, universally, every human being has the responsibility and the opportunity to turn to the light and be "saved." Protestantism has been associated historically with the enlightenment and the rise of capitalism; some Roman Catholics would see that tendency as a slippery slope—from traditional authority based on God to the worship of the human individual.

The question of a Christian economic system and its distribution of material goods is addressed in Chapter 6; at this point the issue is the relationship between Christianity and individualism and community as a social question. Superficially, it may seem to fall into that category of questions to which there is no Christian answer; but that is not entirely the case.

Christianity is not the only set of ideas that must come to terms with those important concepts; Judaism and Islam are also examples. Only tiny minorities in nominally Christian, democratic countries believe in either a pure, totalitarian form of socialism or a pure Ayn Rand form of *laissez-faire* individualism based on self. Neither extreme is readily compatible with Christianity, the former because it denies individual freedom to behave freely and follow one's God, the latter because it is based on a belief in the primacy of self-advancement that contradicts the fundamental Christian belief in service to others and to God. Most contemporary expressions of political ideology (in the democratic West) attempt to find middle ground between communitarianism and individualism, although the tilt is very much towards the latter.

Christianity is both individualistic and communitarian, and neither element can be dismissed without attacking the integrity of the Christian tradition. It is fundamentally individualistic in the sense that each human being is ultimately alone in his relationship with God; only the individual can finally determine the authenticity of repentance and the love of good and truth. Although that statement may seem Protestant, most Catholics would not take exception, although they would press the importance of the church as a necessary intermediary.

More complex is the relation between Christianity and community. The argument here is that, although the acceptance of Christian truth is an individual resolution, authentic community, as distinct from both society and the state which, for good or ill, are no longer communities under the decline of nationalism, is required for Christianity to flourish within the modern, pluralist state. I reject the common mainline view that religion is purely a personal and private matter, that one should live a full secular life independent of one's religion, and, most of all, that Christian children are best educated in secular schools lacking in religious identity. That world view is often underwritten by relativism; if an absolute is accepted at all it is one not closely related to traditional ideas concerning the conduct of our lives. Religious community is required for the practical reason that it is hard for faith to survive in a sea of materialism.

If my argument that God and good are inseparable is accepted, it follows that the traditional Christian emphasis on right conduct is not only appropriate but definitively immutable in its essence. If there are such things as right and wrong, then it is necessary for Christians to determine what constitutes Christian virtue. That process—from right principles to right action—is fundamentally different from the process followed within today's dominant relativism, whereby appropriate human behaviour is considered essentially in terms of its consequences. In some cases, the final decision may be the same, but the origin of and justification for the decision are different. If one truly believes in right behaviour, in virtue, then one acts normatively on principle, the consequences of the action being secondary. If one believes in relativism, principle is nothing more than a flexible. working rule (constantly in need of revision) while the anticipated consequences of different actions are most important in day-to-day moral decision making in the moral domain.

A relevant example is the behaviour of President Clinton which led to his being impeached on charges of perjury. Whether or not he lied under oath is a technical and hotly debated matter, but he appears to believe he did not. If a lie is essentially deliberate, then it is arguable that any untruths were clothed in ambiguity. But no one, including the President, argues that his actions, behaviour, and words were honest, transparent, and wholly truthful; he has apologized for misleading and hurting his wife and daughter. Doubtless, his own statements and those of members of his entourage were made on the grounds that the consequences of total honesty (notably Clinton's possible removal from the presidency) would be extremely damaging. Their relativist calculations have proved correct, and Clinton has retained considerable popularity. Equally evident is it that they were not made according to the principles of truth and moral integrity. When it emerged that the President's top advisor and confidant, Vernon Jordan, a prominent member of a major law firm, had consistently lied under oath on matters of fact in defence of Clinton, it became clear how unprincipled behaviour (however advantageous the desired consequences may be) can corrupt the core of government (as well as the souls of those concerned). Whether or not the entire, politically partisan process leading to impeachment in the United States (involving the cases of both Richard Nixon and Clinton) is desirable and sensible is entirely another question; what is clear is that consequentialist behaviour, uncontrolled by moral principle, however pragmatically defensible, is apt to lead to the spread of a moral stain.

It is important to re-emphasize at this juncture the added complexity that not all liberal Christians actually accept my claim that God represents an absolute, although opponents tend to shy away from the only alternative way of thought, relativism. But there is no half-way, I have argued, between an absolute and its absence. I am unaware of any convincing, logical philosophical statement explaining how relativist individualism can be avoided once the notion of the absolute (which was accepted by both Judaism and Greek Platonism before Christ) is abandoned.

If there is no absolute, then we are left to decide for ourselves which, if any, moral precepts we shall choose to follow. It is argued that "everyone" agrees on the golden rule—that society could not function without it; it is a part of every world religion and set of ethics. But of course, millions of human beings have deliberately chosen not to follow the golden rule, some, like Hitler, Stalin, and Pol Pot, on the grounds that their greater secular god supersedes it, others, such as Idi Amin of Uganda, simply because it is convenient to ignore others' rules when it is to personal disadvantage (when "I don't think I shall get caught").

Relativism makes all moral decision making situational. Ultimately, if relativism is taken to its logical conclusion and every surrounding environmental factor is taken into account, then all behaviour, however wrong most of us may think it, becomes explicable and thereby justifiable—when *all the circumstances are understood.* That is true by definition. It is a common place today to hear it argued that criminals should be separated only to protect the public and to give them the rehabilitation they need; no fault is involved—they are simply the victims of their genes, their upbringing, and their environment.

I am not arguing that personal history and context should never be taken into account in making a moral decision, but I am arguing that principle (based on fundamental morality) should take precedence. Further, alleged motive is often only of partial help in making moral judgment; it is of little account whether or not Hitler and Stalin genuinely believed that killing Jews and starving Ukrainian peasants would have the consequence of improving their respective countries—they surely knew that murder is wrong. If they did not, why did their supporters and they themselves conceal and deny their behaviour?

An assumption throughout this book is that there is right and wrong, good and evil; without that reasonable belief, neither Christianity nor any ultimately sustainable moral (as distinct from amoral) order can either survive or be shown to be true according to reason. Relativists respond that the individual, absolutist or relativist, still has to discern what is good and people will not agree on what they discern. While that is correct, belief in an absolute in which one has faith (and which has been believed and honed by others for centuries) is very different from determining a choice for the occasion without any prior faith in an external good or trust in tradition. Without right and wrong, Christianity and all other religions do indeed deserve to be confined to the dustbin of history.

Virtue, based on right action, is the bedrock of an absolutist Christian morality, but what, it may be asked, has that to do with individualism and community?

It may seem reasonable to assert that relativists may come to choose community as one of their values just as readily as the absolutist; after all, individuals freely choose to join a tennis club, form environmental groups, and to attend church. Don't they thereby join subcommunities—of tennis players, environmental activists, and the church? The answer is no. The term community, as I am using it, does not refer to any group of people who come together for a joint purpose. A community is a group of people who spend time together, who have strong bonds holding them together, whose organization has clear bounds (i.e., there is a clear division between members and non-members), and who hold a common bond of loyalty and commitment to the joint enterprise. Genuine communities are becoming rare in today's fragmented society, and few of us belong to one. An isolated village or small town may still be a community, even in North America. Jehovah's Witnesses, Orthodox Jews, and old order Mennonites, i.e., those whose religion is an integral part of their entire lives, typically form communities. Communities form best when there are internal values shared strongly by members and where there is alienation from the outside. On the larger scale, nation states used to be communities writ large; Japan, Denmark, and francophone Quebec may still be communitarian societies, composed of numerous subsections of the larger community, nearly all holding common values of loyalty, commitment, and patriotism. (In today's political regime, they unsurprisingly have difficulty coming to terms with their respective Korean, refugee, and non-French-speaking minorities). Such large-scale communities are increasingly rare in the modern world, and even those that exist are under attack under the banner of universal human rights.

It is true that there are also communities that are harmful or criminal (some individualists believe the nation state is evil)—street gangs and criminal organizations; there is no automatic association of community with positive values. Nevertheless, while religious communities have frequently behaved badly in the past (and egregious examples today include Sudan, Afghanistan, and Northern Ireland), religious groups are the most evident examples of positive and enduring communities within the pluralist democracies. Not all churches are based on community; and among those that can claim some genuine affiliation, the ties are sometimes other than religious (most often geographical). Despite the decline of community, the fundamental law of western democracies is based on vestigial Judaeo-Christian morality; without some common beliefs, the multicultural society cannot survive.

When relativists form communities, they are usually based on passing political causes—environmentalism being a favourite at the beginning of the twenty-first century. But note that there is (and can be) no clear, founding faith. Although the rhetoric suggests otherwise, no environmental group is really committed to returning the world's environment to its ecology before human development began to change it. Environmental organizations are more like political parties, with some shared interests to hold them together, but many points of separation.

Even as Christian community dies, notably in the secular sections of society where skeptical Christians are most likely to be found, the survival of Christianity depends on community, however limited it may be. The paradox is that community, requiring the shedding of individualism and independence, while easy to appreciate in the abstract, is extremely difficult for the skeptic to embrace. Further, the fact that strong religious community depends on commitment to a belief in an absolute automatically alienates secular relativists outside the circle. The very quality on which Christianity ultimately depends for its survival, I am arguing, separates its communities from the dominant forces of our time. It is ironic that community is not an identifiably Christian property and one does not have to belong to a community to be a Christian, but the future of Christianity depends on the continuity of Christian communities. (Thus it is not surprising that modern churches have much in common with organizations based on passing ideological fashions.)

If community (as a repository of committed, shared belief) is in decline, it follows that the term virtue is obsolescent, because it is difficult for virtue to survive within an atomized individual; virtue depends on integrity, a whole based outside human preference. To the extent that the fragmentation of society implies acceptance of libertarian individualism, then virtue becomes incompatible with a modern form of morality based on what is called "enlightened self-interest."

Virtue depends on others for its definition and expression. Virtue is most clearly evident when it is announced and practised; commitment to a spouse is more easily internalized in a community where adultery will lead to shunning or expulsion than in one where it is considered a normal and acceptable part of life. Modern preachers who announce instant forgiveness for adultery (or ignore it altogether), but not for such ideologically unfashionable misbehaviour as pollution or opposition to bilingualism, eviscerate the traditional meaning of marriage.

Virtue flourishes where there is common understanding of its meaning, and where people have contempt for behaviour that falls outside its realm. The Lord's Prayer asks that we not be tested; being weak, we are all apt to succumb to temptation. Contemporary media glorify traditional examples of temptation. In contemporary Western society, many instances of virtue are sources of amusement, contempt, and disdain. The person who does not take his opportunity is seen as narrowly conventional, moralistic, inhibited, or just plain stupid. *American Beauty* was assessed by critics as one of the finest films of 1999. It lacks character development (there is only a weak attempt in the case of one individual); the plot-line is weak. The acting is unexceptional because not much is required to represent stereotypes. While it does provide some mild entertainment, its thematic development mocks any traditional sense of the good, and condones or celebrates the three characters who live most freely outside convention; one has to assume it is those latter qualities, involving both criminal and immoral behaviour, that most attract the critics. *American Beauty* was a great success—after it received the accolade of Oscars. Even North Americans still require some teaching on how to enjoy the trashing of morality. There are still cases, happily, where critical acclaim of thoughtful films with amoral or immoral subtexts is not followed by public success; *Being John Malkovitch* is a recent one.

Individualism is not necessarily incompatible with a sense of the absolute; there are many cases of strongly individualistic people, some regretting the lives they have lived, turning to search for the light of truth. But the lonely path is a hard one, and most people, like me, turn to community for help and support. Indeed, one of the ironies of Christianity is that Jesus effectively undermined the Jewish community into which he was born by attacking the placement of ritual behaviour before virtue; but the growth of Christianity was to depend heavily on tightly ruled Christian communities, many of which, like their Jewish predecessors, have been far from Christian in their practice, as an astute observer of early Christianity would have predicted.

That irony is re-lived in Christian communities today; Christianity cannot survive in a hostile secular world without community, but strong communities frequently wander far from the path of truth and righteousness; we need authority, but there must be checks and balances, because human authority, even under God's name, always has been and always will be corrupted. The more communities become entrenched, the more unthinking the members follow rules rather than the right way, the more open they are to abusive leadership. As communities weaken, however, the more their members are drawn into the individualistic, self-seeking, secular world outside. That may sound pessimistic, but it is simply an affirmation of our sinful nature. We need community because we are too weak on our own, but communities are open to corruption.

Christian life depends on virtue. Virtue, which must be freely exercised, may cling to the wreckage within an individualistic world but can only flourish within some form of community where there is commitment to its worth. It is not surprising that the churches of evangelicals and fundamentalists, more isolated from the secular world, survive better than the mainline churches contorting themselves to be accepted by the external secular world. It is equally unsurprising that the strong churches are prone to demonize their rivals as much as they do unbelievers.

THE VIRTUES

Alasdair MacIntyre (1981), whose ideas on virtue suffuse this chapter and underlie the book, begins his account of the virtues with classical accounts, particularly with his idiosyncratic interpretation of Aristotle. Christianity arose in the context of Judaic and Greco-Roman cultures, so there is little surprise in a level of compatibility between those two sources with Christian ethics. Thomas Aquinas, centuries later, was to compose a theology melding Christian (including Jewish) and Greco-Roman ideas, a union of faith and reason, on which much of Roman Catholic thought is still based.

MacIntyre begins his account of the virtues with truth, justice, and courage. The meaning of truth (in the sense that God is truth) was discussed in Chapter 2, where I showed its centrality to the good. Truth is concerned with factual honesty (we should not lie about our actions and knowledge), but it also includes spiritual truth. When one says John is true to his wife, one means much more than that he is honest. Included in his true behaviour are loyalty, love, and commitment. When we say we try to be true to God, we do not merely mean that we acknowledge our faults and weakness, but that we accept that the good and the truth should define our spiritual relationships and moral choices, deliberate and incidental, planned and unplanned. Saying one is virtuously truthful because one does not lie is like claiming to have nurtured a child by feeding her twice a day; necessary, but pathetically insufficient.

That does not diminish the value of personal honesty. Personal honesty is the foundation on which greater virtue can be based. The "white lies" told ostensibly, usually, or even genuinely in the interests of the recipient can easily be the beginning of habitual dishonesty, the beginning of the cancer; this is evident in the lives of public figures. There are a few, very few, occasions when leaders of government should lie to protect the state or individual citizens, but it is tempting to confuse one's selfish interests with those of the state. Of course there are hypothetical situations where a lie would be the least objectionable choice for anyone, but they are remote from most of our lives; the problem with most people is not that they speak the truth too much, but that they prevaricate, dissemble, deceive, mislead, and lie. It is increasingly assumed that any sensible politician, lawyer, or child will deny any accusation that would lead to trouble for himself or his associates, provided that there is a good chance of not getting caught. The person who tells the truth unnecessarily is deemed as stupid as the person who lies when the truth will obviously get out: the result of consequentialism, where good and bad are distinguished only by the aftermath of an act rather than by its nature.

Most casual lies are made out of simple self-defence or to avoid trouble, for oneself or for someone else. If spouses or close friends habitually lie to one another about small things, there can be no complete trust; indeed, if a more serious matter arises, each will wonder if the other is lying. "Do you think I am fat?" is an unhelpful question, because "fat" has little objective meaning; there is a polite and a rude answer, but usually no factual answer, because the person who is greatly overweight (objectively fat) does not ask the question, any more than a blind woman would ask what one thinks of her sight. "Do you like my new shoes?" and, "Do you think it's time I watched my diet?" deserve honest, neither dissembling nor rude, answers. Honesty can be used as a weapon, when factual but unnecessary truth is used to wound, but lying is not the better alternative. Honest answers can be phrased that address the genuine, underlying question, if there is one, providing useful information. Many questions are rhetorical, requiring no direct reply, or pleas for reassurance (such as, very often, "Am I fat?"), to which the respondent should provide kind and honest reassurance or not, according to the nature of the problem.

Truth is the focal point of virtue. I was sometimes asked by academics (appalled by my naïve belief in an absolute), "How many absolute virtues do you think there are?" The intent was that I should give a number greater than one, so they could deride my lack of logic; after all, how could any two absolutes not conflict? For the Christian, the answer is easy; God is the only absolute, but there are many aspects to the absolute. Justice, MacIntyre's second virtue, is closely associated with truth, but it cannot stand alone. How can one embrace untruth and be fair? Being untruthful is being unfair.

When I turn to economic systems in the next chapter, it will become apparent that one person's economic justice is another's injustice. Justice can only exist within a system where there is an accepted code of conduct. If they assume that the accused, victims, witnesses, lawyers, and police are all habitual liars how can any judge or jury reach a reasonable verdict? That is one of many reasons why so many court judgments seem bizarre and inconsistent; whom does one choose to believe in a society where lying is increasingly accepted? Justice depends on an apprehension of the good; without that, it flounders in a morass of technicalities, rules, and conflicting rights. The Supreme Court's chief justice recently appealed to lawyers to help the court work out conflicting equality rights; but lawyers are not expert in morality but in rights; they are much more the problem than the solution.

Justice is a vital part of virtue because it emphasizes we should be fair in our dealings with others, and that we should live both within the moral code of our society as well as within its legal code; it must inform our everyday behaviour, when we deal with family, friends, and fellow workers. Justice in Canada is being corroded because judges are increasingly making decisions based on their own personal values. This is not simply a result of their own human weakness, notably their inflated sense of self-worth. There are other factors.

First, there is decreasing agreement on a single moral code (I have used the illustration of honesty). Feminists argue that there are many circumstances in which women are justified in killing their husbands, because their husbands have abused them in the past, because they fear what their husbands may do in the future, and because of the circumstances of their personal and ethnic background, e.g., Métis or Native Indian. Group membership quickly becomes a basis for unequal treatment.

Second, codes of human rights are often vague or contradictory, necessitating that they be interpreted by the courts. Third, elected governments are often only too pleased to have controversial decisions made (in the direction they but not necessarily their constituents wish) by the courts. It is not surprising then that respect for the "justice" provided by the courts is often replaced by anger and ridicule.

The same social changes apply at the individual level, where the traditional code of behaviour becomes weakened and confused. Infidelity in marriage is no longer considered relevant in divorce proceedings, so infidelity is a lesser stain on one's conscience and a lesser inducement to others' disapproval. The concept of bastards (or illegitimate children) disappears in order to avoid a stain on the innocent child, thereby inadvertently legitimating the behaviour that leads to the birth in the first place. Teachers inadvertently reinforce the corruption of traditional values, directly and indirectly. Directly, an example is the use of moral dilemmas where young people are asked what they would do in dire hypothetical circumstances. One obscene case is the once popular lifeboat story where students were asked what they would individually do if the lifeboat were unable to support the entire group. "Whom," from your own or some hypothetical group, "would you discard?" The lifeboat has more recently had another life in the form of the popular *voyeur* television program, *Survivor*, and its successors. An indirect example is the increasing failure to draw a reasonable moral line between justifiable loyalty to friends and the civic responsibility not to look away from theft, destruction of property, and violence; the result is that both disloyalty and support of immoral behaviour increase, all depending on individual advantage at the time.

Thus justice as a comprehensible virtue is losing sense in the modern world; being fair lies increasingly in the eyes of the beholder. It is becoming "unfair" if one gets less than one thinks one should have, and there is little agreement on what one should have (besides more); poverty is generally described in relative terms, with two inevitable results—the better off have little knowledge of real poverty and tend to deny it, and the worse off, increasing in numbers as each generation expects more, have their grievances justified and made permanent.

Is it fair that a black person from a rich family gets a place in university ahead of a more qualified white person from a poor family? The answer depends on whom one asks. Once the idea of appointment by merit is corroded, whatever the eventual decision, some of the rejected will feel aggrieved, and more important, will receive moral support from peers. Governments are first in the race to sue tobacco manufacturers for selling a dangerous product, even though they have drawn (and continue to draw) millions in taxes and the danger has been well known to them for years; they even pass laws to redefine their alleged costs, in order that the fact that they actually profit from early death is excluded from consideration. Smoking is perhaps the area of greatest government and elite hypocrisy; it is an easy area to attack "them" and pretend to virtue, because smoking is a pleasure of generally powerless low income groups.

Law is passed retroactively to accuse immigrants from German-occupied Europe for alleged behaviour half a century earlier when they worked for a totalitarian regime; when the laws prove ineffective, suspected war criminals are deported for having lied when they immigrated, at the same time as new immigrant refugees routinely and acceptably lie for admission (their lies are ruled justifiable on the grounds of their legitimate fears of authority). There is little evidence that lawyers and scientists are concerned about the stain of injustice and misrepresentation that spreads in their respective areas of expertise. Christians are frequently among the proponents of the new secular "justice," with definition changing according to political fashion.

There are minor ways in which justice is corroded as well. Laws are increasingly passed which are either universally ignored, according to circumstances, or which are seen as unfair by the affected groups and their supporters. In Canada, speed limits are inconsistent by local, national, and international standards. Few drivers consistently obey the limits and police patrols are generally seen as the enemy. Getting a speeding ticket is reasonably seen as mere bad luck, part of the cost of driving. Police, expected to demonstrate diligence by issuing large numbers of traffic tickets, equally reasonably decide that it makes sense to find large numbers of people speeding in the most open, safest stretches of road (where stopping vehicles will not be a danger to others), rather than waste half an hour finding a single dangerous driver, who, if she can afford a good lawyer, will probably get off anyway. That kind of acceptable lawlessness easily spreads, so that people feel that avoiding sales tax, cheating the customs officers, and not declaring income is fair, if you can get away with it. Beating the police becomes a game, and our association with them as defenders against crime is weakened.

If justice is becoming individualized, and thereby emptied of consensual meaning, MacIntyre's third great virtue, courage, at least in its moral form, is in danger of extinction. Clearly, there is no value in believing in truth if one lacks the courage to express it. But if all truth is tentative, speculative, and subjective, then why get into trouble for announcing what others will ignore or deride? No one else gets excited about this crime, why should you? Whereas the confusion besetting justice is a part of the modern age, resulting from the loss of consensual values, courage has never been in plentiful supply. For most people, most of the time, yesterday, today, and tomorrow, courage remains the most difficult virtue to demonstrate in daily life. In an age where wild accusations of racism, sexism, and religious bigotry are often made with minimal evidence, how often will ordinary Christians dare to speak out against the politically correct? Indeed, secularized Christians scramble to join the mob, and throw the first stone at anyone, particularly an evangelical or fundamentalist Christian, who refuses to accept the new secular standard. It is hard to imagine a mainline Christian leader speaking out in the year 2001 against a suspended sentence for a native woman who has murdered her husband in cold blood, simply on the basis of her unsupported testimony that he had abused her in the past. But that same leader will be quick to castigate a corporate leader who closes an unprofitable Canadian factory, even if those who gain are workers on the edge of physical survival in Bangladesh. Indeed, that leader will probably object that the workers in Bangladesh have poor working conditions and no unions; let them eat cake. Situational ethics and true virtue are incompatible.

I do not imply that circumstances are irrelevant in making judgments (as will become apparent later), but the Ten Commandments remain valid. It takes courage for a mainline Christian minister to defend the Ten Commandments before a contemporary, secular audience; I have known just one minister make such a defence. Often, ethics are segregated, so that moral rules are only applied in specified cases. The evil becomes not the specific evils of hatred, violence, and theft, but those evils segregated in fashionable secular taboos. We have new laws to discriminate according to the grounds for hatred, as though murdering a man because he is gay or black is worse than murdering him because he is rich, weak, or married to a beautiful woman for whom the murderer lusts.

Truth, justice, and courage are all part of what can be seen as an individual's integrity. Stephen Carter ("The insufficiency of honesty," *Atlantic Monthly,* February 1996) suggests that there are three parts to integrity: deciding what is right and wrong; choosing the right way, both of which require the application of truth and justice; and saying why you are doing what you have decided on. Of the three steps, the last requires the most courage unless one happens to live in a strong community of shared values. The Christian who announces that he is taking an action on moral grounds (in business, in academia, or in personal life) opens herself up to charges of being priggish, snobbish, intolerant, arrogant, and bigoted; if she is a politician she will be accused of forcing personal religious views down the throats of her constituents, while the person who gives consequentialist grounds for a different decision will be praised for being broad-minded and tolerant, always provided that the decision matches currently popular secular ideology.

Prime Minister Trudeau was praised highly, and is still quoted favourably today, as saying that the state had no business interfering in what goes on in the privacy of the bedroom. But what did he mean? Was he suggesting that we should be tolerant of all and any sexual activity in the bedroom, spousal rape for example? Probably not. Exactly what he did mean is far from clear. Doubtless he was approving adultery and homosexual sex, but it is not apparent whether he and his sycophants in the media included such other consensual behaviour as incest, wife-swapping foursomes, sex with or between minors, and sex with animals. Probably he and his followers would draw the line in different places, but they would all agree they favoured tolerance, unlike their bigoted and intolerant opponents who had the audacity to oppose adultery.

In contrast, Premier VanderZalm of British Columbia was excoriated when he said that women who choose abortion should pay for the procedure, just as patients pay for many other kinds of discretionary surgery. One was proposing a relaxation of current standards based on secular preferences of the time, the other was proposing a tightening, based on religious preferences. If tolerance is the preferred answer, why is not Trudeau interpreted as meaning acceptance of the much greater range of sexual activities that may take place in the bedroom? It took no courage for Trudeau to bask in media praise; he did not even have to reach Carter's second stage of determining what was right and wrong—he merely had to say we should be more tolerant. VanderZalm, in contrast, had considered the various positions on the complex topic of abortion and decided that, in a highly contested policy area, his was a reasonable compromise; it took great courage and might well have been accepted by the public (if opinion polls are correct) had he not been drowned by media condemnation for trying to stuff his private values down the throats of everyone else. The public was never invited to consider whose (undefined) values Trudeau was stuffing down people's throats.

There is only anecdotal evidence of the tendency of main-line Christians to cloak their Christianity. I had Christian friends before I became a Christian myself. Rare indeed was the occasion when any made any religious comment in my presence, other than one critical of or skeptical about Christian practice. This was not deference to me in particular (they knew my values were conservative and not worthy of deference in academic circles), but deference to the secular community in which we lived.

As a part of a research project, I interviewed a number of prominent directors of education with different outlooks on education; I was particularly interested in their personal world view and its relation to their professional practice. One said he was a strong Christian, a Presbyterian, but he was quick to assure me that he never let his religious views interfere with his work; it would be very wrong for him to impose his religion on others. Not one expressed concern about imposing secular views on students. Indeed, that same man had no hesitation in imposing child-centred principles (with a strong moral content based on high self-concept) on young people, because, he incorrectly believed, they were government policy. To be fair, it must be said that if that director had tried to implement his own beliefs, he would not have lasted long. We live in a secular society and our public schools are appropriately secular.

The problem of Christians' hiding traditional and advertising trendy values is more complex than a lack of courage, but the tendency to conceal and depreciate one's religious opinions is a major issue in the context of Carter's version of integrity. If for most of one's waking hours, one keeps one's fundamental world view carefully hidden to avoid foisting one's opinions on others, how can one decide what is right, act on it, and explain what one has done? Implicit in that habit is the proposition that authenticity, honesty, and integrity are not subjects for teaching to young people, definitely not by example.

Shortly before retirement (when the judgment of others was conveniently of little concern), I planned and participated in a debate in an academic journal on the place of religion in public education (a discussion with Robin Barrow published in *Interchange*, 24, 3, 1993). During my academic life, I am not aware of any other published article in a major journal on educational policy dealing with the intrinsic merits of religion in education; our debate would not have been published, I suspect, if I had not been able to convince an independent-minded editor with whom I had worked for several years in the past. Over the same period, there were hundreds of articles published based on ideologies such as neo-Marxism and post-modernism, many advocating highly ideological educational policies to be applied universally. Religion was rarely attacked; more often it was trivialized or simply not considered as a relevant issue.

Courage is one of the rarest virtues; over and over one finds professionals—physicians, psychiatrists, lawyers, and accountants—ignoring or covering up the unprofessional activity of colleagues. When I used fictional case studies in graduate classes in education, more than half the class members would say, sometimes angrily, that they would not take any action against inferred immoral behaviour of a fellow teacher involving his students, even though the same educators were quick to advocate action in a comparable situation involving a child's parents. Partly it is a matter of solidarity with colleagues, but it also seems related to the difference between directly confronting the teacher one knows (required by their code of ethics) and indirectly accusing a parent one has seldom met. There is also a traditional tension between parents and teachers, sometimes hostility; close ties are rare in the modern school.

While the problem in the area of truth and honesty has been greatly aggravated by individualistic secularism in modern times, and the existence of right behaviour denied, my sense is that a general lack of courage is an essential human characteristic, that it would be difficult to show that we are more sheep-like than our ancestors. Cowardice is the norm; consider Christ's disciples. The difference today is that children are unlikely to be shown models of courage at all; the hero is replaced by the victim as a subject for moral approval. Traditional tales modeled courage for children more than do their contemporary equivalents and we made mythical heroes of leaders in our past.

MacIntyre argues that modern times have weakened integrity. He writes of the manager, the therapist, and the aesthete as being prototypical modern "characters," with none being responsible for doing anything substantive. The aesthete, unlike the artist, does not produce, the therapist, unlike the osteopath, has no objective standard of wellness and therefore of improvement, and the manager is concerned mostly with process, irrespective of authenticity or truth. So, he claims, the personal life of those characters often becomes fused with their public life, and their own sense of direction, their central integrity, their sense of wholeness, becomes confused.

That is an analogous danger for the mainline Christian active in modern secular life, particularly in the case of professionals who are supposed, above all else, to exercise discretion, to make choices. When one's choices are constrained by a secular code, what happens to one's integrity? It is not simply that courage falters; the whole issue of courage to take the right way is suppressed, because discussion about means and ends is reduced to a consequentialist discussion within an implicit or explicit secular code; courage is implicitly excluded; an act of courage implies strong opposition, and strong opposition is precisely what consequentialist discourse is intended to avoid. If one does not complete Carter's first two stages, seeking and acting on the right way, the question of the greatest courage in the announcement of one's reasons never arises. Moreover, one's cowardice can also become a shield to prevent one even thinking about the first two stages; "Obviously, I could not say the proposed action would be wrong. I'd be fired or committed to a psychiatric hospital. So let's think about the realistic choices and their consequences." I have shown that in a secular society, that situation is inevitable, and not necessarily illegitimate. Christian action is often not legitimate in a secular milieu.

As the church becomes increasingly secularized and politicized, even the Christian temple is infected by modern times. We should bear in mind the title of MacIntyre's classic statement, *After Virtue*.

Some modern Christians will feel uncomfortable with those first virtues—truth, courage, and justice. What about God? Is not loving God the first commandment? Is there not a contradiction between the earlier acceptance of belief in and love for God as the centre of Christian belief and God's omission from a list of Christian virtues? And what about Jesus?

MacIntyre situates the virtues within those "practices" that contain an intrinsic moral character. Virtue is about practice not about religious creeds; virtue stems from the good, but does not subsume it. Right practice emanates from right belief. Dictionary definitions of the usage applied here include: general moral excellence, right action and thinking, goodness of character, a specific moral character regarded as good, and conformity of life and conduct with moral principles. Belief in God, even a sincere claim to love God, is not in itself a testament to virtue. The virtuous person is of good character, feels impelled to act on good moral principles, and in general behaves in accordance with those principles. Virtue requires that one knows the good and acts upon it.

This chapter, and the book itself, are premised on the idea that being a Christian is meaningless if there is no connection between that claim and one's morality and life. This in no way contradicts the equally valid proposition that one should put oneself right before attempting to put others right; it is inappropriate for Christians who do nothing to help the less fortunate themselves to urge government to "care" for the poor, although it may be consistent in terms of secular non-believers' values. There are many on the left who claim that charity is wrong—there is no place for it in the modern state. Every person has a right to support from the state. Whatever the validity of that ideology, it does leave individuals free to pursue their own interests on the grounds that the government should be looking after social problems.

Non-Christians are apt to oppose the Christian appropriation of virtue, arguing, reasonably enough, that some atheists are better behaved than some Christians. They then go on to remove the word from their vocabulary, preferring the less judgmental term, values. The preference for values over virtue makes good sense in the context of relativism, where there is no good or evil, merely shades of grey, and where people do not differ much in terms of an obsolete morality, but simply choose different sets of beliefs. Those self-described tolerant folk are just as vehement, however, about those who oppose their secular values (e.g., the universal right to state-provided child care) as fundamentalist Christians are about adulterers and thieves.

While the first three virtues, from which all others follow, are not essentially Christian in origin, but are nonetheless basic parts of Christian teaching, the following elaboration of virtue is Judaeo-Christian, and in some cases arguably Christian in origin and character. The golden rule lies at the heart of Christian teaching as does, I believe, humility. The golden rule sometimes appears impossible (as in the Sermon on the Mount, for example). "Loving" one's neighbour as oneself is difficult to interpret; if it implies that one should truly love oneself, it is opposed to the virtue of humility. Moreover, the idea that one should "love" oneself is often used to justify the elimination of humility, and substitute in its place self esteem, in Rousseau's term, self-love, and in contemporary educational jargon, high self-concept. Even if loving oneself is interpreted more sensibly as self-knowledge and self-respect, that cannot be applied to others whom one does not even know. If, however, one interprets the golden rule as behaving towards others the way you would like them to behave towards you, as I do, then it derives directly from the first three virtues; if you are true, if you act fairly, and have the courage to do the right thing, how could you defend behaving towards others worse than you would have them treat you?

The skeptic should have little problem with the golden rule; as for humility, however little appreciated today, it is clearly an integral part of the Christian tradition. Extreme forms of individualism and the unwavering belief in *laissez-faire* capitalism do oppose both virtues, but no Christians oppose the principle of the golden rule and few will condemn humility outright, preferring to avoid it by emphasizing instead the value of self-esteem. The Anglican *Book of Common Prayer* makes humility its prime personal virtue. We must "acknowledge and confess our manifold sins and wickedness" and "confess them with an humble, lowly, penitent, and obedient heart." Church members are exhorted to make their "humble confession to Almighty God, meekly kneeling." They do not approach the Communion table trusting in their "own righteousness, But in thy manifold and great mercies. We are not worthy so much as to gather up the crumbs under thy Table." To set oneself high is to set God low. We are never completely in the light; our every day is compounded by shadow.

It is not easy to discern a complete, authoritative list of virtues from the Bible, although the general spirit of what constitutes good and bad conduct is obvious enough. *The Oxford Companion* makes little attempt to determine a biblical sense of the virtues, and subsumes virtue under ethics. Allen D. Verhey (under "Ethical lists") does refer to numerous lists of "virtues," but, as he notes, they are an odd, *ad hoc* mixture of qualities, many of which would not be virtues in the sense used here. Perhaps the most coherent account is provided by Paul in Colossians, 3.1–4.6. He first lists the things one should not do. He then continues with the standards of good conduct, which may be taken to include: compassion and kindness (the golden rule), humility, meekness, patience, forgiveness, obedience (to God and legitimate authority), diligence, and justice. Although there is no sharp departure here from the classical virtues, there is greater emphasis on the softer virtues of humility, compassion, and obedience, while truth, subsumed in God, is only considered indirectly. Overall, it is probably fair to say that the Bible is clearer about proscription (based on the Ten Commandments) than prescription, with the not very helpful suggestion in the New Testament that we should follow Christ, when it is often far from clear what Christ would do in many specific circumstances, in his own time let alone ours.

Contemporary liberal Christianity tends to discard virtue along with sin, notably some of the specific virtues, including those of strong New Testament emphasis—humility, meekness, and patience. The stronger traditional references to humility in the Book of Common Prayer are mainly removed from the contemporary services used in most Anglican churches today. The Ten Commandments are rarely (never in most churches) read in full; a shortened version is occasionally used instead, which conveniently excludes direct reference to adultery and theft, acts increasingly seen as being acceptable or understandable, depending on the circumstances.

It is not unreasonable to argue that the traditional standards of conduct of biblical times should not be transposed without modification to the very different times of today, that we should try to follow the core of Christ's message rather than every detail added by his interpreters. (It should be noted, however, how inconsistent that widely accepted line of argument is with the demand that we should stick to the letter of specified parts of the Nicene Creed, factual claims which have questionable justification in Christ's established teaching.) Nevertheless, although we will nearly all accept that wives should not always obey their husbands, Paul's injunction notwithstanding, we should still determine carefully the status of the traditional codes. There is an important distinction between re-interpreting codes of daily behaviour and re-writing fundamental traditional virtue. It is a big step from removing a one-sided vow of obedience from the marriage vows to eroding mutual commitment.

A major problem with mainline churches today is a lack of clarity concerning which virtues, if any, remain important, and which codes of conduct should and should not be approved. There is little consistency among different churches and ministers and little attempt to codify areas of substantial agreement. Problems arise over specific issues, such as sex outside marriage, with resort to the Bible when convenient, and its dismissal as being old-fashioned and irrelevant when inconvenient. My purpose in this chapter is to develop a code of conduct based on Christ's teaching and on the traditional virtues as represented in the Bible and the Judaeo-Christian tradition. Clearly, no reasonable and justifiable code can direct us in every instance of life, but at least its coherence may give us a general guide.

MacIntyre has successfully married the classical and Christian traditions of virtue. He argues persuasively that the best expression of the Christian version of that union is to be found in the writing of Jane Austen; her writing is the more significant because she is not setting out to teach Christian morality (a fact seized upon by contemporary critics who would like to convert her into a secular feminist); rather her narratives embody it. Fanny is the central figure in *Mansfield Park*. Her character does not appeal to the contemporary feminist, because she is humble, modest, and deferential. (She is entirely transposed in a recent film.) Yet in the novel, she exhibits the key virtues already listed—a transparent honesty, courage, a sense of fairness, consideration of others, and, not least, humility. Three further virtues demonstrated by Austen are closely associated with the Christian tradition—constancy, self-knowledge, and patience. Those three virtues shine in Austen's more important novels, most evidently in *Emma* and *Pride and Prejudice*, as well as *Mansfield Park*.

One of MacIntyre's central virtues has not been mentioned. Friendship seems an improbable virtue in an age of individualism. His interpretation seems obsolete, he would agree. Friendship, according to classical tradition, is the bond formed when people come together to take righteous action; it is forged in the heat of conflict and opposition. In an age when people lay claim to tens or hundreds of friends, that definition seems, to say the least, strange. Yet it does still have limited currency for the Christian. I have emphasized that virtue, possessed by the individual, can only be expressed, can only live, in the context of others. In modern times, the virtue of friendship is to live and congregate with others who are also trying to find the right path. It becomes a strong reason for joining a church where like-minded people can find and follow God. Without any remnant of MacIntyre's friendship, a true Christian community cannot be formed and survive. But that means the church has to stand for something and against something. There's the rub.

There are other characteristics that mark the Christian, but there are issues with respect to virtue that should first be directly addressed. **How is this list of virtues compatible with a single objective good? Why my list, rather than someone else's? Do we not now understand that there is no black and white, merely shades of grey; if so, isn't the entire concept of virtue rightly obsolete?**

The good is singular; God is singular. But the ways in which good (or God's will) is expressed are many. They remain a part of a unity. MacIntyre shows the connection between kindness, the golden rule, and courage. If one believes in treating others as one would like to be treated, how can one be considered kind if one is too cowardly to stand up for a friend because that action will bring disrespect, anger, or, most likely, disengagement from others? It is not enough, MacIntyre suggests, and Austen shows, simply to be of good disposition, to mean well is quite insufficient; constancy requires that one repeatedly do the right thing; one does not turn away, saying, "Well, I tried, but it did not work." Self-knowledge means that one understands oneself, and does not delude oneself by only recognizing the benign part of one's personal motives (high self-esteem impedes self-knowledge). How can one be good if one does not even recognize the selfishness that insinuates itself into every area of one's life? Patience means that one understands in others what one should wish understood in oneself; others cannot be expected to act on one's expectations, standards, and hopes, partly because one's wishes are rarely themselves pure and partly because one should not expect others to live to a standard one cannot oneself expect to achieve. One may retort that there is only one absolute, God; the problem with that simplicity is that one can easily lose sight of the implications of an absolute good if no attempt is made to work out precisely what good, or God's will, means. If one's god is a subjective Rorschach blot, a teddy bear for grown-ups, a comfort in times of sorrow, a scourge for one's enemies, then his death should be welcomed.

The list of virtues is not *my* list in any sense other than that it is recorded in my book. It is a synthesis of the classical, Judaic, and Christian traditions. Those who would scornfully reject the "Holmes" list of virtues had better provide one both superior and equally authentic—or simply deny the existence of good and evil. The reader is right to be suspicious of anything that I have added myself.

At the same time, it would be foolish for me to assert that the list is written in stone and cannot be changed in any way. There are many other characteristics that stem from the good and one could argue for their addition or higher ranking. Such virtues as fidelity, charity, purity, industriousness, perseverance, personal responsibility, and loyalty are clearly linked to the good, but they can readily be seen as derivatives of one or more of the virtues already listed. Fidelity derives from friendship and constancy, charity from consideration for others and so on.

One quick, admittedly superficial, way to determine the centrality of a virtue is to ask if one can have too much of that quality. One cannot have too much of the absolute. One cannot be too truthful (if one relates facts unnecessarily in order to hurt or insult, one is not being true in the sense I have described), too just (if one is overly insistent on one's "rights" one is not concerned with justice but with self), too courageous (recklessness and foolhardiness are not indications of courage but of lack of self-knowledge, lack of consideration, and impatience), or too considerate of others (one is not being truly considerate of one's children if one accedes to each passing whim and makes every path smooth). The secondary expressions of virtue listed above are somewhat more susceptible to the charge of potential excess—too much fidelity (other than to God) may lead to moral blinkers concerning those closest to you, charity to condescension, industriousness to putting work before family and the right, and personal responsibility to pride and hubris.

It is argued that self-knowledge and humility are not real virtues. Success and happiness by that account depend on our having good opinions of ourselves; crime and unhappiness stem from a poor self-image. There is no convincing evidence that having a high opinion of oneself is generally beneficial. There are many examples in my own field of education where the opposite has proved to be the case. For example, it was long asserted as psychological fact that school bullies suffer from low self-concept and poor academic performance; they therefore need praise to help raise their self-esteem. Research suggests that bullies are normal or high with respect to self-concept, but are stronger and more aggressive than normal. They need their aggression curbed, not their self-importance enhanced. It is often announced that children cannot learn if they have low self-concepts, but studies show that North Americans tend to think they are better in school subjects than they are, while Asians tend to think they are worse than they are, and the latter outshine the former academically.

Most people outside a strong religious tradition tend to think that more money and more things will make them happy, yet in fact materialism as a central value is not associated with happiness. Happiness may well be better found if it is not directly sought; one is happier if one has done the right thing, rather than if one has grabbed more for oneself. Most truly happy, mature, Christian people whom I have met possess an enviable serenity. They are not all strongly religious (although most are), but they have a sense of wellbeing based on right behaviour; none is constantly seeking more. Overall, they tend to possess the virtues listed earlier. They are imperfect and all are prone to the inevitable moral afflictions of being human, but those are outweighed by virtue.

I am not attempting to draw a picture of a happy and virtuous life in poverty, compared with the misery of being malignantly rich. It is desirable for all to live in reasonable comfort, to have enough to eat, a secure place to live, and time to think. Virtue can be found in good-living rich people, and greed and dishonesty among the poor. I am asserting that a life built mainly on more for oneself is unlikely to be happy or fulfilled, whether wealthy or poor. That assertion is made descriptively, not in moral judgment; greater wealth brings with it greater responsibility.

Perhaps the most cogent criticism of the traditional virtues is that they are male values, that they underestimate the importance of caring. Many feminists claim that caring is the first value, from which everything else follows. Their argument confuses emotion and behaviour. Some facets of love (including caring for others) are also central aspects of the good. But just as being in love is not more virtuous than not being in love, so the state of caring about others is not virtuous in itself; virtue is dependent on action, not on feelings. This is not to say that emotion, notably in the form of motive, and action can or should be entirely separated from right behaviour; clearly telling the truth or helping others for base motives is unChristian, but emotion without action does not constitute virtue, even when that emotion is clearly related to the good. Actively caring for others is undoubtedly one of the best things the Christian can do, but that caring is greatly restricted if it takes place outside truth, courage, and justice. For example, if one withholds care from those who may bring you into disrepute or from those of a different race from oneself, the quality of care is devalued. Further, one can care too much and make others dependent on you. Simply, caring for one whom one loves is not more virtuous than caring for one whom one no longer loves—although the former has a more vital connection to the good.

In the end, however, the argument has little value. Good has many parts, many interpretations and expressions. It is important not to confuse virtue with the good itself. There are aspects of the good that do not have a neat corollary in virtue; aesthetic beauty is not necessarily an outcome of or connected with virtue—but it may be. No one will dispute that caring for others lies at the heart of Christianity, but there is a reason, a legitimacy for the caring.

Some people will reject religious tradition and name some of their own preferred "universal" values. The problem with "universal values" is that they have no rock on which they are based; they are simply personal preferences. The universal values nominated by non-Christians are not necessarily drawn from all religions, which they usually consider archaic. They are more often *ad hoc* values selected for the point at issue.

Contemporary relativists may give two responses: first, that their list is just as valid as mine, and second that even Christian morals are inevitably relative because no Christian can reasonably claim to know God's will. Yet Christian virtues provide a set, a moral code, with a source in tradition. Secular values are insulated, free standing, and flexible.

For example, a popular secular value is that men and women should be treated equally; the Christian tradition is denounced for its history of sexism. Most Christians today would agree that women have been treated badly on the basis of their sex, by Christians, pagans, Jews, and Muslims. They would assert that all people are equal in the sight of God; abuse of women is wrong, just as the abuse of men and children is wrong. At the same time, most Christians would assert that treating all women and all men in exactly the same way, within the family, for example, is neither definitively Christian nor necessarily right. They may not even be treated exactly the same under the law. Some countries have reasonable laws concerning maternity (but not paternity) leave and the treatment of the fetus. The argument that the Christian tradition traduces women's right to have total control of their own bodies lacks merit; no one has total control of their own bodies—there are laws for example against the possession of certain drugs.

The word "equally" is used ambiguously, one moment to mean a right to identical treatment, the next to equal standing. Christians support the latter, but not always the former. There are reasons and occasions to discriminate by sex without denying equality of standing (i.e., equal human dignity). For the most part, men and women compete in separate teams in sports, such as boxing, tennis, hockey, basketball, and track events. Where I live, there are many women's reading groups, none for men. Should I have a right to join? Surely not. Solomon would not be able to determine exactly when separation is justifiable and when not. Establishing a "universal" principle makes little sense; one thing is certain—it will not be universal for long.

The problem of singling out a certain fashionable value for extraordinary attention is that it tends to distract from virtue and to distort both law and morality. Christians abhor the idea that one race is superior or inferior under God, while not necessarily wanting to take up the banner of anti-racism—a concept that is confused and sometimes becomes discriminatory. Violent or unfairly discriminatory behaviour is wrong when it is directed against people of one race, one sex, one nationality, or one religion, but it is divisive and unhelpful to become obsessed with one single example of our ability to behave badly towards one another. The deliberate genocide perpetrated by Germany during the Second World War against Jews is one of the most horrific acts in history, but it should blind us neither to Nazi murder of the disabled, political opponents, and Poles, nor to Stalin's genocide in pre-war Ukraine, or to the more recent instances of mass murder in Cambodia and Rwanda. There is nothing to be gained by implying that the murder of a person on the basis of Jewish religion is worse than murder on account of disability, murder in a German gas chamber worse than murder in the Cambodian killing fields. Fashion has no place in the discussion of evil.

One of the most popular examples of what MacIntyre calls emotivism (poorly-founded values that become mini-gods) is environmentalism. Extreme believers oppose almost all proposed human activity outside cities (as well as much behaviour within) on the grounds that it damages the environment; in a sense they are correct. Every human being affects the environment, and the richer we are and the more there are of us the greater the effect. Christians do believe, it is true, that human beings are of special status (by virtue of their knowledge of God, their recognition of good and evil, and their personal responsibility), but they vary greatly with respect to enthusiasm for extreme environmental causes.

Most Christians would situate environmental values within the broader scheme of Christian belief. George Grant posed the useful and generic Christian question, "What is its *due*?" The question is usefully addressed to animal life. How should we treat the animals we have domesticated for our purposes—pets, pigs, cows, and chickens? How should we treat the wild animals over which we have increasing control? It can be extended to plant life and to the earth itself. That is not to endorse a mushy pantheism or to suggest that damaging a human being, a cow, and a grain of wheat are moral equivalents. But, if we consider the good of others, should we not also consider the good of the planet that we inhabit? If we admire, as we should, the well-kept home, the well-kept garden, and the well-kept farm and factory, should we not also respect the well-kept countryside and forest? It is not reasonable to isolate the condition of human beings from the condition of that which surrounds them. A simple consequential example is that the child who begins with cruelty to cats is likely to extend the behaviour to human beings.

We are returned to the central motif of Christian behaviour, of integrity, "What is the right thing to do?" We should ask the question, determine the answer, and explain why we are doing it. Of course, there will never be total agreement on the answer, but recognizing the importance of the question (instead of applying some scrap of secular ideology in terms of rights) helps us reach accommodation. The secular path is either to announce the special, sacred value of green environmentalism (at an extreme, to be defended by violent action against people who disobey the strict rules) or to consider the environment only as a physical resource for sustained economic development. Examples of some possible answers to Grant's question include: We should not keep domesticated animals (e.g., chickens and pigs) in factories where most natural activity is excluded and where they are maimed; We should (reasonably) maintain a gene stock of wild and domesticated plants and animals; We should treat agricultural and forested land so that it will maintain its fertility and capacity for future use; We should set aside areas of the natural habitat where human activity is strictly limited, and help less affluent countries do the same; We should think of ourselves as stewards rather than rulers. But that does not translate to not using resources or to avoiding all further change in the natural environment.

Humility, however, should keep our belief in our ability to control the earth within reasonable bounds. There is false pride in human pronouncements that imply that we have, or ought to have, complete control over natural forces. Most obvious is our fantasy that we can control future climate on the basis of pseudo-science that disregards the enormous climatic fluctuations that have occurred within historic times, even more within the geological record. The alternative is not greed, profligate use of resources, and despoliation, but judicious application of the question (and implicit range of answers): What is its due?

OTHER ASPECTS OF CHRISTIAN CHARACTER

There are qualities, not within the definition of virtue, that are clearly Christian. Foremost among them is the characteristic of hope. *Hope* is mentioned again and again in the New Testament. Hope should be distinguished from optimism and pessimism. The optimist believes things will turn out for the best; mainline Christian optimists may assert that a reasonable prayer for a favourable outcome will be positively answered by God. I have argued that the inevitable disappointment from that form of faith is based on a misapprehension of the nature of God. In contrast, the pessimist believes that most things will turn out badly. The mainline Christian pessimist is likely to see the devil in every bush, and is often overly ready to spot evil in others, particularly in unfashionable groups of the time—today, Muslim and Christian fundamentalists. Pessimism is at its worst when it degenerates into cynicism, when human behaviour is systematically attributed to selfish motives.

Christian hope is not just a whim or fancy; it is not a fantasy about winning the lottery. Hope is above all realistic; one does not hope for thirty days of sun and warmth for one's vacation on the west coast of Ireland, or that one's children will all behave perfectly towards their siblings and parents for the rest of their lives. Hope is based on the recognition that there is good in the world, and that one's life is not just based on random patterns or pre-ordained fate. We know that we and others can affect the future by our action, by following God's way. Christians do hope that their children will lead good, fulfilling, and happy lives, that they will marry and love their spouse and children, because they know those things are possible, and because they know their own behaviour and their children's will influence, but not determine, the course of events. Hope is grounded in our knowledge of God; if there is no good, hope quickly becomes silly, sentimental, or even greedy. We should not hope for things that are not "expedient" for us.

Closely connected to hope is the habit of mind described by Jacques Maritain (a Roman Catholic philosopher of education) as an *openness to life*. Hope is not a recipe for sitting in an easy chair and expecting that good things will come one's way. Openness to life is an active extension of hope; it means making and taking opportunities. It is a habit that should not be confused with recklessness, greed, excessive ambition, self-indulgence, or even an appetite for life. Those characteristics imply or easily lead to a promotion of self, a passion for more—possessions, consumption, titillation, entertainment, gratification, and experience as an end in itself.

Openness to life is not the same as fulfilling oneself, although at its best it will bring fulfillment. Fulfillment, like happiness, is more easily found when it is not sought; it is less the property of the activity in which one is involved, more a property of the attitudes one brings to the activity. Spending one's life always looking for novelty and gratification is more likely to bring discontent. Openness to life means that one does not think one is finished, complete, when one has married and raised a family, or has become a Christian, or has earned respect in one's work, or retires. The human being is an unfinished project and one gains from pursuing different aspects of life and thought. Openness does not mean that everyone ought to try everything, or that everyone should be, in the conventional sense, well-rounded. It means that one should not close oneself off, from lack of confidence, from convention, from a false sense of respectability, from fatigue, from boredom, or from self-satisfaction. It means one should take an interest in life around one. Christian openness does not mean that every activity must be measured in advance according to a scale of virtue measured in steps along the Christian path, although of course it should be limited by one's integrity and sense of right; openness implies recognition that life is unpredictable—we cannot know where every path will leave, but we can travel in hope and good spirit.

A third quality that a Christian should exhibit is *trust*. Trust is not a virtue. It is an imprecise term, related to the good, often used indiscriminately—like love and beauty. Sometimes it is used as a synonym for faith in God. Faith and belief in or love for God are clearer terms. Trust in God may indicate a naïve and innocent optimism that God will personally attend to one's genuine needs; the empirical evidence against such naïveté is overwhelming. If it were truly the case, there would be no place for hope. What could or should one hope for if one trusts that God assures that what happens to you is always for the best? That interpretation of trust falls into the trap of predestination; if one has total trust in God's handling of one's future, what difference does it make what one does? It also requires belief that God is also responsible for the bad things that happen. One's trust in God is that he will not be vanquished.

The desirable version of trust is that it be placed in other people. That does not means that one should trust all other people always; that is the way of the fool. Everyone has experience of people who are not to be trusted, sometimes over trivial matters, sometimes in important things. To continue to trust people who have stolen from and lied to you is neither wise nor prudent; it also encourages their bad behaviour—you are entrapping your acquaintances, perhaps even friends and family. Further, if none is without sin, it hardly makes sense to put final and complete trust in anyone, just as it would be unwise for others to have final trust in you. Can anyone be trusted always to do the right thing, never give way to temptation? Of course not. The only object worthy of complete trust is God's goodness, and even there it is important not to confuse any human interpretation with the absolute itself.

That qualification of trust represents a limitation of the golden rule, superficially a contradiction. You want to be trusted, so how can it be legitimate not always to trust others? It must be kept in mind that there is but one absolute; all the virtues and Christian values are simply ways of addressing that absolute. They are not rules to be applied without thought. Consider the case of a child who frequently denies offences, even when the evidence of the misdoing is conclusive. It is a foolish parent who pretends to believe the denials and continues, again and again, to show a trust that is constantly betrayed. Quite the reverse, parents should neither place temptation before their children nor ignore the unpleasant consequences of misplaced trust. The child or adult whose untrustworthiness is overlooked is unlikely to change track. If we are honest with ourselves, we should recognize that we should not want others to trust us where we are not trustworthy. There are situations in which I would prefer not to be placed.

Despite the obvious limitations, the fact remains that we should normally trust others. Suspicion and cynicism corrode morality; when we assume that nearly everyone will take advantage whenever the opportunity arises, will always lie when convenient, one of two things is likely to result. We may become proud that we are the only true Christians around, the only ones without sin; or we may become so convinced of the universality of wrongdoing (lying, cheating on income tax, overlooking a mistaken payment in our favour) that we join "everyone else" with the comfort that "everyone is a sinner" and "we are no worse than anyone else." Both results obviously denote a separation from God. The underlying principle is that we should act with integrity. We should not distrust others without good reason. It is unfairly prejudicial to assume that all used car dealers and politicians are dishonest. In my experience, I would deny the validity of either, even as a generalization. At the same time, it would be folly for a rich white person to walk the back streets of Harlem flashing gold chains, furs, and expensive rings, saying, "I have no prejudice against poor black people, so why should they steal from me?" That behaviour has little to do with trust, more to do with temptation. It is also wise to be careful when dealing with people whom we do not know but who badly want something, most often money, from us.

Finally, *forgiveness* should be a normal habit of the practising Christian. Few ideas are more confusing in Christianity than that of forgiving. It is too vague a concept to be a virtue, except insofar as it is represented by the golden rule, perhaps best expressed as behaving to others as you *ought to* want them to behave towards you. Christ did not absolve everybody for all misdoing, and neither should we. He did two things. He said we should not be quick to judge others, while overlooking our own faults. And he said we should turn the other cheek, not respond to every appearance of insult with anger and revenge. Those are really examples of the golden rule, and forgiveness should be seen in that context. Forgiveness does not mean that either the state or the individual should ignore all crime and moral misdoing and it certainly does not justify the view that we should absolve our children of immoral behaviour on the grounds that not too much should be expected of "innocent" children. It does mean that carrying slights, grudges, and wrongs through life harms ourselves as much as it does those whom we, rightly or wrongly, accuse.

Virtue or values: conflict and resolution

The above discussion touches upon the obvious point that the various Christian attributes are not free standing; they are interwoven and will at times conflict. There are few rules that should not in some circumstance be broken. The secular argument immediately ensues that therefore everything is relative. If we cannot speak with absolute certainty about what is right, if all judgments are provisional and circumstantial, if there is potential conflict among some of the virtues, then that means there is no such thing as virtue, simply individual values, many of which happen to be widely held.

I have heard clever relativists argue that some values are indeed universal; they then go on to define "universal" only in the context of educated, thoughtful people like themselves. This kind of argument is often found as a defence for the imposition of "universal" human rights on all cultures, by people who deny God or any absolute foundation, instead believing that the new Western elites who have developed sets of rights have found a better replacement for God. The secular argument against virtue takes us back to the fundamental article of faith that runs throughout this book, a faith in good and a belief in good and evil, where evil is represented by a deliberate separation from God. No logic can finally resolve this fundamental dichotomy, between those who believe in good and evil and those who do not. It is a real and sharp divide that should never be lost sight of in any discussion of morality and right conduct. At the same time, it does not follow that individuals on either side of that line must have totally different interpretations of what they consider good and bad behaviour; they grow up together in the same culture. But their starting points are different, with absolutists beginning with a perception of the good, and relativists starting from some kind of social and intellectual consensus on what works for them (which inevitable owes a huge debt to our common culture and traditions).

While it is possible for individual relativists and absolutists to share almost the same values, the differentiation is still important. Overall, absolutists in North America—Muslim, Christian, and Jewish—have a stronger sense of the virtues than do relativists. They have a secure and rigid base for their beliefs. That said, there will be times when the skeptical Christian will be closer to a secular than to an extreme fundamentalist interpretation. I am arguing, however, that the problem with much of mainline Christianity is that, in a wise attempt to avoid the hatreds and prejudices of the past, it thoughtlessly casts aside the singular source of a guide to right conduct.

Although there is no final proof of good and virtue, the evidence for their existence has already been described. In the context of moral conduct, the evidence for virtue is this. Our entire lives are built on "common sense" assumptions of truth. We take an umbrella knowing that the weather forecast may be inaccurate, that a gale may blow the umbrella inside out, and that, if it really pours, the umbrella will capitulate. We assume that other people and objects exist, that they are not simply parts of our own subjective world, although we know there is no final proof. We go to friends and relatives with personal requests and confidences, recognizing that people are not always loyal. We vote in elections aware that election promises are sometimes broken and that the party we vote for only partially reflects our own world view. Nearly everyone knows about right and wrong; indeed, the courts even today base guilt on an assumption that the accused knows that difference. (That should not be confused with knowing the law; ignorance of the law is not a legal defence, whereas the inability to distinguish the difference between right and wrong is). Throughout history, human beings have acted on the assumption that they know the difference between right and wrong.

In modern times, sophisticated arguments are widely accepted that there is no virtue, no ultimate right and wrong. Even then, I have argued, relativists frequently try to erect their own "universal values," which they seek to impose on others just as rigorously as Christians seek to impose their code of traditional Christian behaviour and virtue. If there is no virtue, why does almost every value community try to develop (and given power impose) its own code of conduct? If there is no virtue, then nihilism or a code based on the mutual self-interest of the powerful makes most pragmatic sense. While there is plentiful evidence of the spread of codes of self-interest based on power, hardly anyone publicly announces that credo; it is automatically accompanied by an argument that others will benefit. If there is no virtue, it is passing strange that those who deny it try to substitute, indeed to impose, fundamental beliefs in feminism, anti-racism, environmentalism, marriage as tyranny, or the evil of smoking. Chesterton was right; most of those who deny God do not then believe in nothing; rather will they believe anything.

Christian teaching and prayer have reasonably been removed from the public schools, on the ground that one faith should not be imposed or given preference. Instead, however, secular egalitarians are demanding that all children be compelled to attend comprehensive, secular schools, John Ralston Saul, philosopher-husband of Canada's Governor-General, going so far as to propose the abolition of independent schools. There is no god; in his place we should worship the egalitarian and totalitarian state and everyone's children should be compelled to absorb its values. Statists, drunk on their new power, imitate the ancient Christian monopoly which for centuries attempted to impose its version of good on everybody else; the new statists are quite as certain of their god as Christians were of theirs. I am arguing of course that the pluralism of the modern democracy should be recognized in politics, the media, and education, where strong religious belief has become sacrilege.

Notwithstanding the reality that we cannot know the good with final certainty and that different expressions of virtues sometimes conflict, the good can still be ascertained with some confidence. There is an important distinction between traditional virtue developed and believed over centuries and its modern replacement, enlightened self-interest. Virtue—truth, courage, justice, humility—requires the renunciation of self, not its endowment.

Secular moralists develop elaborate stories to test moral thinking based on improbable conjunctions of imagined conflicts. Lawrence Kohlberg, a leading thinker in the teaching of value relativism, developed an elaborate six-stage scale to test the level of an individual's moral reasoning. But there is no relationship between being expert at moral reasoning and being a moral person, to which anyone who has worked on a university faculty can attest. The sophistication of a level six individual is characterized more by advanced intellectual powers of reasoning than by the identification of right and wrong and choice of the former.

Most of the time for most people, the right way is clearly evident. Every day we see the contortions public figures, particularly politicians, make in order to justify a decision or action they have taken. In most cases, problems do not result from moral conflict, but rather from efforts to conceal what they have done, or to find a publicly acceptable motive for action taken for different reasons.

A lovely story from educational research tells of a ten-year-old girl who objected when another girl tried to join in a game during recess. Later, back in the classroom, the teacher calmly described what had happened and asked her, "Would it be all right if someone pushed you when you tried to join a group?" "Yes," she answered, equally calmly. The teacher calmly repeated the question several times, each time eliciting the same response. Finally, the teacher asked, "Is that the right answer?" "No," the girl replied. Most of us are like that girl. We distinguish between what we think is right, and what is generally held to be right. Sometimes our distinction is based on a genuine, well-established inner morality; other times it is based on personal convenience for the occasion—as was probably the case for the girl in the narrative.

Even so, there are cases where there is genuine conflict among the virtues. Is it right to abort a fetus if it is the result of rape, or if it will never live a fully human life? Is it right to abort a child if its birth will seriously inconvenience the parents or produce another unwanted child? Is it right to attack, even deliberately kill, a person as the only apparent way to prevent a serious, violent crime? Was it right for the Allies to carpet-bomb Munich and Dresden and use atomic bombs on Japan to shorten World War II? Is it right to increase welfare payments to help the poorest members of the community if one subsequent effect is to increase the numbers seeking and to prolong dependence on welfare? Some such issues are addressed in the next chapter in an attempt to place Christian morality in contemporary contexts. The point here is that sincere Christians will take differing positions on complex problems. That fact in no way refutes the existence of virtue. Belief in virtue provides a base to address those problems. Without virtue, self-interest soon fills the vacuum. Virtue requires an attempt to consider issues in a wider framework than self.

In addressing the most complex moral problems, one must first accept that in some situations there is no right way. The

239

systematic development and study of moral dilemmas in narratives has the effect, well beyond understanding, of undermining virtue by implying that there is no simple right answer to most important questions. Discussing complicated situations may be fun and intellectually exciting, but it is of little help to the average person in finding the right way. Some moral dilemmas are based on situations that result from previous immoral behaviour; a sequence of immoral behaviour may well lead to an impossible confrontation. The idea of virtue is that one attempts to construct a moral world of right behaviour. No such world will ever be completed (because we are all imperfect), but the goal is valid. It is irrational to conclude that, because we are imperfect, there is no point in trying to do the right thing, and that we may as well do whatever we feel like. That is to suggest that the good of others is not for us, a contradiction in terms. That self-serving simplification only makes sense if we have first determined that an external good is a fantasy and that our own idea of good is simply a construct from circumstance and experience.

In authentic (not contrived) situations where there is no right way, one has to seek the outcome that is least morally offensive. That consideration does indeed involve careful thought, involving both consequences and principles; but it should never be resolved solely on the basis of the former, because that would be a denial of virtue. Experts in decision making ask students to choose an option based solely on sets of consequences (they call them criteria which each person should construct individually); if pressed, they say that virtue can be classed as a criterion if that is important to the individual.

Consider the case of Robert Latimer. Most Canadians know of the Saskatchewan farmer who murdered his own severely disabled daughter. At first sight, murder seems the most unlikely sin and crime to require careful judgment and there are many, Christians and non-Christians alike, who see his act as a straightforward criminal act of extreme cruelty.

Latimer seems to have been a reasonably caring family man; his wife tacitly supported him in his terrible act and during his trial. His daughter, Tracy, lived in great pain. She had spent time in a home for the disabled, where she apparently became emotionally distraught. The effect on the family was one not uncommon in the case of the severely disabled. Life revolved around Tracy, to the point that there was little time for others.

To some there is no moral quandary. Murder is always wrong; Latimer should have made the best of the situation at home. He should have full punishment under the law.

But consider the circumstances. He claims that he could not bear to live with her continuing suffering. It is clear, even if his motivation was significantly selfish ("he" could not bear, but could Tracy?), he was at the end of his tether. His options were: to stay and bear it, which he felt he could no longer do; to return her to external care, under which he believed she would die in physical and emotional pain; to abandon the farm and his family and start a new life on his own in another province. We know that many husbands (and a few wives) do run away from such situations. That last option is not virtuous; it involves the absence of courage, consideration for others, and constancy. It is hard to see what good consequence could come of it for others than himself, but it would have been legal. The greatest legal wrong is not always the greatest moral wrong. Law and morality are associated, but they cannot always work in tandem.

Probably most men in Latimer's circumstance would, with their wife's agreement, have returned Tracy to the home, washing their hands of the whole affair. That option, like abandonment, is not criminal, but it is, at least, morally questionable. It means knowingly leaving her to almost certain death, a death that would be as horrible as any she could face, in extreme physical pain and mental anguish, deserted by her family.

No sophisticated person would choose the option of murder. But would that be a result of morality, of abhorrence, or of fear of the consequences—a likely charge of murder? Latimer showed the police exactly how he had murdered his daughter (but not until his first explanation had been rejected).

The conventionally correct answer, to stay at home and continue to care for the whole family, including Tracy, might also have had severe consequences—the neglect of other children, the fraying and eventual collapse of the family and the marriage; we cannot know, and neither could Latimer for sure. It is still, by our fifth grade teacher's account, the right answer. But there are circumstances where failure to choose the right answer should be judged with particular compassion. (Even in the fifth grade story, the girl who continued knowingly to give the wrong answer, may have had compelling circumstantial reasons for her reply).

It is possible that of the three options that Latimer not unreasonably thought were open to him (two involving cowardice and one murder), the one he chose was the least morally offensive, if it is assumed that Tracy's remaining life would have been unbearably unhappy. Consider the golden rule. As my vet said to me when I took my senile, much-loved dog to be killed, feeling a mixture of sadness, relief, and guilt, "Don't you wish you had a loving person able to make that decision for you?" (My answer is ambiguous). Irrespective of the morality, Latimer was legally guilty. He had committed the most serious crime, but the circumstances are such that a Christian might well exhibit unusual mercy. If in a court, a jury were to be confronted with an impossible choice between a sentence of twenty years and acquittal, the latter, though wrong, might have been the lesser offence against morality.

The law distinguishes between murder and manslaughter (Latimer's crime was clearly the former), but life is less simple.

Those who judge him harshly, on the grounds that any commutation of sentence announces open season on the disabled, should at least be confronted with the options he faced. How many of the rest of us would have made the correct answer? Most of the sophisticated people who judge him harshly would have returned her to public care (as I would), refusing to sacrifice their other children, their wife and themselves to the care of the one. Many families and individuals are faced with the demand that they sacrifice the fullness of their own lives, and perhaps their children's and spouse's, to others; some agree, others do not. We should be cautious in passing judgment on those who refuse to make that sacrifice. Even when a married couple has had a long life of loving partnership, one partner may reasonably and fairly decide to have the other committed to a hospital or placed in a home, knowing full well that the result will be one of angry unhappiness. That may well be the least bad decision, compatible with the golden rule, in some circumstances. But surely some observers will say the wedding vows have been broken.

It is similarly justifiable to commit one child to residential care if keeping that child at home will severely curtail the meaning of the marriage and the full lives of other children; one may be forced to choose which child or children should be sacrificed. At the same time, one has to be careful not to use other children as an excuse for one's own selfishness. There are some sacrifices one should make for one's child, others one should not.

There is no clear Christian answer to the Latimer case. My own is to choose "innocent" over "guilty" of murder, if those are the stark choices. I should prefer there to be more gradations of murder—capital murder (for crimes of extreme bestiality where there is certainty of guilt), first degree murder,

second degree murder, and third degree murder, for cases like
Latimer's where the circumstances are extreme. Third degree
murder would retain the essential moral stain, but with a com-
paratively light sentence, possibly community service. Would it
not be right for Latimer to have been sentenced to a period of
care for disabled children?

Two points arise from this discussion. First, even when the
right way is clearly visible (which it usually is if we are open
and honest with ourselves and if our hearts are imbued with
the Christian virtues), it is easy to be distracted by a consideration of unpleasant consequences for oneself and others. It is
appropriate to consider consequences, but only in the light of
the playing out of virtue. Second, the right way is, much more
rarely, difficult to distinguish, as in the Latimer case, either
because what seems to be the right way is beyond one's physical or psychological capacity, or because there is, most unusually, a genuine moral dilemma.

When teaching, in school or at home, it is better to dwell
on the ninety-nine per cent of decisions where there is a right
way, than on the occasional exceptions. I have used the
Latimer case to show that even in the case of the most serious
crimes, there are sometimes exceptional circumstances. That
does not mean that everything is relative; murdering Tracy was
wrong; Latimer is not innocent.

PUNISHMENT

The case of Robert Latimer raises the issue of the Christian
view of punishment. The Bible can be used to support extreme
positions on two sides. Traditionally, Christianity has pre-
scribed strong punishment for moral transgressions, not too
different from the codes found in strongly Muslim countries,
ones condemned as primitive and barbaric within a modern,
secularized, and liberal Christian perspective.

Many mainline Christian churches avoid the use of the term punishment altogether, emphasizing instead mercy and forgiveness. It is sometimes argued or implied that the Jewish tradition in the Old Testament saw God as a being quick to anger and punish, while the later Christian tradition emphasizes a God of love and forgiveness. Both assertions are premised on an anthropomorphic God who makes decisions based on human behaviour, a perspective not shared in this book. Fire and brimstone were not in short supply in the Pauline letters or in most versions of early Christianity. It is likely that the modern view of a personal, sentimental God who forgives everything and slathers everyone with love, knowing nothing of hell and damnation, is derived from criticisms of traditional Christianity, beginning with the philosophic Enlightenment, with minimal biblical support.

If one believes in good and the virtues, it follows that deliberate acts against the good are wrong. The relativist secular view is that, because there is no ultimate good, behaviour differs only in its degree of social and personal acceptability and consequences. If there is no ultimate right and wrong, no such thing as evil, it makes sense to try and make misbehaving people good, and apply therapy directly to those who commit socially unacceptable acts, as foreseen in Samuel Butler's *Erewhon*, where the sick were punished and the evildoers cared for. The underlying assumption is that people who do wrong are morally sick or ignorant; if so, they need help and education, not punishment. There are major practical problems with that idea. One is that without a standard, there can be no such thing as improvement. Therapists escape that trap either by asserting that the patient is better when he feels better (says he does not want to commit more crimes) or by administering a psychological test, one which is readily manipulable. Another problem is that rehabilitation simply does not work; overall, following release, therapeutic treatment produces no better out-comes than no treatment in the case of sociopaths, who form the majority of hardened criminals.

The Christian view is that people choose to follow God, or choose not to. If none of us is perfect (and none is), then we all err (or sin). Many, perhaps most, Christians still believe that those who commit serious illegal and immoral acts should be punished. Punishment is not at all the same as therapy (or reha-bilitation). If human beings have free choices, then externally applied rehabilitation is not the answer; they should choose to do the right thing. The first and crucial purpose of punishment is to demonstrate to the criminal and to the public, society's dis-approval of the offence. The essence of punishment is that it is a response to the harm done to society by the criminal.

Secularists argue that there are three valid reasons, and one invalid, for convicting and sentencing criminals: to protect soci-ety from further harm; to rehabilitate the criminal; to deter the person involved and others from crime; and, inappropriately, to take revenge. Socially sanctioned revenge is clearly illegitimate, they continue, to Christians and secularists alike, so only the first three reasons stand. Secularists ignore (and usually fail to understand) the point that punishment publicizes and responds to the behaviour that is morally wrong. Many do not under-stand it, wilfully or not, because they do not believe that human beings are capable of deliberately and knowingly choosing the wrong way; they believe the inappropriate behaviour results from past mistreatment or inadequate training and upbringing. Note that the secular interpretation implicitly denies human freedom; people do wrong because they have been badly treated; treat them right and they will reform—there is no question of choosing the wrong way; thus jails become correctional insti-tutes. So, organizations for rehabilitation make criminal people well again, just as state medical care return the sick to good health. Criminal behaviour is the result of background factors in the same way as disease; there is no personal responsibility in either case (except, for many secularists, in the case of smoking-related illness which is also the fault of the tobacco manufacturers). But it is not the individual's fault, except, one infers, in the case of corporate leaders and politicians. In effect, certain groups of people cannot be held guilty of wrongdoing while others can. That point-of-view inadvertently diminishes criminals from the disadvantaged classes to an inferior status, people incapable of knowing right from wrong, in need of being re-made.

The traditional Christian approach recognizes three reasons for, in their case, the punishment of crime: to express society's distress at harm done to it; to deter the individual and others from further crime; and to protect society and its individual members.

Rejection of rehabilitation does not mean that criminals should be treated in the most unpleasant way possible short of brutal abuse. But there is a subtle difference between rehabilitation, which is based on the assumption that kindly therapists can turn wrongdoers around, and the belief that criminals should be given both an opportunity and an incentive to reform themselves; there is a fundamental difference between inviting criminals to simulate rehabilitation, and providing opportunities for genuine contrition (which will be judged, in the first instance, only in their relationship with God, not by psychologists and parole board members). Rehabilitation is a matter for public reward (early probation) on the basis of a psychologist being convinced that her theory has been validated, contrition a private matter for criminals, their god, and their conscience, separated from the reward of early release.

Criminals should be given considerate, fair, and decent treatment, healthy and useful work, and increasing levels of trust. They should be given reasonable levels of training generally available to others. At the same time, imprisonment should denote punishment, not therapy. There should be limited remission of sentence for good behaviour (courtesy and obedience to rules), none for being announced "cured." The Christian way does not accept that criminals can be molded into acceptable patterns of behaviour by psychological treatment; choosing the right path requires a genuine freely-made choice. That decision is initially known only by the individual, although gradually, after release, friends, relatives, and the public will come to recognize the change if it is genuine.

Most modern prison systems combine practice of malign neglect with a naïve theory of treatment. The outcomes among prisoners are obvious: cunning, deceit, hypocrisy, aggression, manipulative behaviour, and a significant rate of recidivism. Perhaps the worst consequence for society is that criminals themselves are often convinced by the system that their criminal acts did not result from their evil behaviour, but from their unfair environment, by parents who did not love them enough, schools that did not teach them enough, and a society that did not provide opportunity enough for fulfilling, well-paid work. Rehabilitation helps to erase the one thing that would most help them, an active conscience, a sense of personal responsibility.

The assertion that punishment reflects evil does not mean that every time a child is "punished" she has performed a pernicious act. The word "punishment" has usage outside the law as well as the context of a formal response by legitimate authority to serious misbehaviour or crime. However, the general principle does apply to children when they do something that is morally wrong; for example, deliberate lying by children over the age of six or seven should not be treated lightly. Aside from the deprivation of loving care, perhaps the worst thing parents can do to their children is to erase their sense of personal responsibility, by excusing their bad behaviour on the basis of alleged mistreatment by others or some other misfortune beyond their control; in other words by ignoring or excusing badness and substituting treatment for standards.

The application of Christian conduct to the raising of children is considered further in the next chapter. My purpose here has been to lay out a framework of Christian conduct, based on a long tradition of virtue. Parts of the tradition can be seen as being almost universal, consistent with my argument that the good is accessible to all. In detail, the expression is distinctly Christian. Just as following the way of God is an individual and free choice, so the decision to follow a pattern of Christian conduct, to be virtuous is equally individualistic. Paradoxically, virtue cannot be expressed by the atomistic human being living in physical or psychic isolation; virtue is expressed in the context of others, in some facsimile of community, which is too often limited to the nuclear family. So far, I have attempted to define Christian virtue, by examining its whole and its parts, and by examples of exceptional dilemmas and of deviance. Virtue should not be seen as a set of vague principles that we should all take into consideration. Virtue is the practical realization of belief in God. If hell is separation from God, then sin is the concrete renunciation of virtue—consisting of the acts that sever our connection with God. Mercy, forgiveness, and contrition are elements that serve to wipe out the stain of our bad behaviour; they do not however provide a licence to go out and sin again, rather are they premised on the assumption that we shall try to stick to the right path, knowing at the same time that we are inevitably imperfect. This investigation of Christian conduct is extended in the next chapter to a study of a few selected areas of modern life.

CHAPTER 6

CHRISTIANITY IN
THE MODERN WORLD:

FAMILY LIFE, THE WORKPLACE,
AND GOVERNMENT

Most non-Christians as well as many liberal Christians
rationalize their behaviour something like this. "Of course, I
believe in moral behaviour; I'm opposed to lying and cheating just as much as the next person. I abhor violence. But the
traditional virtues do not really make sense any more. Life is
far too complicated to be lived by applying simple rules, of
which many young people today are ignorant. Those rules
were made in culturally different times. Naturally we should
draw the line at doing anything really immoral, like supply-
ing children with heroin, but in the real world we have to
accommodate ourselves to a variety of lifestyles and ethical
principles. If we jump up and refuse to do all sorts of things
because it offends some obscure principle suited to biblical
times, we won't last long in today's economy. It is not our
place to be forever judging our fellows as though some label

as certified Christian makes us superior. We should all accept that people differ, and the rules that our grandparents may have learned are not necessarily the best for our children and grandchildren."

There is more than a grain of truth running through that argument. When we take a job, we are accountable to our employer. There is not much point in taking a job in a fast food restaurant and refusing to serve fatty food; or taking a job in automobile sales and refusing to persuade customers to buy a car. We should not impose our personal principles on everyone around us. Others make their choices and we do not all share the same values. Additionally, few Christians try to follow every rule and admonition from the Bible.

The problem with that plausible rationale is that it justifies almost everything—it is an authentic slippery slope. Persuasion may give way to deceit, deceit to misrepresentation; devious behaviour at work can lead to cheating at home. Once one discards in principle the specifics of the Ten Commandments and the way of life advocated in the Gospels and the Pauline letters, one is left with one's own wishes, inescapably influenced by the fashions of the time, as a guide. It is one thing to accept that we do not all agree, another entirely to decide that no restrictions apply to ourselves.

It helps to return to Carter's interpretation of integrity: deciding the right way; acting on the decision; and explaining why one has acted that way. The relativism of modern life makes it easy to replace "finding the right way" with "rationalizing my way." One important starting point to avoid that temptation is to listen to George Grant and give all people their due. We should try never to treat other people as objects, however angry we may be with our own treatment, if we believe that all people deserve dignity and respect (that we are all equal in the sight of God).

Three different areas of modern life are briefly surveyed in an attempt to show what it could mean to be a true but skeptical Christian in a contemporary, pluralist, and predominantly secular society. The three topics are: raising and educating children; the workplace; and making choices about the economy.

RAISING AND EDUCATING CHILDREN

Relatively few people live in communities that are identifiably Christian. Those who do usually hold strong and inflexible beliefs. Old Order and traditional Mennonites, Doukhobors, Seventh Day Adventists, Mormons, and Jehovah's Witnesses all hold strongly to their faiths, and attempt to pass them on to their children, but they are few in number. The price of inflexible versions of truth is the likelihood of rebellion, although they bring success expressed in terms of most children following in their path, always provided that the firmness of the upbringing does not descend to fanatical rigidity and is combined with love and kindness.

Most children accept their parents' teaching, firm or flexible, at least initially; a minority rejects it entirely—and for those few that means, if they are in a religious community, leaving the community, and, in all probability, their parents, either directly by expulsion and shunning or indirectly by the spiritual and ideological chasm that emerges between family and child. The stronger the teaching, the greater the success with the majority, and the greater the chance of rebellion with the minority. The tragedy is that there is little room for compromise. In the West, where religious communities are exceptional, the external temptations lead to numerous sad separations. Those generalizations work within a wider social context. Strong teaching opposed to the external culture is more likely to lead to rebellion than is similar teaching consistent

253

with it. In our secular, individualized society permissive treatment will more easily take root than will the inculcation of a strong moral code. Nevertheless, it would be a great mistake to downplay the potential effect of parents' teaching, both direct and indirect.

Strong mainline Christians of all denominations may live effective moral lives in the tradition within a much looser Christian community of people who generally share their beliefs. This is particularly true of Roman Catholics, notably in small towns and rural areas where there are also Catholic schools, and of many evangelical Christians, whose stricter rules separate children from much of the secular life of contemporary adolescents. Similarly, Conservative Jews usually live in communities more porous that those of the Orthodox, but still not overcome by secularism. In addition, there are numerous networks of Christians, sometimes of the same denomination, sometimes of various denominations, birds of a feather flocking together. For the network to coalesce and endure as a form of pseudo-community, the common adherence to Christianity should outweigh the other interests and beliefs that bring people together—sports, clubs, work, and charitable organizations, or keep them apart—long working hours, hobbies, television, politics, and family obligations. Obviously, there is no hard line; those latter activities may be compatible with or supportive of the religious community, but it would be foolish to ignore the fact that other obligations, however desirable in themselves, frequently compete with and displace the development of a spiritual life.

Skeptical parents to whom this book is primarily addressed are unlikely to be members of either strong communities or even weak religious networks. Indeed, some will have rebelled against the inevitable and necessary ties that bind any community; it is the necessary conformity and commitment, the lack of room for individualism, that made them leave in the first place. The following passages assume that the reader is not strongly attached to a religious community.

Joining a church

One consideration is whether or not it is sensible to be a member, or quasi-member, of a religious community, at least in part for the benefit of the children. That question is not the same as that of attending church. One can attend church, as an individual or as a family, and not become a member of the church community, even if there is one, and most urban and suburban, mainline churches have little or none of the commitment and bonds that are prerequisites for community. That is not necessarily a fault; skeptics are justifiably wary of a church that wants to take over members' entire lives. Most mainline churches welcome new members on their own terms; even those with some form of community typically accept that some members do not wish to participate except at the margins.

The easiest church for the skeptic to join is one that is not a community. Such churches are the norm in urban and suburban areas; although nearly all have a core, a clique perhaps, of key members who help the minister run the church, most are content for a family or individual to maintain a separate identity. A more likely problem is one of perceived unfriendliness—where families join a church looking for fellowship, support, perhaps even half-hoping for community, but finding anonymity. Many marginal Christians are ambivalent; on the one hand they want the benefits of friendliness, support, and inclusion, on the other hand, they want to maintain their freedom to follow a way of life without being judged by others; in short, we want to have our cake and eat it, the benefits of community without the price. Many would love their children to become involved and to move in a set of Christian children, but are resistant to actually joining that set themselves, in the same way that parents used to send their children to Sunday school to get a dose of religion, while being too busy to attend church themselves except at Christmas and Easter.

Unfortunately, the church that is most accessible to skeptical parents may be least effective for their children. Part of the motive for parents joining a church is the desire to give their children a sense of Christianity (at least enough to give them enough knowledge and understanding to make an informed decision later) and to find them some healthy peers. That requires a church where is there at least some semblance of community, where you are noticed if you come, or don't come, and where there is a real attempt at inclusion. An abstract dose, didactic or *laissez-faire*, of Christianity is unlikely to have much positive effect (it may inoculate the child against religion). It helps enormously if there are other children whom your children like and respect and who have some commitment to Christian values.

There is no right or wrong way, but going it alone as a Christian in a secular society is very hard. Most children, particularly adolescents, do not care to be seen by their peers as being different, particularly if that difference is seen to be disinterest in typical secular activities such as adopting fashionable dress, listening to trendy popular music, hanging around with the in crowd, going to movies favoured by the group, and participating eagerly in sex and illegal drugs. Some parents, both religious and non-religious, do manage to withstand the common cry that everyone else is going to the rock concert, or wearing cut-off, torn jeans, or going out on dates—at the age of fifteen, or twelve, or ten, as the case may be. Others attempt continual compromise, asking helplessly, "Where do I draw the line? What is 'everyone else' doing?"

The busier the parents, the more important it is for them to be part of something approaching a community to support their standards. The rub is, the busier they are, the more difficult is it to find time for community. If both parents work, if the children attend secular public schools, and if the children participate in numerous, secular activities (e.g., music, sports, swimming, skating, and gymnastics) and Christianity is a one-hour, one-shot deal on those Sundays when the other activities do not interfere, the battle is, to say the least, uphill. A half-hearted approach to church may be the worst option; parents pretend to themselves that the church is looking after their children's moral and spiritual education, but it cannot. This is particularly likely to be the case if the chosen church is itself half-hearted, where traditional morality is ignored as old-fashioned.

Christian schooling

It is all too easy to imagine or pretend that "secular" means morally and spiritually neutral. That is often not the case. Today, most young people know little or nothing about Christianity. In a secondary school classroom, it would be a rare teacher who would admit to Christian leanings, for fear of being accused of being discriminatory, but not unusual for one to express disdain or contempt for Christian behaviour; after all, most teachers want to form bonds with their many difficult adolescent students, and what easier way than to sympathize with "rebellion" against a disintegrating authority.

Skeptics also draw back from the church because they fear that their children will be taught a simplistic faith that most educated Christians have long abandoned for themselves, with sentimental stories about Jesus loving children, lambs, and puppies. It is much easier to tone down the extremes of church-school education than it is to try to fill a vacuum.

There is little harm in very young children believing in a humanoid God; that fantasy can be dealt with at the same time as Santa Claus, with which it has something in common. Nevertheless, it is vitally important that nine-and ten-year-olds come to understand the true nature of the skeptic's beliefs, before they quietly picture Christianity as entirely hocus-pocus, recognizing that even their parents do not believe much of what they, the children, are being taught. A greater problem than an overly literal interpretation of biblical stories is the absence of the teaching of virtue in many church-schools; so that becomes a do-it-yourself project. Daily reading and well-chosen books make the ideal vehicle. Unfortunately, many Sunday schools have it the wrong way round; they teach the Bible stories as fact, and portray God and Jesus as kindly father figures dispensing sentimentality based on turning the other cheek (which very few Christians believe in doing on a systematic basis, i.e., they are neither pacifists nor supportive of the abolition of prisons). Virtue is forgotten.

Even if the skeptical parent manages to become attached on the margins of a community, and some of the children's friends are at least nominal Christians, the responsibility for the Christian, religious, and moral upbringing remains largely that of the parent in today's secular world. Anyone who imagines that the public school will teach the basic tenets (the Ten Commandments, for example) of Judaeo-Christian morality—or teach them the core virtues (say, truth, justice, courage and constancy) is dreaming. That is not to say there is no moral code in the school. Most principals and teachers do try to live by and hold students to three important standards: tolerance, non-violence, and the golden rule. Unfortunately, usually added, if not actually foremost, is the value of high self-concept (the opposite of Christian humility), which causes numerous problems, both academic and moral.

There is nothing wrong with that basic triad, although tolerance easily leads to looking the other way except in the most extreme cases of inappropriate behaviour. But it is sadly insufficient; consider the virtues that are implicitly excluded: truth, justice (beyond one's own immediate circle), courage, humility, constancy—let alone such other Christian attributes as hope, openness to life, forgiveness, and trust.

Perhaps the most dangerous omissions from secular life in school are truth and trust. If the assumption is made, by teachers and students alike, that it is normal for students to deny any misdoing of which they are accused, then dishonest denial becomes the norm. Parents (and teachers) should instead assume that a young person is telling the truth, and punish dishonesty harshly. That trust should not be confused with the pernicious practice, referred to in the previous chapter, of unwavering trust in one's children irrespective of contrary evidence. One of the most vital tasks of the parent is balancing an assumption of trust with its justified withdrawal. It is equally wrong to announce either that one would one always trust one's child or that one cannot believe a word he says. As with all virtues, the primary virtue of truth must be modeled, taught, demanded, and reinforced. To withdraw all trust from one's child is wicked; to continue total trust in the face of its evident abuse is morally destructive.

In practice, public schools at best try to ensure that students adhere to minimal standards of physical behaviour (avoidance of violence and insult, completion of school tasks); lack of commitment to the virtues goes unnoticed. Indeed, it is a cliché for teachers to say that it would be wrong for them to impose "their"—a code for traditional, Judaeo-Christian—values on students. As teachers are no more likely to uphold Christian values than the rest of the population, Christian parents should often be pleased if the teachers' values are not imposed. Inconsistently, however, secular teachers are generally more than willing to preach secular values, even those that are not shared by some parents: the evil of smoking by adults; extreme versions of environmentalism; opposition to capitalism; and the right of educators to determine alone the ideas, texts, and materials to be taught in sex and family education, social studies, and literature.

The teaching of literature in the secondary school serves as an example of the problem of the contradictory ethics in secular schools. Educational leaders in the field hold two strong opinions. First, they assert that only they should choose the books to be studied. They are experts and are qualified to choose a range of works written from a variety of perspectives that will give young people a broad and balanced outlook on literature and life. (Any parental intervention is dismissed as attempted censorship). Second, they claim that literature should not be taught at a superficial level, simply looking at character, plot, and style. Rather teachers should engage students in the ideas and underlying meaning of the text. The more progressive teachers go further and argue that text should be "deconstructed" so that the writer's ideas and prejudices may be examined and so that the critical reader can make her own interpretation (which usually turns out to be the teacher's). The two arguments, both superficially convincing, are inconsistent. The first makes an implicit claim to objectivity; there is such a thing as an objective sense of the world, free of bias—that is the traditional liberal idea of "great books." The second assumes an inevitable subjectivity. The meaning of a book is what the reader perceives (with help from liberated teachers, perhaps). But, if students are to be subjectively engaged in the underlying meaning of literature under the guidance of the teacher, then parents should surely be involved in (at least notified of) the selection of the ideas and ideologies with which their children are to be engaged. It is wrong for educators to claim both that experts have objective knowledge, authority, and values and at the same time that books have important underlying ideas with which young people should become subjectively engaged with teachers' help.

It is no secret that the great works of writers in the Judaeo-Christian tradition, notably Jane Austen and Joseph Conrad, have been substantially supplanted in high school literature courses by modern writers whose ideas owe more to left-wing ideologies, subjectivism, and existentialism—Samuel Beckett, Joyce Carol Oates, Margaret Lawrence, Margaret Atwood, and J. D. Salinger. It must be acknowledged that those liberal Christians who reject traditional codes of conduct, who consider the Ten Commandments outdated, rejoice in the change, as they do most other changes welcomed by the secular elites. Coming "on-side" has the advantage of earning them acceptability in the eyes of the intellectual and artistic elites which generally view any religious statement as threatening, naïve, or irrelevant. The experts see such "broad-minded" parents as being admirably tolerant, as distinct from the "narrow-mindedness" of those parents who do not share their values.

Clearly then, even if parents are able to assume the task of being teachers of moral education, not just by modeling the virtues they wish their children to learn, but by explaining, preaching, illustrating, and taking opportunities for developing a moral sentiment from music, literature, and art, they should recognize that the time spent outside the home, necessarily increasing as children pass from childhood to adolescence is likely to be providing very different instruction from that consistent with the virtues outlined earlier in the chapter.

Fortunately, choice of school is increasingly becoming a practical reality; where there is none, increasing numbers of parents are opting for homeschooling, an extremely ambitious undertaking. Overall, choosing a school is an individual task, and the moral environment of the school should be considered as much as the academic. I generalize about public schools, but they all differ, as do individual teachers and principals. Similarly, one should not imagine that an independent school, with perhaps a tangential Christian connection, is necessarily free of trendy secularism.

Luckily, strong academics and a moral atmosphere frequently coincide. The teacher is the most important element, but it is not practical to choose a new school every year based on the available teacher, even if the school will (or can) provide the information as to who will teach which class in advance.

In general, skeptical Christians are best advised at least to consider a Christian school, irrespective of its denomination. It is easier to moderate denominational or sectarian teaching than it is to counter the indifference or hostility of the public school. Bear in mind that there is no shortage of counter-balancing influence opposed to religion (from television, magazines, pop music, and neighbourhood friends). In Canada, particularly in the case of publicly supported religious schools, parents will find they are far from being the only skeptics. One of the problems facing publicly-supported Roman Catholic schools is the increasing secularization—not caused by a flood of non-Catholic parents, but by secularized Catholics, both parents and teachers.

Against that choice, it is argued that young people should be provided with the widest possible context of belief systems, so that they can reach their own conclusions as mature and knowledgeable adults. After all, a fundamental and revolutionary aspect of Christianity was and has remained, reinforced by the Reformation, that one must choose, not blindly follow, the right way. That argument made some sense in 1950 when Christianity was a majoritarian religion, but is much less sensible when children can and do grow up without ever hearing a reasonable explanation of Christian life and ethics.

Young people have only a limited capacity to sort objectively through competing belief systems and choose a right way. They need guidance and a chart, even more than adults do, because they are still learning in all areas, and they are inevitably ignorant in all or many of them. The more parents and teachers try to get out of the way so that their children can supposedly "make up their own minds," the more other influences flood in to fill the vacuum.

Suppose parents and teachers were to combine to provide the most objective, i.e., factual, account of the world's religions and ideologies attainable. (The thoughtful reader will immediately object that that is a hypothetical supposition—few parents or teachers can be entirely objective when it comes to fundamental beliefs; neither should they be). Most children would learn from an attempted objectivity that it does not matter what you believe because adults disagree, thereby making it even easier for the informal peer group value systems to creep in, ones that may well be internally inconsistent, self-centred, and strongly influenced by sexuality and materialism. In practice, children will absorb their family values (not necessarily the intended ones) with some degree of accuracy. Modern parents can then pride themselves that they gave their children free choice of values and they had the wisdom to choose their parents'!

Some will argue that, instead of teaching dull facts about the world's ideologies, leading to disbelief in all of them, we should teach a set of "universal" values acceptable to all. Any such set will inevitably be *ad hoc*, and almost certainly based on current enthusiasms among the powerful groups deciding what is universal. Belief in fundamental human rights is perhaps the most strident rallying cry of Western elites today; but there are many religions and ideologies, many nations, to which a highly individualistic, Western manifestation of rights with little or no mention of obligations is unacceptable.

Interestingly, despite the chatter about teaching objectively about the world's religions and, inconsistently, subjectively about this month's "universal" values, very little of this is actually done in today's secular schools, except according to the opinions of the individual teacher. Religion is generally ignored or treated with condescension and contempt, and the values practised, as I have said, are, not unreasonably in the context of a secular public school in a pluralist society, the minimal ones needed to get the school peacefully through the day.

The argument here is not that young people should simply be given a set of rigid rules to memorize and regurgitate (although the Ten Commandments make a good point to begin), and then left alone. In the first place, the virtues described earlier are far from rigid; they require development, understanding, and intelligent interpretation. In the second place, a list of virtues is of little value if it is not accompanied by a sincere attempt (by parents) to model them. No parent is perfect and the inevitable errors should be openly admitted— example is not a substitute for explicit teaching, but it is a necessary accompaniment. Thirdly, there is a strong case for external support, from the school and the church, for the teaching so that young people can see that it is not just a question of imposing an arbitrary set of behaviours that "our family" happens to believe. Friends, books, and film are also powerful teachers.

That does not mean that one should only mix with people who live by one's own values, or that all books and films should be checked to ensure compatibility with one's own beliefs. Obviously, if there is a short list of boring, approved books and a longer list of the provocative and disapproved, most adolescents will make for the latter. The point is that it is valuable to discuss books and films in the context of one's world view on a regular basis, just as it is important to discuss some of one's own and others' moral dilemmas and place them in a context of virtue.

The occasions may be once a week or once every six months, depending on the age and interest of the children and the happenstance of spontaneous opportunity. Every discussion should take place in the context that when young people become adults (at, say, the age of eighteen) they will be independent and will have full responsibility for their own moral choices—in the context of post-secondary schooling or work. At the same time, as they move towards adulthood, they should have increasing freedom in their own choices, of reading and viewing.

None of that implies an intolerance for or denigration of other religions and ideologies. Every opportunity should be taken to illustrate where other religions or perspectives share many of our Christian virtues. Where they do not, it is important to recognize difference of emphasis and circumstance. Similarly, one should never pretend that the Christian tradition is pure and unstained, or that there is consensus among all right-thinking people on every aspect of right and wrong.

A hundred years ago, it is likely that children were overly indoctrinated in the one right way. Today, the situation is very different. Too many children are never given a chart to guide them as to how they should live; even those who attend mainline churches rarely if ever hear the entire Ten Commandments (the implications of the abbreviated and isolated first two are open to wide interpretation and even they are only occasionally mentioned). They hear a variety of rules and exhortations from different sources, but they are rarely embedded in a meaningful, coherent body of truth.

Problems of adolescence

Conservative and traditional Christians are accused of being obsessed with sex; a strange accusation if one looks at the secular world of popular novels and television. Sexual behaviour is important however for the contemporary parent, because of the media's obsession, because immediate gratification of all desires and sexual desires in particular are an important part of the secular culture, and because obsession with sexuality is not abnormal in the adolescent irrespective of culture. Just as the popular argument is that you should not preach to young people because they will do the opposite, so it is said that because large proportions of young people engage in sex, therefore one should accept it, and merely try to ensure that disease and unwanted pregnancy are avoided.

Both arguments are based on the false assumption that parents and other adults cannot and do not influence young people's behaviour, or at least not by conveying their opinions directly. Clearly there are societies in the world where most children do follow the rules and there are small communities in Western democracies where most children follow the rules; they are characterized by lower levels of individual freedom. There are also millions of young people in Western countries who do not have sexual relations during adolescence. Underlying the obviously false argument that "you may as well accept it because there is nothing you can do" is the even more dangerous view, often voiced by "experts," that it is normal and desirable for children to experiment with consensual sex, provided there are no ill-effects.

Rarely discussed are the limits. The implication is that adolescents will make up their own minds; a heterosexual couple who "love" (never defined) one another may decide to have sex, in which case the only thing that matters is that it be consensual and "safe" sex. The experts rarely talk about the inadvisability of sex between siblings or with partners, say, eleven-years-old, or with older adults, let alone the inappropriateness of sex with animals. One explanation is that they are reluctant to develop a new, but more liberal, set of rules to replace the traditional ones. Another is that they simply do not conceive of the slippery slope, just as early advocates of easier divorce never thought of a future of serial marriage and the proliferation of troubled blended and single parent families. The liberal parent today announces, "Of course my son would not have sex with his little sister, she's only twelve" with the same naïveté that a Victorian parent would have remarked, "Of course my daughter is not pregnant, she is not even engaged."

Permissive adults give the impression that it is all a matter of common sense—sex is acceptable unless one party does not want it or disease or unwanted pregnancy will result. They are at the same time reluctant to admit that: it is impossible to prevent either pregnancy or disease when there is frequent sex between fertile adolescents; that homosexual sex is even more likely than heterosexual to lead to disease; that even intended pregnancy among young girls is usually socially undesirable and individually unhelpful; that the long term social and personal effects of promiscuous sexual activity are usually unpleasant and harmful; and that marriages following cohabitation more often lead to divorce than do traditional marriages. They congratulate themselves that, "My daughter had a trial period before she got married and I am so glad because they are very happy" without regard for the many young people who have many trials without marriage or for those who marry after a trial and find the relationship entirely changed after the wedding—and not for the better. In practice, although marriage is less common among young people in today's permissive society, the divorce rate remains high.

The answer to all that is usually the repetitive, "But they are going to have sex whether it affects your moral scruples or not. They always have, and they always will." Bullying, smoking, and shoplifting are also both common and inevitable, but we do not turn round and decide we should accept and promote those activities, because preaching does not always work.

There can be little debate that sexual activity outside marriage has not been acceptable within the Judaeo-Christian tradition (and in many other cultural traditions as well) and there is no obvious reason why a Christian today should feel pressured to accept it. While it is true that there is no guaranteed way to prevent it among one's children, there is clear evidence from surveys that sexual activity is less common among families where it is actively disapproved. Lying, aggression, and unkindness are all common among young (as well as older) people, but we do not decide they are therefore acceptable or desirable. Clearly, it is easier to prevent sexual activity if adolescents live substantially within a context where the traditional values are shared, but there is no need to be put off by statistics showing that 50 or 60 per cent of young people have had sex by the time they are eighteen. With only about one quarter of the population of Canada actively religious, it would hardly be surprising if the percentage were higher.

It is important to distinguish between having had sex and being sexually promiscuous. There will be occasions, even in the ideal family, where an adolescent will be overcome by passion; pregnancy may or may not result. The more permissive society becomes, the more promiscuity increases. "Make it easy for them to do the right thing" is a too frequently overlooked precept. Some parents argue that refusing to leave one's son alone in the house with his girlfriend is a sign of distrust; perhaps it is, but one would not leave a steak on the kitchen counter alone with even the best-trained dog. The Lord's prayer asks that we not be led into temptation, in an alternative version that we not be put to the test. Surely, it is perverse for parents to believe that their children will be immune to the urges to which normal adolescents are subject. We must all learn to resist temptation. Even wise, happily married adults carefully avoid situations where they may become close to attractive people of the opposite sex.

If a person is determined to do the wrong thing, nothing can prevent it, but sensible parents reduce opportunity to a reasonable minimum. Any parent who claims that his son will never do the wrong thing however great the temptation is either dangerously naïve or his son unusually inhibited.

The arguments here have been consequentialist; the chances of unwanted consequences of sexual activity and promiscuity are too high to justify it. Those arguments are emphasized to counter the secular rationale that sexual activity among young people gives them pleasure, fulfillment, security, and high self-concept. Nevertheless, it should be clear that seeing sexual activity as being essentially centred on the relationship between husband and wife, is highly consistent with the virtues of truth (being true in one's sexual commitment), the golden rule (it is unusual for a spouse to enjoy hearing of her partner's previous or current sexual involvement with others), constancy, fidelity, purity, and personal responsibility.

It should not be necessary to add that the argument that young people should be taught that the authentic place for sex is within a marriage based on mutual commitment does not mean that anyone who has sex outside marriage is destined for hell and eternal damnation. If, as I have argued, even murder may in an extreme circumstance be treated mercifully as a lesser or understandable evil, how much more is that true of sex, whether between mature same-sex partners or besotted young lovers. The basic teaching for young people should be that sexual relations, both heterosexual and homosexual, are matters to be decided as mature adults (over eighteen, say) when both partners can fairly be seen to be taking serious, personal responsibility for the consequences, whether they be moral guilt or caring for, deserting, or aborting an unwanted child. The killing of an unborn child, one with the potential to live a full and loving life, is a morally wrong form of birth control; it speaks to casual, uncommitted sexual relationships, but there are circumstances where abortion is justifiable as a lesser wrong; the cases of conception by rape or incest, a severely damaged fetus, and danger to the mother's physical health are examples.

Sex is used here because it is probably the single most difficult area for parents of adolescents today. The Christian must be prepared to take an unpopular stand, and to draw a line not drawn by all other loving parents. There are of course many Christians who take a permissive line in the rearing of children. There can be no simple litmus test for Christianity. Even so, Christians should be prepared to meet the challenge of how being Christian affects their conduct. There is a real danger that Christians attached to the mainline churches align themselves with popular secular ideological trends first and then rationalize their chosen behaviour in terms of a flexible Christianity.

The argument in this book is that while there have been enormous variations in Christian doctrine from the earliest times, the basic maxims of personal conduct did not vary nearly so much, even from the Judaic Ten Commandments, before the ages of reason and modernism which themselves define a departure from Christianity leading to the denial of God. The liberal, flexible Christian code of the twenty-first century derives far more from secular doctrine than it does from a fundamental re-examination of what it means to be Christian. Indeed, it is reasonable to ask why one should be a Christian at all if being so puts no limits on one's behaviour that have not been already determined by progressive society.

Towards the end of the nineteenth century, progressive Christianity began to take on the form of the socialism of the time; today, liberalism has largely replaced the narrow confines of socialism and Marxism and many Christians appear most concerned about such liberal ideological issues as environmentalism, feminism, abortion rights, and homosexuality, at the same time being suspicious of or hostile to any discussion of limits and prohibitions. If one uses currently popular moral codes for a guide, it is wrong for a man to cut down ancient forests, but all right for his wife to deliberately damage or kill her fetus at any time before birth; it is wrong to condemn sexual activity among adolescents, but all right to excoriate adults for smoking cigarettes; it is wrong for a mother to slap her child as punishment for defiant disobedience, but all right for her to abandon her husband and children in a search for personal fulfillment. How is this new morality justified by traditional Christian morality? If traditional morality is to be abandoned, then what is left of Christianity? The new morality places good in the minds of modern, progressive thinkers, with the notion of God as good ridiculed and traditional morality eviscerated.

Sexual issues should be discussed openly in the family, preferably as they arise. Sex is not shameful or dirty, but it is an activity that is best expressed within a committed and loving marriage. Other moral issues, large and small, should be dealt with similarly in the family—sharing of work within the household; civil treatment of siblings, other relatives, and friends of the family; sharing of money earned by adolescents; problems with friends, e.g., when to be loyal and when to report them to an authority, i.e., how to draw the line; dating; time spent on homework and other activities; access to television; access to family resources, e.g., food, telephone, and computer; vacations. While I advocate open discussion and openness to suggestions from all members of the family, young people should understand from the beginning that it is their parents who take responsibility and make the final, important decisions. They have authority as parents, they provide the money, and they are responsible for how things work out. Consultation should never be confused with democracy (decision by majority vote), but there should be no consultation if there is no room for flexibility.

Perhaps the most insidious infusion of secularism is the idea that freedom is the most important condition for even the youngest children. One of my children once told me blithely that her young child did not understand the meaning of "no." I had to bite my tongue not to reply that it was time she learned; "no" is one of the first words the youngest children should come to understand, for their own safety as well as for the equanimity of others. The idea that there are and should be restrictions on our behaviour is fundamental for the Christian. The popular idea that it is impossible to spoil a young child is nonsense; anyone who has observed the relationship between children and their parents, before they are even able to walk, will understand how they learn to control the behaviour of others, most evidently in terms of getting attention and eating habits.

The acceptance of aggression in children and their failure to follow reasonable norms of language, eating, sleeping, and manners are the surest way to produce a child who will be disliked by others. The child who is raised by parents who believe that self-concept is one of the most necessary qualities is one destined to put self first, the antithesis of Christian teaching.

As children reach an age of reason, usually about ten, instruction should gradually give way to advice. Bright children are good at reasoning (i.e., arguing their interests and point-of-view) long before ten, but they are not usually as adept at considering the position of others abstractly; still, it is never too early to deliver a reasoned, Christian message to an attentive audience. By the time children go to school, they should be learning to share.

Modern, progressive parents claim that it is wrong to give advice—to adult and even adolescent children. Followers of Rousseau, they believe that children are naturally good and will make wise choices if left alone. The reason why so many liberal Christians have totally secular children is that their parents have given them almost total freedom, in the naïve belief that they will make the right choice eventually if left alone. Indoctrination, they claim, is totally wrong. Indoctrination is a complex topic that I have dealt with extensively in *Education for the pluralist society*. The point here is that no clear line of distinction can be drawn between alleged secular objectivity and religious indoctrination; teaching takes so many forms that it is ridiculous to refrain from formal teaching of what is right for fear of impinging on adolescent "autonomy." More direction is not always better than less; parents should be sensitive to adolescents' reasonable resistance to continual instructions, but it is the height of folly to go to the other extreme and remain silent about one's own convictions.

Often the belief in adolescent autonomy results in the peculiar situation where adolescents with a great deal of freedom feel a wave of discontent when they have done something they know that their parents do not like; they become irritated and frustrated because they only find out after the event what it is they should not have done, and even then indirectly. Before the event, they may have a vague feeling of, "Mum and Dad won't like this" but will quickly reason that they have never been told not to do it. The parents will later tell their friends that it is obvious that they did not want their child to catch a sexual disease, come home at four in the morning, or get hooked on cocaine; but the path to those mistakes is easy to travel if all they have said is, "We want you to make up your own mind and we don't believe in rules. Just make sure that you don't harm others." It should be obvious that that kind of vacuous chatter is impossible to translate into concrete behaviour. Does it mean that the adolescent should do nothing that will upset her parents? If so, it would be sensible to explain in some detail what will upset them. If not, the advice would appear to permit, among numerous other things, drunkenness, alone or in consensual groups and stealing provided that the person does not know he has been robbed—for example taking money out of the purse of someone who does not keep an exact count. It would certainly permit staying out all night without advance approval.

Wise advice, kindly meant, is not interference in another's autonomy. Far from it; advice is respectful, because it is given in the knowledge that it may or may not be acted upon. Advice is quite distinct from instruction, and one's children, by the age of ten, should always know which is intended. It is vitally important not to express a wish in the form of advice and then, after the event, behave as though it had been an instruction. (As a school principal, I got caught on that. I was given advice by a superior which I did not take and immediately received a written reprimand—without there being any negative consequence from my action.) Some parents do not explain their values clearly and explicitly to their children, not wanting to interfere or indoctrinate, and worried because they have been told, wrongly, that giving children advice or instruction usually has the opposite effect. Even the seventeen-year-old sometimes requires clear and strong instruction; he has to do his share of the housework; he may not use the car without permission; he must pay his share of the telephone bill, and so on.

It is sensible on occasion to give instructions, to lay down rules, even in matters over which parents cannot have close control. One can ensure that one's children do their housework and pay their bills. But parents may also reasonably direct, not simply advise, their children not to take illegal drugs or have sex. The danger in giving commands where one does not have control is that it may lead to the concealment of increasing proportions of activity, and increasing numbers of infractions of the rules. Whether to give instruction, to lay down a rule, or give advice depends on individual judgment, and on the nature of the relationship with the adolescent concerned. Numerous instructions easily threaten a relationship by unintentionally encouraging lies and deceit.

Some Christian parents retreat even from strong advice, let alone laying down a rule, giving generalized virtues, with the possible result that clever reasoning may give adolescents far more leeway than their parents intend; adolescents in the company of peers are unlikely to stop and ask of themselves, like the fifth grade teacher of the stubborn child, "Is that the right answer?" They should have been told the right answer.

Simply stated, one cannot and should not have complete control over an adolescent's life; increasing freedom and autonomy inevitably mean that mistakes will be made, sometimes ones with serious consequences, which may include death or serious injury. Bad things do happen to good people, but they happen more often when parents are self-indulgent, immoral, dishonest, selfish, lazy, uncaring, indulgent, thoughtless, authoritarian, unloving, overly protective, or permissive. As adolescents become young adults, reasoned advice, talked through at the appropriate moment, is likely to be more effective than either long lists of rules or vapid clichés.

That pattern of upbringing is inconsistent with modern, progressive dogma. "You cannot control the life of adolescents even if you want to. Giving them advice and preaching to them only annoys them and makes them want to rebel. The stern, hypocritical, moralizing parent always has the worst children. If you bring them up to love and trust you, they will probably make fewer mistakes and will at least come to you for help. Most young people today do try drugs and do have sex before marriage, so you may as well accept it. Encourage your children to bring their friends home to stay overnight, and put sex in a safe and loving environment. Don't make them furtive and guilty. Leave them to make up their own minds and most will be sensible about it."

There are, of course, grains of truth in that argument. Children are likely to behave better if their parents model the right behaviour. Adolescents do need constant assurance that they are loved, particularly because their behaviour sometimes makes them hard to love. But overall the claims are false. Most young rebels come from permissive environments, not strict ones (although, as I have said, extremely strict environments will produce a minority of strong rebels). More obviously, encouraging or condoning sex increases sexual activity and increases the probability of disease and unwanted pregnancy. Sending one's young out into today's secular world without a moral and spiritual chart is unhelpful as well as wrong, unless one is perfectly satisfied with the dominant values and behaviour expressed by society to the young adult, by the media, by commercial organizations, and by the peer group. Those values and their attendant behaviour, however, cannot be mistaken for Christianity in action, by anyone's standards, liberal or conservative, high church or low, fundamentalist or skeptical. There is no such thing as total autonomy; if we are honest, we can identify the various influences on ourselves at different times in our lives. Adolescents, whose world view is rarely fully formed, are more open to influence than are their parents and grandparents.

Once again, we are returned to the central problem of the Christian in the modern, secular world: integrity. Discerning the right, doing the right, and explaining why one is doing it. Secular ideologies based on relativism make even the first step confusing; peer pressure constrains adolescents from taking the second step; and fear of ridicule or being considered a prig or holier than thou precludes the third. And yet the third step is the most effective way of dealing with pressure. "I am not going to shop-lift because it's wrong," ends the discussion, while consequential excuses ("There's nothing I really want," or "They have strong security in this store") only postpone the moment of truth. Of course, the third step, as the adolescent will be quick to retort, may also end the friendship—which is why so many adults balk at that important point. After all, we are living in an age, "after virtue."

For most Christian parents, raising children is the most important task of their lives. There is no second chance, no way to revise their effect. Earlier I used the metaphor of a flowing river of good, on which we draw and to which we contribute. The heavenly after-life is our contribution to its waters. Our children are the most obvious manifestation of most people's contribution; moral leaders like Mother Teresa, Dietrich Bonhoeffer, and Alasdair MacIntyre, who contributed Christian service, principled self-sacrifice, and teaching virtue respectively—are not in plentiful supply.

In the early years of childhood, we do indoctrinate in the sense that we teach clear rules and prohibitions that are not to be questioned. We teach children rules to avoid harm—the hot stove, the busy road, and deep water. We teach them the fundamentals of living with others—helping, sharing, good manners, and telling the truth. And we teach them limits—time for bed, breakfast, school, and quiet, and the various things they are not allowed to do. We put the basics in place; they are not suggestions, not advice, not requests—they are the rules for life in the family and within society. As their minds develop the power of reason, we gradually increase our explanations of right and wrong, moving from simple consequences, "John will not play with you if you always hit him and snatch away his cars," to an understanding of virtue, "You should tell the truth even if it will get you into trouble." As they move towards adolescence, the rules become more substantial, more complex, and more understandable within the circumstances. The basic virtues remain the same, but their interpretation is not always as immediately obvious, as discussed in Chapter 5.

Continuous instruction gradually gives way to advice. Dependence makes way for independence as externally imposed discipline is replaced by self-discipline. Part-time work for the adolescent is crucial in a society where the possibilities of children helping their parents in their work are few or non-existent. Permissive parents, whose children stay at home semi-dependent until their thirties, waiting for a "fulfilling" and well-paid job to arrive on their doorstep, are apt to be lacking in self-discipline. Indeed, it is an interesting irony that post-Christian parents who have substituted a permissive autonomy for a more rigid sense of virtue frequently first notice failure in the absence of independence in their adult children.

CHRISTIANITY AND THE WORLD OF WORK

A crucial conflict is that between the secular workplace and personal religious belief. In one way, this serious and often insoluble problem is obvious. Most people today are not religious in any genuine sense—they do not attend church on a regular basis or seriously consider Christian values when they make difficult decisions, although the vast majority claims vaguely to believe in God, to be a member of a denomination, and to have a set of spiritual values. Work is organized according to business principles, not religious values. There are overt difficulties for Jews expected to work on Friday evenings, Sikhs wearing turbans, Muslims being unable to pray regularly, and traditional Christians working on Sundays.

In a more important sense, the real problems are insidious and concealed. Not only do many modern Christian parents not like to inflict their religion on their children by means of what they term indoctrination, never mind evangelizing in their workplace, but they do their best to camouflage their religion and appear to be the same as everybody else. They try to avoid being "judgmental" and "intolerant";

if pressed, they may retort that if Jesus did not condemn sinners, surely they should not. That self-satisfied response implies both that they themselves are never contaminated by workplace ethics and that their unwillingness to blow the whistle on unethical behaviour by others is not a moral issue.

The physical aspects, prayer, dress, and everyday discourse (including profanity, prejudice, and lack of consideration for others) are superficial manifestations of the crucial spiritual dilemma. That dilemma is whether or not one leads a separate public and private life. The nature of the dilemma varies greatly with the kind of work in which one is involved. It is no coincidence that members of the strongest religious sects and denominations, e.g., Pentecostals, Orthodox Jews, Seventh Day Adventists, Old Order Mennonites, tend not to be fully involved in the modern workplace. By fully involved, I mean fully involved in a moral and spiritual sense, not just in terms of hours and place of work. They are typically either employed in traditional independent occupations (often farming) which are integrated with their religious and residential communities or they are employed in low-level jobs where the work is more manual, technical, or mechanical, in which the basic values do not conflict with their religious values, e.g., honesty, personal responsibility, justice, constancy, humility, perseverance, industriousness, and courage.

It is interesting that those two approaches (working within one's religious community or living in a religious community while being a part of the material world) mirror the two patterns of early Christian life, being separated from the world or a part of it. Both approaches, however, can be successful in maintaining a full Christian life. Many will see the former pattern (living entirely within one's community) as being closer to the true spirit of Christianity (falsely in my view, or I would not be writing this book). Leo Tolstoy's story, *Walk in the Light*, gives a vivid picture of that traditional interpretation, based on an early Christian manuscript called *The Didache—The Teaching of the Twelve Apostles*.

However, the tradition of living as part of the world and bringing the word of God to it, is equally strong from the earliest times. While some mainline Christians carelessly refer to the values associated with the single community as somehow being more valid, the reality is that hardly any try to emulate it; total community is an option for only a tiny fraction of the Western world. I am not centrally concerned in this book with that choice. There are practical, spiritual, and ideological reasons. Practically, if one takes the demands of the totally faithful community at face value, even old order Mennonites scarcely qualify (most use money). Few Christians are or have ever been totally opposed to violence in any form; most of us believe in restraining and imprisoning violent criminals (not simply turning the other cheek and asking them to sin no more) as well as in "just" wars (even if we find it harder to agree on the definition of what is a just war). Fewer still abstain completely from the money economy. If survival were dependent on small, self-sufficient communities, urban and suburban populations would have to starve, or follow Cambodia's leaders into the killing fields.

Few if any readers of this book genuinely aspire to that segregated version of Christianity (although some may pay occasional lip service). Most of the thoughtful but doubting people reading this book will not even belong to the less restrictive Christian communities still defined by their close allegiance and shared worship.

Employed Christians may be divided into two categories: those who work in manual, technical, and mechanical jobs where there is little conflict with their religious beliefs; and those who work in sectors where the application of values, including their discretionary use, is an important part of the job. Even the self-employed, for the most part as subject to the whims of clients as the employed, also fall into one of those categories, although there are a few freelance writers who are truly free to integrate work and belief, insofar as their paying readers will permit.

Ironically, the more successful, the more ambitious, including those who work in jobs with little apparent discretion, are also more prey to value-conflict than the less successful. The ambitious person who works at installing car tires may be tempted to recommend replacement of brake pads with as much as twenty-five per cent wear remaining. Those who stimulate the most business may be highly regarded and rewarded by the manager. Because success is defined in material terms, one is inevitably tempted to place continued progress ahead of Christian virtue: honesty, justice, humility, and constancy are not always rewarded in a commercial marketplace based on the ethic of "more." Even courage may lead to shunning, demotion, or dismissal, when it involves an uncomfortable truth, whistle-blowing, or a stand against perceived injustice. If lying is rarely officially approved, deceit is often condoned.

Those working in the professions, which are by definition involved in discretionary choices, and in a managerial capacity, are most obviously confronted with the central dilemma of being a Christian in a secular world. Lawyers work to free accused whom they may inwardly believe or even know to be guilty of the most heinous crimes, or to defend corporations guilty of unpleasant or dangerous practices affecting their employees or nearby residents. Physicians and nurses help girls gain access to "safe" sex and subsequently (consequently?) provide third trimester abortions, and turn away patients with undiagnosed problems from crowded emergency rooms, according to regulations. Teachers avoid any favourable mention of God and do not teach or model virtue (unless a particular value is required by enforced regulation); indeed the term virtue is avoided and the value of high self-concept given prominence; they strike when so instructed by their union, whatever the harm they perceive to their students; and they avoid reporting suspicions they may have of unethical behaviour of colleagues with individual students. Accountants help the richest people (particularly the richest people) find legal loop-holes to reduce their taxes, and look the other way if they suspect that income is being illegally concealed over-seas. Psychiatrists fail to report colleagues when their patients talk of improper treatment. Corporate leaders help their orga-nizations survive and grow by reducing the pay of the least-skilled, most easily replaced workers and by increasing effi-ciency by contracting out, perhaps to other countries where workers living in extreme poverty can be paid less. I am not referring primarily to illegal behaviour (although some of it may cross the line), but to actions that raise moral doubts in those not involved and by those who may be disadvantaged.

It is important to note that in the cases mentioned above the individuals generally are acting ethically, defined in terms of their contractual employment; indeed, continued opposition to the activities is likely to lead to their resignation, dismissal, fail-ure, or disgrace. By secular standards, those activities are justifi-able. Most readers, I suspect, like me, will indeed justify some of the above listed activities, carefully defined and limited, while arguing that others are simply wrongful activities which either should not be permitted by law or are simply wrong. Being human, we are apt to draw the lines that are most convenient for our own and our friends' and family's circumstances.

Many of the mainline Christians who do not work in busi-ness themselves particularly despise the last example. They vil-ify corporate leaders while accepting or overlooking equally or more suspect activities on the part of professionals, because the existence of codes of professional ethics implies some "higher" value than profit, even when the codes are self-serving. The problem of capitalism for the Christian is dealt with later, and many of the activities deplored by mainline Christians are inseparable from it—there is no such thing as a kindly, humane capitalism that systematically puts employees and the disadvantaged before profit.

It may be generous for a rich capitalist to donate money to worthy charitable causes, but that action does not purify the source of the wealth. Indeed, if a capitalist corporation improves its image by donating money to opera or a Christian charity, one may ask whether it is morally justifiable to transfer money from its customers and shareholders, without their prior approval. In short, one cannot endorse the fruits of capitalism without accepting its inherent values.

There are problems when a professional teacher inculcates a set of secular values not formally endorsed by either the teacher's employer or the students' parents, justified on the grounds that it is expected by other educators (the English literature team perhaps) or by vociferous interest groups (e.g., environmentalists). Some teachers do maintain their integrity by announcing their values (as grounds of possible bias) when appropriate and by never denying them. Others do not recognize a problem. They defend their action by justifying the cause in question. Professional teachers face an impossible dilemma in a school where all belief systems are to be considered equal. On the one hand, as authentic teachers, they should be open and honest about serious questions that arise. But immediately they explain their own position on a controversial question, they are likely to influence those students who like or respect them. They open themselves to the charge that they are teaching their own values, which are likely to conflict with some of the students' and even more so with the students' parents. (That is why it is important for a caring parent to

283

choose a school with a belief system reasonably compatible with her own.)

At this point, let us assume that the reasonable, skeptical Christian accepts the secular arguments for many of the moral choices listed above; every accused deserves the best possible defence; it would cost too much to provide every emergency room with enough beds for any conceivable calamity; a secular public school system is desirable and necessary in a pluralist society and teachers should not impose even majoritarian Judaeo-Christian values; corporate efficiency is necessary because inefficiency leads ultimately to losses on the part of workers, shareholders, and citizens alike. Does being a sincere Christian living in the world therefore require that one separates one's religion from one's worldly activities? To what extent should one simply accept that living in a modern democratic state entails carrying out activities that are not entirely compatible with one's religious beliefs? Or should one decline to participate in employment which is not organized in accordance with one's beliefs? What does the Christian ethic demand?

It is important to make distinctions within the professions. Law and medicine are individualistic professions (although decreasingly so as they become bureaucratized by government). Lawyers can refuse to take on and choose to drop clients whom they do not feel they can ethically defend; physicians can (and often do) refuse to be involved with those activities they consider unChristian. University professors still have a high degree of academic freedom, even though that freedom is under attack from several sources—the influence of research funding, the power of secular ideologies dominant in the humanities and social sciences, the need to publish, the unionization of faculty, and the secularization evident in all aspects of life.

Teachers have much less discretionary space. State organizations impose their secular ideologies, informally as well as formally. As a teacher of teachers, I heard the mantra, "It would be wrong for me to impose my values on students" over and over again. What they referred to were not usually "their own" authentic values but rather their code for religious and traditional values. They were quick to insist that it was legitimate for them to teach against: sexism, racism, and smoking, and in favour of environmentalism. At the time, the traditional Judaeo-Christian values were included in the Ontario education act (although generally considered a technicality); they were rarely mentioned, and then dismissively or derisively, even by Christians trying to ingratiate themselves with a predominantly secular audience—mention of purity and sobriety would always guarantee an easy laugh.

Public education is perhaps the most difficult area of all for the sincere Christian. If a sincerely religious person decides not to go into education, she is abandoning the whole educational enterprise to the secular majority. If she chooses to teach but decides to separate her religion from her working life (as most do), then she is falling into the trap of the secular world. That trap is obvious in the cases of those who allow their convictions to influence their public actions. Consider the educator who introduces religion as a factor in a course on sex or family life; in most urban areas, he is risking ridicule and castigation, perhaps an informal reprimand.

MacIntyre refers to the process that ensues from denying or putting aside one's personal values as being the fusion of one's "character" as a worker with one's private life; the tendency is for one, over time, not to wear two hats (although that does happen), but to become the part one plays at work. He uses three typical, modern occupations to illustrate his argument— the aesthete, the manager, and the therapist. All three live off the world, off other people; the aesthete does not produce art, the manager does not produce a widget, and the therapist does not produce a cure (in the normal, objective sense of the word). The trend then, in a world without virtue, is for jobs to be removed from any founding ethical virtue and to be justified in their own terms. The aesthete defends art as a subjective experience, not to be judged by a set of external standards, but still somehow susceptible to expert interpretation. The manager is justified in terms of successful innovation, carefully avoiding any thought of whether the world is better or worse for that change. The therapist is justified when the patient claims to feel better after the therapy, unworried by any effects on others, or any objective evidence of symptoms. If one lives at work within the ethic that process is more important than virtue or principle, it is unlikely that, over time, one will continue to apply rigid standards outside work; to do so would make one's work a fraud. That is not to say that all aesthetes, managers, and therapists are of that kind, any more than teachers, lawyers, and physicians are more immoral than others. Nevertheless, the problems and compromises are evident enough.

Some compromise is possible and necessary. Good Christians do survive within the secular world, even in teaching and government. But it is hard. Everyone recognizes, including young people themselves, that adolescents find it difficult to resist peer pressure. Less obvious is the way in which adults themselves submit to the pressure around them. I recall the highly respected director of education who told me in an interview, with some pride, that he never let his religious (Christian) convictions interfere with his work. I would not want to single him out for criticism, because he was aware of the two hats he was wearing, and each was worn with care. More problematic are those who blend with their working environment without becoming aware of the gradual surrender of values they once held. Nevertheless, one must ask what happens to society and individuals when leading professionals with strong religious convictions feel they must spend their working life putting aside their moral and religious convictions. The easiest path is to change one's values.

It is possible for the Christian to maintain integrity in most modern working environments. One should keep in mind the basic tenets of one's faith, applied to conduct. That means frequent rehearsal, for which one can no longer rely on regular church attendance. If one has determined the virtues, rehearsal becomes easier—truth, justice, courage, the golden rule, humility, constancy. When faced with difficult decisions, Carter's definition of integrity is practical. Teachers, for example, even in the most secular environment where religion and virtue are a joke in the teachers' room and the classroom, do not have to deny their faith; certainly they will pay a price in personal relations in the short run, but they may be surprised at the respect shown for their integrity over time. The lawyer who refuses to succumb to popular causes will be passed over when it comes to promotion to judge, but will be appreciated by valued clients. The physician who treats patients with honesty and integrity will receive angry complaints in the short run, appreciation over time. The person who works in a capitalist corporation should accept the principles necessarily involved within his world view. That done, he should, for example, practise the golden rule and be honest in his dealings with others. If he does not understand that he should be let go if his work can be done more efficiently in some other way, then he has no business taking the job in the first place.

The precise way in which holding fast to one's core of meaning is practised varies from individual to individual. At one extreme, linear rationalists have to work through decisions, constantly checking to see if self-interest is subtly guiding the choices. At another extreme, some strong Christians have so internalized the right way, they scarcely have to consider; they intuit the right way. Most fall somewhere in between, sometimes acting intuitively, on other occasions having to stop and deliberate.

Most adults (if they think it important to act virtuously in the first place) will say that they try to do the right thing, but it is enormously difficult, standing alone, without a church or companionship for support. Many find support in a spouse, personal friends, selected colleagues, and family. But increasingly ours is a lonely world, with many individuals finding they have no genuine friends, and with families consumed with their own lives and problems. The advantage of a religious community is twofold. If carefully chosen, it provides company in which religiously-based conduct is not considered odd, arrogant, judgmental, and provocative, but right. It also provides a retreat where one can think over one's individual problems, and come to terms with sometimes unpleasant consequences.

If the implication that even doing the right thing usually has negative consequences sounds gloomy, it is misleading. The traditionally religious sometimes say following God's way leads to peace and success, but that is forgetting the biblical God who brought doom and destruction. The skeptic will put it somewhat differently. Being right with God can provide a sense of peace with oneself, although there is often a price. While acting with integrity frequently enhances self-respect and even grudging respect from others, there is no iron law of optimism. Doing the right thing does not always have happy results, and bad things do happen to good people. Nevertheless, the outcomes overall are likely to be better than those arising from doing the wrong thing. How could it not be so? How can one feel good about having trampled on one's core beliefs? Put in the more spiritual terms of earlier chapters, choosing the right way is not a matter of accumulating gold stars to justify oneself in the sight of God; rather one does the right thing because one believes it to be right; one is justified, straightened out, by following the right path.

To the extent that an authentic act of moral discernment is correct, it is likely to have good results, expressed in terms of contributing to the store of good in the world, but not in terms of more money, more popularity, or more gold stars.

CHRISTIANITY AND GOVERNMENT

Socialism and capitalism

Although Jesus carefully distanced himself from the civil government of his time, modern Christians are more involved. In the United States, the Christian fundamentalist and evangelical right represents an attempt to install conservative local, state, and federal governments that will favour such policies as making all or most abortion illegal, providing state support for Christian schools and the restoration of prayer in public schools, firm treatment of criminals, and the censorship of violence and provocative sexual expression within the arts. In Western English-speaking, countries, the mainline Protestant and Roman Catholic churches tend to support left-wing policies such as greater government control, higher taxes, increased financial redistribution, and generous welfare programs. Do God and Jesus prefer capitalism or socialism? Is there a third and more Christian way?

Glenn Tinder strikes to the heart of these issues in a perceptive essay review of a book by Richard John Neuhaus, a Christian capitalist, entitled *Doing Well and Doing Good* (Doubleday, 1992) ("Capitalism versus conservatism," *Atlantic Monthly*, December 1992).

Tinder observes that social change is the demand of mainline leaders:

But social change is hardly a simple matter... What direction should it take? Who answers these questions?... what should be done about people who don't want to change? How much force can legitimately be used? All these questions raise issues of power. 'Social change' probably has agreeable connotations for most people, and 'power' disagreeable connotations. Yet social change... depends on power... The project of transforming society completely implies totalitarian power (p. 143).

Neuhaus wants change through freedom; he believes in the "subjectivity" of society, by which he means a society of persons, "who, because they are persons, are subjects of action not objects." Neuhaus sees it as axiomatic that the only answer to poverty is greatly increased productivity, which in turn is dependent on capitalism. Human dignity is therefore adequately maintained only when there is freedom to work in response to one's own inclinations and talents.

But is capitalism beneficent? Neuhaus believes that while it is not necessarily so, it can be. The freedom of which we must be consistently aware is not, according to the Christian Neuhaus, an end in itself (which it is to libertarian supporters of capitalism), but an "indispensable prerequisite to living constructively in the world." The challenge to the Christian capitalist is to use capitalism to improve society, to render life more decent and just for everyone, and to bring about historical progress.

This commentary does not imply that Tinder (and I) believe that capitalism is Christian, but it does counter the prevailing tendency among mainline Christians to see it, at best, as a necessary evil, at worst an essentially harmful set of ideas. Tinder's own views on Christianity's relationship with politics and economics is found in his book *The Political Meaning of Christianity* (Harper, 1991). Although far from accepting the socialist alternative and the denial of freedom that it entails, he is less optimistic than Neuhaus about capitalism. Poverty, he believes, is a much greater concern today than it was in the past precisely because it afflicts only a minority in the affluent countries, and because of the enormous gap between the rich and the poor countries. At the same time, that greater significance does not make it curable:

> For Christians, there are no human capacities that enable us to construct and inhabit a good order here on earth, not even an inward and spiritual order" (p. 204).

Tinder distinguishes between Christian and secular radicalism. "Although Christianity is suspicious of the established order, it is fearful of disorderly human inclinations." It does not see ruling groups as having a monopoly of evil. "Secular radicals typically depict the oppressed as entirely innocent" (p. 207). One may infer that Tinder is pessimistically accepting a retreat from society to an individualized or separated communitarian spirituality, but that would be wrong. Although he has no faith in revolution (it usually brings tyranny) and little in governments, the best of which display "ineptitude and deception," the worst corruption and terror, he is an advocate of Christian action, both within the community and as an individual. Skeptical of civil disobedience, justifiable only when obedience would require the clear disavowal of God's law, he believes strongly in the importance of taking right action within one's own sphere of influence.

Those looking for the truly Christian political and economic ideology, the third way, will be disappointed by Tinder. Not only is there no right ideology, but any approximation of it is certain to conflict with God's truth. We should see political ideologies as being inevitably flawed and corrupting, because they set up a series of ideological tenets that come to replace or corrupt the right way. Thus in economics, neither capitalism nor socialism can be seen as being inherently Christian, and manifestations of both will inevitably and fundamentally (not just because they will be imperfectly applied) lead to conflict with the good. While it is true that the socialist and the capitalist must compromise (or abrogate) their principles to be Christian, it does not follow that there is some Christian compromise implying an ultimately knowable set of economic and political principles. Rather is it that any human project is necessarily consumed by spiritual error, partly because secular projects are definitively not Christian, and partly because all our actions are compounded by error and selfishness.

My own leaning is more to capitalism than to socialism, for many of the reasons advanced by Neuhaus, and accepted to some extent by Tinder. I do believe in trying to improve the human condition, and that this cannot be done by severely repressing human freedom and by tightly regulating human social and economic activity. At the same time, I would not describe capitalism as Christian. Modern processes—railways, the Internet, large-scale agriculture, mass production, and government itself—are not Christian, but they are all, like capitalism, tools that can be used to make a good life possible for more people; by good life, I mean in this context good in both the material and the moral senses. I am sufficiently secularized to accept that the two are not entirely separable.

Lester Thurow describes the apparent problems of contemporary capitalism within the corporate structure in an essay in *The Atlantic Monthly* (June, 1999). Of relevance here is his picture of work in the contemporary knowledge-based economy. How can one build a career in a system where there are no careers? Even highly-skilled employees quickly become redundant for reasons well beyond their control. The entire production unit may be closed because the product can be produced more cheaply elsewhere or because the product itself becomes obsolete. There is no beneficence on the part of the employer, and the employee reciprocates with minimal loyalty.

His commentary is prophetic in the light of the collapse in high-tech in the winter of 2000–2001.

At first sight, employment in that kind of workplace appears to be a Christian nightmare; but is the situation really any worse than most working environments through the centuries? Further, Thurow exaggerates the prevalence of that pattern, typical of the high-tech world, one which tends to attract highly individualistic employees in the first place. Hardworking, productive employees remain valued by most companies and once again I caution against strong claims concerning the nature of other people's, or even one's own, motivation. After all, it is a universal truth that people, today and yesterday, stop working for their employer when the employer ceases to pay them. The essential character of the highly developed and bureaucratized world of work is contractual—that is the nature of modern organization; it is one of the reasons why I believe that the family, the extended family, the community, leisure activity, and the ideal school should remain substantially non-contractual.

In the early years of management "theory," D. M. McGregor (in *The Human Side of Enterprise*) wrote of organizational patterns 'x' and 'y', the former being a bureaucratic, hierarchical model, the latter, which he of course favoured, the new cooperative, informal model. However, he, unlike many of the enthusiastic experts that followed him, admitted that the manager, irrespective of organization and personal style, who behaves honestly and stands up for those who work for him is the person who is successful. Since then, management theories and styles have come and gone, but the standing of the authentic manager, who is straightforward, transparent, hardworking, considerate, firm, open to advice, and true (to both authority and subordinate) holds; there is no guarantee of continued employment for such an individual, and there never has been. Doing the right thing has never been a guarantor of reward.

A relative of mine worked for Shell, a major oil company with a paternalist reputation of looking after its employees. He was intensely loyal to his company, singing the qualities of its every product. Although I do not doubt his integrity, enormous commitment to a corporation, which is necessarily committed first to profit, can easily lead to a blind devotion that sees no evil. In a situation of supposed benevolence, moving out becomes disloyalty, blowing the whistle unthinkable.

Another man I met worked for a very different oil company, Texaco Canada, in which there was little mutual loyalty on the part of either employer or employees. He knew that he would be let go if he did not produce, but he was well paid as long as he did. It is difficult to see how the Shell relationship is intrinsically more moral, less open to corruption, than the latter. Most people may well find the first environment more comfortable, but comfort and right are not habitual partners. A comfortable environment for employees can readily be accompanied by unsatisfactory treatment of clients—notably the case in schools and social work.

Models of management are rarely strongly related to ethics, but ethics should be the first test of any corporate behaviour because we should all follow the virtues, in our working lives as much as in our private lives. Hitler is said to have loved his dog, but that is not enough. Corporations must make money, but they must do so honestly. Enlightened self-interest is not necessarily superior to other forms of self-interest, because the enlightened path will only be followed as long as it does not threaten the self. Enlightened self-interest is often favoured because it works better in the long run, a commercially valid but not a moral reason. Clearly, the individual's motivation is often ambiguous, sometimes moral, sometimes practical. Equally obvious is the fact that we all like to think we are acting on moral motives when we are in fact working for our own long-term best interests.

Significant issues for the Christian are: Is the work I do, and the organization I work for, carrying out work that is legal and helpful to neighbours, to society? Am I free, where relationships are part of the job, to develop true relationships, based on integrity, with my colleagues, superiors, and subordinates, my clients, and the public? (That does not mean we should be friends with everybody; to the contrary, the test of true business relationships is that they are extended to all, not just those close to us). Of all people, the Christian should recognize that there is never a guarantee of peace, prosperity, health, and success. Those who believe they can build a utopia on earth do not recognize human propensity for good and evil.

Can one then be a strong socialist or a strong capitalist and still be Christian? That is an unanswerable because meaningless question. The answer is positive if one inquires as to whether some in each category call themselves Christian and attend church faithfully. The answer is negative if one investigates all the practices each advocates and carries out and checks them for one hundred per cent Christian content. But the second standard is senseless; no Christian is without error and sin in some areas of life; and many persist in denial, ignorance, blind belief, or wilfulness. To assert that corporate or political leaders are or are not Christian on the basis of carefully selected acts or areas of life deprives the word of meaning. How many in any occupation would survive that test? The accusation comes closer when applied to the core of activity; as a generalization neither socialist nor capitalist activity is either Christian or unChristian.

Far more useful than labeling individuals or ideologies unChristian is the identification of right and wrong behaviour, first in ourselves and our friends, and second in those whom we may seek to influence. That is not to say that there are no ideas that are unChristian in their essence; racism, the belief that some races are inferior before God is one such proposition, as must be any belief that deliberately denies classes of human beings their freedom and dignity. Any ideology used as a fundamental guiding principle inevitably conflicts at some point with the Christian God; there is only one absolute. Some ideologies defy God in their very foundation. Whether social- ism or capitalism is more likely to be congenial to Christian expression is a matter of reasonable disagreement. It is fair to state, however, that when ideology approaches fanaticism, when it becomes an idol, Christian belief and behaviour are, by definition, displaced. True Christian behaviour requires that one puts Christian principles first; if the capitalist and the socialist put their political ideals before their Christian moral- ity then they jeopardize their faith.

But what does all this mean in practice? If all human insti- tutions, political and economic, are inevitably weak, ineffi- cient, and lacking in Christian values, if socialists and capital- ists have equal legitimacy in calling themselves Christians, and if the Christian actor still has a responsibility to take legitimate steps to improve the political and economic environment, what should a person do?

Crucially, it comes back as it must to the ideals of Christian conduct, to the virtues. The most pressing and evident problem facing the Christian economist and politician in the West today is that of poverty, i.e., lack of the basic necessities of life, both among a small minority in our own countries (probably under ten per cent) and also in much larger numbers and proportions in the less developed world. First, we should humbly remember that universal problems are probably not curable, certainly not quickly. Revolution and grand plans have not worked in the past and are unlikely to work in the future. Second, we should remind ourselves that right action demands that we do what we can, that which we could reasonably hope for if we were among the poor. Third, we should observe that simply promoting socialism or capitalism is most unlikely to address the problem in a serious way; there are obvious examples of countries where neither socialism nor capitalism appears to have done much to remediate poverty, indeed where they have aggravated it. Consider for example the old Soviet Union, much of eastern Europe, North Korea, Kampuchea (Cambodia), Tanzania, and Nicaragua under socialism, and Kenya, Brazil, Guatemala, Pakistan, Indonesia, and, again, more recent Nicaragua, under some simulation of capitalism. Both sides will fairly claim that their list of countries never implemented true socialism or capitalism, but that is the point; true socialism and true capitalism, as described by their most enthusiastic and idealistic supporters, will never be implemented. If we look at wealthier representatives of their ideology, Sweden and Ireland perhaps, we are no closer to determining the way to utopia; it is the practice of democracy and their relative affluence that fundamentally distinguish those two countries from the others; they are more like each other than they are respectively like North Korea and Brazil. Overall, the last century suggests that poverty is endemic and enduring in socialist more often than in capitalist countries, but there are contrary examples.

At home, there are several, different approaches to a reduction in poverty. Equality of educational opportunity should be defined as providing educational choices to parents within the legitimate limits of a democratic, pluralist society, and to ensuring that school programs for the most part lead to work or to higher education; as children grow older they will increasingly operationalize those choices themselves. It should be possible for all young people to compete fairly for places in post-secondary education, and to be funded, by parents, their own work, grants, and loans, in such a way that no young person is denied access to education simply as a result of parental poverty or unwillingness to help. There should be clear and public standards of achievement and behaviour required for high school graduation. Those principles are neither capitalist nor socialist. One could make a case for a strongly centralized state system—to make things more the same, or a system highly reliant on publicly supported independent schools, to provide genuine choices. My own view is that the first has conspicuously failed in pluralist countries, not least because parents do not all have the same educational goals for their children. The public emphasis on material goods and their distribution as being the only criterion for judging an affluent country has the effect of ensuring that poverty , expressed, as it usually is, in purely relative terms, can never be mitigated.

Incentives should be provided to employers to select young people for jobs in times of high unemployment by encouraging self-supported early retirement and by financially discouraging work after a determined retirement age.

A distinction between the deserving poor and the undeserving poor should be re-introduced, with generous support for individuals and families whose poor circumstances result from factors that are external and beyond their own control or irremediable, but less generous support of limited duration in the case of those whose difficulties should be temporary. It is vitally important for human dignity and self-knowledge for people to take responsibility for their own lives and mistakes. Blaming others for all misfortune, excessive self-pity, is unhelpful. One does not have to assume motivation (laziness, for example), but it is possible to determine if a person is reasonably capable of doing an assigned task. The principle of providing lifetime financial support for individuals able but unwilling to support themselves corrodes personal responsibility by explicitly denying it.

For those who are in large part responsible for their own condition (e.g., those who refuse available work; single women who give birth and continue to give birth without prospects of support for the children), help should be minimal and conditional on enforceable requirements. Further, those who have a history of behaving irresponsibly should be helped more in kind than in cash, until they can demonstrate sound use of their resources. For example, food stamps and accommodation vouchers should be important parts of their state support; accommodation vouchers would also make it easier for them to find housing, as owners would have minimal fear of default (although they would still be concerned about vandalism, sometimes a quality of those lacking personal responsibility and self-respect).

Clearly, those are personal ideas that do not stem ineluctably from Christian virtue; I would argue, however, that they are highly consistent with Christian belief. Sapping people's independence responsibility is morally corrupt. There is superficial inconsistency between the value of independence and the endorsement of food stamps and accommodation vouchers. There are two answers. First, independence cannot be taught by simply giving irresponsible people large amounts of other people's money—the alternative promoted by many advocates for the poor; handouts teach dependence. Sensible parents, who want their children to become self-supporting, do not teach their children to be responsible by giving them abundant freedom and material goods at a young age, but rather by having them share the responsibility for the upkeep of the home and their own wants. Second, in the case of needy adults with children, society has a special obligation to help the children escape the poverty trap; it is not fair to give parents money in the knowledge that the children will still suffer deprivation because the money will be spent in inappropriate ways. Clearly there should be limits on interference within the family, but the provision of directed aid for accommodation and food is well within those limits. Consistently, I oppose food banks because they sometimes make little distinction between the genuinely needy and those with wants, and are almost never in a position to judge the worthiness of the need. In addition, they promote continued dependence.

None of this is to claim that the mainline churches are being unChristian when they demand that government spend more on those on welfare; it is to reject their claim to certitude, to speak for all their members, when they assume that their policy is the Christian one and, worse, that those who wish to limit and target expenditures on welfare are unChristian. Making an able-bodied person, perfectly capable of working, a ward of the state or of a private charity, is to rob that person of her fundamental dignity, however well-intentioned the policy. As an analogy, I believe it is equally wrong, perhaps worse, for parents to support their able-bodied, employable adult children (except over a short-term emergency).

There is no question that Christians have an obligation to help those less fortunate than they are, as individuals; but that general principle still implies wisdom in its practice. Should the Christian give a twenty-dollar bill to an alcoholic neighbour who regularly gets drunk and then assaults his wife and children? I think not. It is another matter entirely to argue that it is, as a matter of principle, the Christian duty of members of government to spend other people's money in a cause, say universal increases in welfare payments, about which both Christians and non-Christians reasonably differ, both because the spending of the money is often ineffective (when it erodes independence) and because there is no moral merit in spending somebody else's money on one's own cause. Yes, it is a disgrace to an affluent society when children are brought up degraded and in extreme poverty. But it is also a terrible thing if government tempts able-bodied people to become wholly dependent on welfare, and young dependent women to have more children at the taxpayers' expense, at the same time discouraging them from entering a marriage for fear of losing their government cheque. No one, Christian or not, can sail securely between the Scylla of total self-reliance and the Charybdis of excessive government control. We should not imagine that government policies can be neatly characterized as right or wrong; Christianity speaks to our individual lives, being right with God, being right with our neighbour. It does not direct our view of government policy on a day-to-day basis.

There is no reason to believe that more government is more Christian than less (or vice versa). There is no reason to believe that distributing other people's wealth is more Christian than allowing people the freedom to increase their own, and perhaps others', wealth (within the limits of human dignity and a sustainable environment); indeed, obsession with secular intervention in other people's lives is likely to interfere with a Christian life. The Christian does not see government as the answer to every problem; many problems are insoluble and others are for us to overcome ourselves, alone or with others.

Clearly, a Christian life is more possible in a country where all people are treated with dignity, where all have access to work, where personal freedom of belief and expression is safeguarded, where all children are fed, cared for, and educated, and where there is social order, than in one where there is widespread disorder, poverty, crime, and degradation. But the way to reach that more desirable state is the crucial area of dispute among political ideologies. Furthermore, the inevitability of human weakness and, with power, corruption makes any grand plan suspect. The first duty of Christians is to reform themselves and help those around them, not to save the world by enforced recruitment, by regulation or government propaganda, to a secular cause.

Does this mean that Christian politicians have no responsibilities other than those covered by their political ideology and party loyalty, seeing no political manifesto is clearly Christian? Quite the opposite. The first responsibility is to live a Christian life based on truth, justice, courage, the golden rule, humility, constancy, and personal responsibility. One's integrity is inevitably tested in a democracy.

Ultimately, the politician should accept Edmund Burke's maxim that one should behave according to one's own sense of right, bearing in mind but not being directed by the wishes of one's constituents. On the other hand, there are many occasions for honest and open compromise or deference to sustained public will. Suppose one believes that all (or nearly all) abortion is wrong, but knows also that the majority believes in abortion in numerous circumstances. It would be wrong then to pressure or compel one's party to ban abortion in all conditions, to force one's own minority beliefs on a people, many of whom are not Christian. One's own conduct is a different matter, and one may choose to vote personally against the popular will or to abstain. Essentially, on matters of deeply held religious and moral conviction, the Christian should push for free votes, without party discipline, and for referenda and plebiscites.

There are important conditions for dependence on expressions of public opinion. There should be a few clear choices, with no important alternative excluded from the ballot. Further, referenda are not a legitimate means of acting against the legitimate interests of minorities. Examples of illegitimate referenda would include a vote: to increase income taxation of the rich; to fund francophone or Pentecostal schools; and to make the trapping of wild animals illegal. Examples of legitimate subjects for referenda would include a vote: to create a crime of capital (i.e., worthy of the death penalty) or third degree (one with a sentence based on mitigating circumstances) murder; to develop humane standards for the treatment of farm animals; and to abolish casino gambling or slot machines.

The Christian should accept the will of others not to be Christian, in the knowledge that the choice of the right way is definitively a free act. Compelling everyone else to do everything we consider morally right is unChristian, but there are and must be laws to prevent harm to the state and the person; they are often appropriately based on traditional morality—they disallow those acts that are clearly wrong and harmful to social order—murder, assault, and theft.

A major responsibility of Christian politicians is not to allow the party ideology and platform to override fundamental principles of ethical conduct. Even the best political ideas, taken to an extreme, become authoritarian and damaging to those caught in the wave. One must always be aware of the decent people hurt in the rush to change.

Does this mean that government has the responsibility to mitigate the worst side-effects of capitalism? Of course. To place unlimited individual freedom before public order and decency, before consideration for others, is to make the individual person a god worthy of self-worship. But at the same time, socialist principles that require nearly all parents to accept a state-run, secular, and spiritually offensive educational program, in the pursuit of some impossible version of equality is to make a god of the state, in which government and its agents are deemed wiser and more true than its weakened and pliable citizens. Government has the responsibility to mitigate the side effects of all economic and political policy, where people are seriously damaged, within the limits of what is feasible, practical, and apparently in the best interests of society.

The problem of poverty has been referred to; what of the problem of affluence, of the rich? Is it not difficult for the rich to find the right way? Rich and poor will always be with us, for the simple reason that those categories are increasingly in the West relative more than absolute descriptors. There will always be envy of those who have more, whether deserved or undeserved. There is no essential problem in being rich (or not so rich); there is a problem in being consumed (whether one is advantaged or disadvantaged) with becoming richer, getting more. The sight of an affluent person, worth millions, expressing his greed is more aesthetically unattractive than that of a low income person always on the lookout for self-advantage, but the two moral vices are comparable.

Most of us in the West are rich compared with our ancestors and our fellow human beings in less developed countries, but we are not necessarily more corrupt or wicked. The objection is not to technology, cars, or television, in themselves but to the doctrine of more and to the distraction from our moral and spiritual lives. But a democratic government cannot prevent or punish greed, in rich capitalists or in poor laborers, except if they are known to steal or cheat, just as they cannot prevent parents abandoning their spouses and children in pursuit of some personal sense of fulfillment. What they can do is draw a line to prevent the excesses of some and the extreme deprivation of others; as more sharing usually means a smaller pie to share, people work less hard for others than they do for themselves and their families, that judgment requires the wisdom of Solomon.

But is it not Christian, some will press, for government to promote less difference between rich and poor than there is now? To even that apparently easy question, there is no ready Christian answer. Less than what? Do not even small differences become great in the circumstances? Are not children as upset about being given fewer candies than their siblings as their parents about having a smaller house or car than their friends? Do not well-rewarded ministers of government compare the area, furnishings, and aspect of their offices? There is no right Christian ratio between high and low income. At the same time, the display of wealth and waste, whether by public officials (which is worse) or private citizens, the individual concern with more, with greed, and the absence of care for others are all to be condemned. But government cannot make us good; it can only set up circumstances where people have a reasonable opportunity to do the right thing, where there is not easily avoided temptation, where property is secure, where there is order, and where education and truth flourish.

I wrote earlier that it is easier to live a Christian life in a democratic country where the individual is free and respected than in one where there is a constant struggle for survival, against the human and physical elements. Ironically, however, Christianity is being leached away in the most affluent countries and growing stronger in many developing countries where Christians face hardship and oppression. It should never be thought that making things easy for people makes for strong Christians. Becoming an integrated part of a wealthy, secular democratic society clearly weakens one's religious faith. The right choice is easily made, if that is what the individual wants; but there are many other choices, temptations, to distract and seduce.

Christianity has little (but not nothing) to say in direct policy terms about the economy and politics. Neither socialism nor capitalism is Christian, because neither is identified with Christian ends or Christian conduct. And taking half of each of two sets of non-Christian principles, even if it were feasible, does not make for Christian policy. Christianity no more tells us the truth about helpful and unhelpful ideologies than it tells us the truth about science; either may conflict with Christian principles (when, for example, science is used to kill the enemies of those in power, as in Hitler's Germany and Stalin's Russia), but in essence they consist of ideas that frequently operate outside the spiritual realm. But that absence of clear prescription does not give individuals *carte blanche* to pursue their plans thinking they can separate their secular lives from their religious lives. Socialism falsely assumes that government can do most important things better than individuals and their communities can do for themselves, that elected and appointed officials are less prone to human weakness than others. Capitalists and libertarians falsely assume that the more individuals are free, the fewer the limits and restraints society places on their behaviour, the more progress and happiness we shall all enjoy; freedom becomes the purpose of life. Both freedom and government regulation are false gods. Neither the world nor our country will be put right either by central planning or by removing limits to freedom, because both policies put human beings, in the form of government or in the form of the individual, before God.

What Christianity tells us all, whether rich or poor, whether leader or led, is how we should live our own lives, raise our children, and live with our neighbours. In that sense, Christianity speaks to economist, financier, and political leader; it tells what they should try to become and what they should be. It does not usually tell us which politicians to choose (we should of course shun those few who are persistently and deliberately immoral and deny truth, who continue to deny or trample on virtue), but it may on occasion suggest some questions to put to them and some ways to judge their actions. We should not, however, join the popular pastime of claiming that all politicians are liars and crooks. I have seen no evidence that politicians are less moral than those in other occupations; their decisions are simply more visible. On the other hand, political power, like all forms of authority, does tend to corrupt.

Violence

Crime and punishment become an even more difficult moral issue because the tradition is sharply divided. Extreme positions on crime and punishment, as well as violence in war, can be justified within the Judaeo-Christian tradition. It is important that

Christian leaders do not announce **the** Christian position (on war, and capital or corporal punishment, for example), when they describe their personal Christian interpretation.

There is an important distinction between the nature of Christian attitudes to sexual activity and attitudes to violence and theft. In the case of sexual acts, the core of the dispute concerns the acts that may be accepted, condoned, and permitted within the church membership and within the ministry. Should a minister who has had a pattern of consensual sexual relationships with members of the congregation and others be permitted to remain in the ministry, either in that church or another? Should the choir director who has left his spouse and moved in with a member of the choir remain director? There will be incomplete agreement. But few Christians will want to retain a minister who habitually steals or resorts to violence.

The difference (between attitudes towards sexual and violent acts) also arises in the treatment of violence and theft by the law. There are some Christians, usually living in segregated communities, who disapprove all violence. They are consistent, whether the aggression is against a member of the local community, or an enemy in time of war. While there are many passages in the Gospels that would support total nonviolence, there are as many in both testaments that are equally bloodthirsty. Pacifism is supported by a tiny minority of Christians, and is only a minor part of the tradition. While no one is going to accuse pacifists of being unChristian, few will join their ranks.

In practice, therefore, most Christians are faced with decisions concerning the circumstances that justify war and other forms of violence. Christians as a whole are rightly conscious of our unwholesome past, where the church has supported and joined in wars that, in retrospect, were wholly unjustified. They are aware too of the contribution of religion to the ongoing violence in Northern Ireland and the Balkans. In addition, Christians have approved or condoned slavery and the regular beating of wives and children.

There is no coherent consensus among Christian churches on what makes a just war. So, Christians disagree on the violence in which the West has been recently involved, the two attacks on Iraq, and the invasions of Haiti, Somalia, Haiti, Panama, and Serbia (Kosovo), together with the involvement in Bosnia's occupation. It seems to me that a Christian community in the West may justifiably support or accept violence by the state to protect itself and its important interests, and to support its nation's democratic allies in similar situations. At the same time, there must be practical, consequentialist considerations—notably, that the violence will not have the effect of doing more harm than good; there must be a good probability that it will succeed. Earlier, it was argued that there are important areas in the life of the state where Christian input is not of much relevance—the times when we should give to Rome what is Rome's. There is enormous political disagreement among Christians and it is often difficult to define coherently the Christian nature of a proposed action; Christian individuals may have strong opinions, but the objectively right Christian choice is not always obvious. A case can be made that inter-state violence is an example of the impossibility of agreement. Paradoxically, it also seems strange that Christians should have nothing to say about the prosecution of war. The Pope does speak clearly, and reasonably consistently, on behalf of Roman Catholics, but it is far from certain that a majority would consistently share his political judgments.

A hard test for the Christian is the case of Rwanda. The genocide committed by the majority Hutus over the effectively ruling Tutsis was foreseeable and there was a United Nations presence in Rwanda at the time of the carefully planned attack.

Indeed, Canadian General Dallaire requested help from the UN and has since condemned the UN for inaction, claiming that the bloodbath could have been avoided. He has attributed inaction to racism, contrasting the failure to intervene with the intervention in Bosnia and Kosovo. Superficially, it appears that a conscientious Christian should condemn the failure of governments to act.

Once again, we should be careful not confuse government with the individual person. The condemnation, after the fact, has been of the governments of the United States, France, and Britain, the only ones with military forces capable of mobilization in Rwanda at short notice. I do not doubt that those countries' leaders understood that genocidal warfare was possible or likely; they only had to read the newspapers at the time. But were they wrong not to send heir troops? Citizens of other countries, such as Canada, are criticizing the leaders of states with military capacity for not doing something that would cost themselves nothing.

Consider, too, that while in medieval times, leaders usually led their troops into battle at great risk to themselves, civilian leaders today give orders from a safe haven and even generals may be far from the field of action. The Iraq wars and the attack on Serbia over Kosovo are examples of the trend towards vicarious warfare on the part of the most powerful. The leaders are not risking their own or their own children's lives (very few contemporary leaders have experienced action in warfare themselves), but those of anonymous others. It is analogous to citizens saying government should spend "its" money on this or that purpose—democratic leaders do not have money other than that they raise from us; the soldiers to be sacrificed are rarely their own sons and daughters. There is a problem in accepting the death of many of one's country's citizens when the success of the project is doubtful and when the interests of one's own people, whom the soldiers morally contracted to defend, are not threatened. In other words, a high tech war with little fear of loss to one's own armed forces and a ground war with a probability of heavy losses are both morally problematic, in different ways, if there is little threat to one's own country and its allies.

The West had almost no direct interest in Rwanda. The bitter enmity between the Hutus and Tutsis (in Burundi and Rwanda) is of long standing. There is no line on the ground separating the two peoples and they are sometimes difficult to tell apart from appearance; neither is a pure race. Civil wars are typically the most bloody and horrific of wars. In those circumstances, would it have been moral for the leaders of those three Western countries, singly or collectively, to have attempted to maintain peace by force, to have sacrificed their soldiers' lives? I believe the leaders were correct.

Subsequently, the genocide ceased when an army of exiled Tutsis invaded from Uganda. As they drove the Hutu army back, France did intervene, in effect saving the Hutu army—the perpetrator of the genocide—to fight another day; by the time France intervened, there was a rough line between the two armies and the territories controlled by each. The French action raises the question as to how impartial a UN force could have been, with France traditionally linked with the Hutus, the Americans and British perhaps more favourable to the Tutsis.

In the same way, the UN forces in Bosnia and Kosovo, with the exception of the French, appear to have singled out Serbia as the wicked enemy from the beginning. Serbia did behave the worst, but possibly only because it was the most powerful participant; Croatians and Muslims committed their own atrocities given the opportunity. All problems are not solvable, and one has to be wary of asking others to sacrifice their lives for one's own moral beliefs.

One thing is sure—there will rarely be a strong consensual Christian voice, but that does not mean that individuals should stay silent, not even trying to convince others of what they believe their faith or ideology demands. It is important that we judge our actions on what we believe to be Christian principles, rather than on the basis of ideological principles which we convince ourselves are consistent with Christianity.

Many liberal Christians supported intervention in Kosovo more strongly than they did intervention in Kuwait, despite the considerable loss of life (and ruthless aggression) on both sides of the Kosovo conflict, the infringement of national boundaries, the deliberate killing of Serb civilians, and the West's lack of direct interest. Indeed, they see intervention when there is no self-interest as being particularly praiseworthy. That is a sign of the decline of family and community as positive values; most people, most juries, even today, would justify parents' use of unnecessarily, extreme force, even if it were fatal, to deflect an attack on their child more than they would that by a disinterested bystander. While Jesus, in the case of the good Samaritan, was opposed to excessive clan loyalty when it was a matter of disregarding the golden rule, the Bible as a whole—including parts of the New Testament—must be seen as being strongly (indeed, overly) supportive of tribe, community, and family.

There is a difference between defending one's community right or wrong, and defending it right. In Somalia, the West was trying to bring peace in a country involved in extended civil war; it was never clear what could be achieved without massive occupation over a long period of time. The cases of Bosnia and Kosovo are somewhat similar; in both cases, we had less self-interest than in Kuwait and were trying to install a multicultural society (in our own image) which appealed to none of the combatants when they were in positions of power. A question we might ask is: Can we achieve some positive advantage for those concerned at an acceptable cost to our own people? The answer, even with the benefit of hindsight, is unclear in the cases of Bosnia and Kosovo. In the cases of Rwanda and Somalia, it is probably negative.

It is important to note that, for those who reject total non-violence, pacifism, it is axiomatic that governments do and should follow different rules from individuals. But that does not exempt them from applying the test of right and wrong, from distinguishing what is best for society and the world from what is best for oneself.

Conclusion— Christianity in everyday life

It is clear that the foundation of this book is a belief in the good, which necessarily requires a conflict with bad; as there is no dark without light, so there is no good without evil. On the one hand, our prime purpose is to find the right way; on the other, particularly as parents raising children, especially in adolescence, we have to make them aware of the reality and consequences of their choices.

Christians are prey to two opposed kinds of error. Those on the right are susceptible to a certainty of rectitude both in morality and in theology; it is easy for them to exclude from the ranks of Christians large numbers of sincere and good-living church members based on differences of doctrine. Those on the left are subject to the melding of their religious and secular ideologies in such a way that those who simply disagree with them on the application of Christian principles to matters of government policy (e.g., those who support rules limiting welfare, who support rigorous, non-therapeutic treatment of criminals, and those who oppose greater income distribution through the tax system) are, at best, seen as ignorant and misguided people in need of more Christian education, at worst dismissed as unChristian rednecks. Many Christians fall to neither temptation, but those Christian leaders who stick to one of those stereotypical extremes are likely to be welcomed by the media, which are inhospitable to nuance and subtlety.

Dwelling too much on these meaty issues is as bad as pretending they can be papered over. We too easily fall into the secularist trap of defining our faith only in terms of the currently popular secular concerns. I may have made that mistake in this chapter; the reader should bear in mind how inconclusive is the application of Christianity to complex policy issues; in contrast, in our daily lives its is for the most part easy to discern right from wrong related to our own behaviour; most of us never have to face Robert Latimer's problem.

The fundamental issue above and beyond the examples of Christianity's moral ambiguities in today's world is not whether our government terminates or imprisons for life the worst criminals, accepts divorce after one or three years of separation, bombs outlaw states, increases the size of the economic pie instead of sharing a smaller pie more equally, or supports homosexual practice as a basis for marriage or its "equivalent." The real issue facing us is whether we live our lives based on a substantive idea of God representing the right way, or if we live our lives free of external constraints, picking and choosing our own charts from currently popular, secular ideologies—materialist capitalism, universal human rights, environmentalism, fashionable emotivist causes, progressive control by a powerful state, and libertarian individualism. Another way of defining the choice is to decide whether we should first live by determining what is right, our Christian duty, or live by what our secular enthusiasm tells us we should exhort others to do. There is a divide between government, where individually we have little influence, and private life. Simply, we have to decide if the prime enemy is we, and people like us, or mainly those wicked others, them, whom we love to disparage. I am dismayed when ministers choose examples of wrongdoing by those outside their church—typically drawn from churches different from their own or from government, ignoring the sins to which their own congregation are drawn. This is not to deny a place for voicing a clear opinion where there is a clear Christian alternative.

How should we live our lives?

In Chapter 5, I outlined a statement of virtue and ethics based on the Christian tradition. In this chapter, those ideas have been applied to a few examples of contemporary life. There should be no seam between the two. If conduct lies at the heart of Christianity (and any religion), the skeptic will reasonably wonder which path to follow. There can be no satisfactory answer that will please all Christians, but it is possible to give a few examples of what follows, at least in terms of the kinds of considerations the Christian should take into account, placing principle, truth, before immediate consequences. The purpose here is to bring together the two chapters.

A forceful consequentialist conclusion concerning Christian conduct is that there are advantages to parents raising their children as Christians, in giving them a Christian education, at home and at school.

Young people raised within a Christian family and school are in some respects better behaved. There is evidence that they are less likely to indulge in sex and illegal drugs during adolescence (and therefore unlikely to suffer the unhappy experiences that so often follow). It may be objected that there is nothing wrong with youthful experience with sex and drugs and that the statistical relationship does not stem from Christianity but other aspects of the typical Christian home. Both objections are irrelevant to the point that I am making. Those who have no respect for good, traditional Christian conduct are not going to be swayed by any argument that places conduct at the heart of Christianity and family life. Others may interpret the spiritual aspects as leaving individuals free to order their lives as they wish as long as they do not "hurt others" in some ill-defined way (typically according to trendy secular thought). The traditional virtues are virtues precisely because they provide an order in the relationships between individuals and their God, and individuals and other people—a theme throughout this book; among other things, they usually do reduce the probability of hurt.

Those who support divorce and abortion on demand, the value of the single parent family, and cohabitation before marriage, deny the obvious hurt to which these values so often lead; but then most wrongdoers have always rationalized their behaviour, however obvious the empirical facts. The usual trick for contemporary rationalization is to compare the problems of current practices with some extreme version of traditional oppression.

One reason why one should honour truth is that dishonesty is in itself hurtful, to those to whom the lie is told, to the community and society which depend on good faith for survival, and to the liar. The assertion, "I lied, but it was for their own good," is nearly always offensive. One may be pretty sure that the lie is advantageous to the liar (in maintaining an image or avoiding trouble). Consequential reasons why sixteen-year-olds should not have sex are that it may spread disease, result in unwanted pregnancy, cause emotional turmoil, lead to promiscuity, and interfere with the development of a mature and enduring love. More simply, Christians should not be ashamed of stating that bringing purity to a marriage based on love and commitment is a reason in itself; loving sex within marriage is right. There are few people who are not moved by a true marriage based on love.

The precise reasons why Christian families tend to produce more virtuous and civic children are obviously complex;

clearly, if parents, Christians or not, are themselves sensible and virtuous people, their children are likely (but not certain) to learn from them. It would be perverse, however, to suggest, as many liberals do, that parents should refrain from teaching, from "indoctrinating," their children, because that will make them rebel. The evidence goes the other way. Sound education, promoting the ways and ideas one wants, makes more sense than miseducation or a vacuum of so-called "freedom." Parents who believe that individual freedom is the highest goal act on that assumption, and give their children as much freedom as reasonably possible from the earliest age. Clearly, adolescents who believe their individual freedom is of the greatest importance are less likely to pay attention to a version of Christian virtue that restricts their freedom, putting an abstract God before self. The idea that preaching anything to young people simply incites rebellion is false (although young people will always rebel against some rules and some balk at almost any limit).

The implication is that parents should generally favour a school that supports rather than undermines their beliefs.

The education one wants for one's children's education speaks to what one wants them to become. The skeptical Christians to whom this book is addressed are likely to want their children to grow up as decent citizens, good people, who will want to marry and raise a family. They will want them to be educated in terms of their interests and abilities and to become independent, diligent, and responsible. They will want them to understand and sympathize with different world views, but not succumb to the intellectual's temptation of believing that clever argument is more important than right action. Most of all good parents provide moral and religious education by means of what they are, and by how they try to live their lives. What is true inside the family is equally valid outside. The way

316

we treat our friends, strangers, relatives, and fellow workers is more important than the values and beliefs we announce.

But how do we determine which are the fundamental values, and how they should be applied, for our children, and for ourselves? The Ten Commandments are all very well, but they were written in simpler times; today's society is much more complex, internationally, in the workplace, and in the family.

Previously, I relied on a history of the origins of Christian morality to sketch the foundations of our faith in terms of implications for conduct. Interestingly, Meeks ends his book with conclusions about Christian morality, not just as a historical museum piece, but as a living ethic (pp. 213–219). In quoting his conclusions, I do not suggest that the first few centuries were a golden age for Christianity; historians have done an effective job of debunking any idea that early Christian leaders, such as the popes, were good-living models for us all. The point is that the narrative drawn from the first centuries has, for a great many Christians, substantially stood the test of time. The skeptic should not dismiss them out-of-hand.

Meeks develops seven theses, six of which are generally consistent with the narrative in this book. His first thesis is that **making morals and making community are one dialectical process**. Virtue only makes sense in the context of others. We find our morality by being right with God; we practise virtue by being right with others. We skeptics often begin within the community of our family and a small circle of friends and neighbours. Meeks discards rationality as an alternative to the moral community, pointing out that no form of rationalism "has succeeded in finding a place to stand outside" the human community and its tradition, nor a first premise purified of interest. Certainly, every community requires "frequent criticism." And a fanatical community devoted to a relatively good principle "can produce great misery." He acknowledges the important point made by Alasdair MacIntyre that Christian ideas are inadequately captured by symbolic expression; virtue must be grounded in social practice. That is the point I have tried to sketch in my outlines of the implications of Christianity for public and private life.

The next thesis is that a **Christian moral community must be grounded in the past.** Postmodernists claim that the one thing we have learned is that all the great traditions are false. They flirt with nihilism while typically subjecting some traditions (notably the Judaeo-Christian Western tradition) to especial calumny. They often implicitly select a grab-bag of values, drawn from their own interest and a pared-down Marxism. Christians should base their moral code on scripture and tradition; this does not mean that an imperfect code must be frozen in time, but that there must be a starting place; we should not be so arrogant as to believe that we can construct a new truth for ourselves from scratch. "The elementary rule," according to Meeks, "is that Christians must know the church's past in order to be faithful."

The third thesis is that **Christianity's roots in Judaism is an integral part of the tradition.** Christians have often constructed a chasm between the two religions and have ignored or denigrated the Jewish tradition. It is not only intolerant and offensive to separate Jews from the common tradition, it is also intellectually dishonest. When one inquires as to the differences between the teaching of Jesus about how we should live and that of the Jewish traditions of his time, there are few if any easy answers. There may be differences of emphasis. I have emphasized two major Christian traditions concerning the context for moral conduct (living outside the material world and living within it), but equally there are, and were, parallels within Judaism. Just as Pentecostals separate themselves significantly from the secular world and mainline Christians do not, so with Orthodox and Reform Jews. There are differences between the two religions, I have argued that Christianity gives greater emphasis to humility, but it is important to remember that Jesus, speaking from his own Jewish tradition, did not preach a novel ethic of conduct.

Meeks continues that **"faithfulness should not be confused with nostalgia."** It is unhelpful to imagine that we can base Christian interpretation solely on an emotional attachment to the myth, ignoring both new knowledge and contemporary life. I am not repeating here the ignoble, false but all too often chanted cliché that change is inevitable and so the church must embrace it. There is nothing inevitable about the church embracing any particular fashion of the time; indeed, there are many fashions that the church should fiercely resist. Many Anglicans reject change by clinging to the *Book of Common Prayer*, over four hundred years old. I, too, prefer the language and expression of the ancient rituals, without believing that we can rebuild our faith and community as though we lived in the sixteenth century. We cannot replicate a golden age because "there was no golden age to replicate." Jesus did not proclaim "a complete, systematic, and novel Christian ethic, nor even a compact set of fundamental principles." "There has not ever been a purely Christian morality, unalloyed with the experiences and traditions of others." There is no contradiction in asserting both that we are alone and should take personal responsibility for our faith and that we should base our beliefs in the past.

The fifth thesis is particularly valuable from the perspective of the Christian skeptic: **Christian ethics must be polyphonic.** There has been continuing talk but far less action in recent decades concerning ecumenism. While it makes sense for Christians to speak as one when it is feasible, it is absurd to imagine that, in a time of increasing dissent on almost any principle, the denominations should or could come together, either on doctrine or on conduct. "Obviously there can be no community and no tradition if everything is permitted" and community depends on a degree of coercion. "Yet unity coerced is unstable." Meeks quotes Saint Paul, "For why is my freedom judged by a conscience not mine?" "Our creative polyphony," he continues, "needs the voices of some sects, some orders, some traditionalists, some experimental communities, some radical prophets."

Skeptics should choose their church thoughtfully, but be wary of one without core beliefs based on the past. The number of literal facts accepted in the Bible is a totally inadequate criterion; what matters is the church's vision of the truth. But where does one draw the line? Some Christians will begin by placing me beyond the line, a heretic, yet mine is in many ways a traditionalist voice, a voice trying sincerely to express the strength and universal truth of the Christian tradition. Many mainline Christians effectively exclude fundamentalists, arguing that they give Christianity a bad name, that their flat earth beliefs are contrary to all common sense (at the same time that they themselves express dogmatic belief in the literal story, or selected parts of the story, of Jesus). I occasionally feel closer to fundamentalists (although I would never survive living in a fundamentalist community) than I do to those liberal Christians who support secular ideologies such as sex before and outside marriage, divorce and abortion on demand, socialist control of the economy, and the abolition of censorship of any form of human expression.

Meeks argues that "common sense" must determine the line. It is "shaped by common lore, common tradition, common practices, by our memory and experience—no other way." Note also that, as a heretic, at no point have I objected to traditional liturgies within the church.

The sixth thesis, where I begin to part company, continues from his dependence on common sense. "**Moral confidence,** not moral certainty, is what we require." I have more reservations about this thesis than the earlier ones. It is true that if one believes in the absolute good (it is not clear whether or not Meeks does), one perceives it through a glass darkly. No person can ever accurately define the dimensions of God. On the other hand, I have argued earlier that there are certain attributes of the good, expressed in virtue, that it is impossible to separate, as a minimum, truth, justice, and courage. It may be often difficult to discern the right way when different qualities of the good appear to conflict, or when there is no right way. Even so, I cannot accept the absence of any moral certainty; there are acts that are definitively good, and others that are definitively bad. At the same time, while one cannot be too good (too truthful, too just, too courageous), it is easy to have too much moral certainty, and many of us do. Meeks does agree that even moral confidence is too often lacking, that reflection alone cannot produce it. Moral confidence "emerges only from moral communities." While I accept my one interpretation of the thesis, it is likely that others will interpret it in a different way; some will transform it into a defence of relativism. A hundred years ago, Christians might have had too much moral certainty, but today they have too little moral confidence based on lore, tradition, and practice.

The problem with that sixth thesis is that it may have the unintended effect of strengthening the relativists, who deny any apprehension of an absolute good. Nonetheless, most skeptics will agree with him that, if communities are to gain more confidence, they should do it less by reflection, more by "trying to do what they are here for." Attendance to one's own spirituality is incomplete without at least equal attention to one's conduct.

So far, I have attempted to relate the theses to my theme. It is possible that Meeks would not accept all my comment and interpretation, but in general there is consistency. (Those who want to check will have to read the last chapter in Meeks).

The last thesis, only indirectly related to moral conduct, superficially appears to be inconsistent with my world view, as well as being unrelated to Meeks' own theme (i.e., the relevance of early Christian history to us today). **"God tends to surprise."** Readers may interpret surprise as coming from the humanized God whom skeptics find irrational. I do not share the God in human psychological form, who chooses, decides, punishes, loves, rages, rewards, and thinks. It is not at all apparent how or why God as the all-powerful, all-knowing, and all-loving designer of the universe would decide to let so many species perish or so much harm come to good people, or to surprise them.

Yet, as Meeks continues, his point can be read in a very different way. He writes of people's surprise as the truth of God emerges—the action, the apprehension, and the perception are all on the part of the human believers. God is not then thinking, "It's time I gave these smug people a jolt." Rather is it that those who seek God may be taken aback by what they discover. One of his "surprises" is that God has not finished with Jews, as Christianity emerges and develops. Meeks asserts that both Christians and Jews should "find ways to affirm the narratives and rhythms of yet other peoples and traditions, once again revising and rehearsing, but not abandoning, their own." In that sense, the weather may surprise us without having any conscious intent to do so; surprise describes our behaviour, not any intention or plan on the part of meteorological physics.

That Meeks and I share an interpretation of the meaning of God is unlikely; but the extent to which we are able to agree on the importance of the roots of Christian conduct is illustrative of the general principle that agreement on the precise dimensions of God and the historical truth of various sections of the Bible is not required for harmony within a contemporary Christian community.

In terms of conduct, Meeks may perhaps be more content with the *status quo* at the beginning of the twenty-first century than I; he sees the context of the historical picture more vividly from his far greater fund of knowledge. His sixth thesis, that confidence rather than certainty is required in terms of Christian conduct, could imply that most problems of the Christian religion, at least in the West, emanate from those, particularly fundamentalists, who pronounce their faith and their rules of conduct with certainty rather than confidence; that may or may not be what Meeks intended. It is nonetheless how mainline Christian leaders interpret that idea. In practice, the more certain evangelical Christian churches are the only ones that are maintaining their numbers; indeed, the rate of decline in Christian congregations appears to be directly related to the level of liberal thinking in the denomination and the individual church, possibly resulting in part from a lack of affirmation of the line between faith and conduct. Evangelicals argue that we should therefore shore up traditional doctrine. Meeks might argue that we should examine one another's differences within the faith with more tolerance; while agreeing with Meeks, my argument is that we should at the same time rebuild traditional codes of conduct.

CHAPTER 7

No Final Answer

It would be comforting to believe that there is just one sensible and right answer to the questions surrounding religious faith. No skeptic can make that claim. All the skeptic can do is try to find truth and live by the best available standard. There follow responses to questions and comments intended to highlight some of the choices to be made, and their consequences. None of the commentators is based on any person whom I know or on any living being. Their voices are inevitably filtered through my own miasma. "Matthew Bishop" is a liberal voice from a mainline Christian denomination; "Lucia Knox" speaks from a conservative, traditionalist, but still mainline, perspective, and "Bernard Hume" is an atheist and rationalist.

Matthew Bishop: Your version of Christianity has it all wrong. You discard the essentials of our faith, the Virgin birth, the miracles, and the Ascension, while you give undue weight to moral standards that are essentially a product of their times, often in the past based on a misunderstanding of human nature superseded by modern science. The first error is the more grave. Your god appears to be nothing more than a philosophical figment; the Christian God is personal, a being with whom true believers can communicate, and gain wisdom, insight, courage, and comfort. What support can a person facing affliction or death gain from your god? You remove the mystery of belief and remove the essence of religion with it. How can a person claim to be Christian if he denies the Christian God, and the truth of the Gospels?

Lucia Knox: I agree with much of what you say, Bishop, except that I cannot accept that moral standards should change with the times and the discoveries of science. Once we leave the essential truths of the Gospels, in terms of both conduct and the creeds, we are on a slippery slope that leads to disbelief. In the end, our religion will only be saved if we stick with the fundamentals. Look how Christianity flourishes in Africa, Asia, and Latin America, where ordinary people accept the traditional words of God in the Bible. The more we analyze, dissect, question, deconstruct, and reconstruct our religion the more laughably pathetic it becomes; ours is a reasonable religion, but it is fundamentally based on revelation and faith; without faith in a divine Jesus, there is nothing. Look how the Unitarian sect descended, first denying the Trinity, and then gradually abandoning any semblance of the Christian faith; today it is just another cause-loving political action group. Some of the more liberal sections of our mainline denominations would have us go the same way, step-by-step down the slippery slope, losing huge chunks of their membership as they go. Holmes goes even further.

MH: You both hark back to the mystery, miracle and, authority on which the church, but not Christian truth, depended in different times. The secular voices of the last two hundred years have destroyed that form of belief in virtually all educated thinking people, and you both know it. The influence of the church has dwindled almost to nothing in the English-speaking West, and most church members have their own sets of belief and unbelief; that goes equally for large numbers of ordained ministers and priests. Do either of you believe literally in the entire Nicene creed? Do you believe that Jesus sits physically at the right hand of God? Do you believe that heaven and hell are actual destinations that we shall all experience after death, and that all people who have not been believing Christians are destined to everlasting perdition? Do you believe that Jesus, as man and God, individually judges everyone who dies, consigning non-believers, animists, Buddhists, and Muslims to torment and hell? I am sure you have some metaphorical explanation for those ideas. Pope John Paul, an admirable and conservative Christian leader, defines hell as being separated from God, a definition with which I concur, but hardly consistent with details in the New Testament.

You rely heavily on consequentialist arguments, Bishop. Do you really mean that people should say they believe in ancient legend and magic because they bring comfort? I have no wish to destroy the simple faith of large numbers of Christians, particularly the elderly who dominate many mainline churches. I am at least as tolerant as you of fundamentalists, for whose code of conduct I have greater respect than you. Nevertheless, if we claim, and I think Christians must, belief in the truth of God, then we should be honest and straightforward about the nature of that truth. I have said I am perfectly happy with traditional forms of worship; indeed, unlike you I prefer the authentic early English versions from Cranmer rather than more recent versions.

Bishop: Yes. That is ironic. Why would you prefer the more literal and less accurate interpretations? You like the difficult language yet hope to attract more people to a more skeptical version of the faith. It doesn't make sense.

MH: The traditional worship has several advantages. The language is aesthetically attractive. It captures the humility of our faith much more strongly than do modern versions, and humility is the aspect of faith most lost in the more liberal, contemporary churches, more interested in trendy self-concept than traditional submission. I attended a service in Fredericton cathedral one morning. A senior cleric sang to a guitar with the children. He sang about a butterfly with the theme, "I'm glad to be me." The theme was unintentionally underlined by the fact that the minister had a microphone, enabling him to drown out the children's voices.

It is also easier to recognize the myth and metaphor in an ancient telling of the narrative than in a modern one, where the contemporary language may give the appearance of matter-of-fact accuracy. Probably to accommodate the Roman Catholic church, with which union was once hoped for, the modern Anglican version asks the congregation to pray for the dead. Neither the traditionalist nor the skeptic should see any sense in praying for the dead. Whatever the destination of the spirit after death, it is determined before those meaningless prayers are offered. In the ancient version, we remember the dead.

I do not have principled objections to modern versions, particularly if they actually do appeal to young people; but a good modern version should underline the truth, not a set of alleged facts that has little currency today. My point is that we should either choose a traditional version for its truth and beauty, recognizing the omnipresence of metaphor (on the details of which we disagree), or we should use a more plain-speaking version that will not alienate young people by pretending to facts that large number of Christians no longer believe in. The liberal churches have fallen into a trap of their own making. They abandon the traditional code of conduct (arguing it is obsolete and filling the vacuum with secular flavours of the year) and cling to the virgin birth (although that belief is weakening), the miracles and divinity of Christ, and the physical resurrection of the body.

There are many other things we could do to draw in young people, but that is not the topic of this book. It is worth mentioning, however, that by the age of ten, many children are unwilling to believe in a bearded god sitting up in heaven loving and forgiving them. Unfortunately, because the religion seems to them, not unreasonably given their experience in church, to be dependent on accepting unbelievable facts, they, during adolescence, reject the whole thing. They consider the church (if at all) as being irrelevant to decisions they make about their conduct. The result is that the mainstream church tries to recapture them by saying in effect, "We don't really care how you behave, as long as you believe in Jesus Christ who loves you whatever you do." A Faustian contract; if they do behave as they want, they are separating themselves from God. It is the leadership of the liberal church that has things the wrong way round, trying to capture souls by not caring about how their owners live in the world. But what is our soul? Surely it is our character, the qualities that make each one of us different from others. That character is built up, not from what we say we believe, but from who we are and what we do. The reality is that these easy entries to Christianity do not even work; it is so easy to say you have found Christ, so difficult to become and remain a Christian.

Jesus did not tell people to go on sinning, but rather to go and sin no more. It is sad that parents bring their children to church because they think a moral foundation is important. Too often their children are taught stories which their parents long ago ceased to believe as factual belief; conduct, if it is taught at all, consists mainly of secular teaching such as tolerance, consideration of the other person, and high self-concept, the same minimal ethic that they receive in the secular public school. Little children believe the stories at first, just as they believe in Santa Claus and the tooth fairy, only to abandon them all later.

A monthly service in which children and adolescents play major parts based on accessible language is something that I like to see. At such services, the emphasis on conduct, missing in some mainline churches today, should be greater rather than less. The core teachings, including all the Commandments, in a context of humble submission should be central.

Just as liberal leaders are quick to disavow fundamentalists, in order to ingratiate themselves with secular friends and acquaintances, many also disapprove or even disown many of their own members. The Anglican church in Canada has its traditionalist prayer book society, evangelicals, and Anglo-Catholics—all disapproved by the dominant secularized hierarchy.

You, Bishop, use parts of the Nicene Creed as a basis for questioning the legitimacy of the skeptic's claim to Christianity. I do have some sympathy with your trying to limit Christian membership (even if it leads to my own rejection by your church). Forty years ago, even had I believed then what I believe today, I would not have called myself a Christian. In those forty years, I have changed, but so has the church. Although there have been skeptical and dissenting members of the Protestant churches for over two centuries, it is only in the last forty or so years that such dissent has become open and almost respectable. Today, Bishop, you know well that I am far from alone in the Protestant mainstream in rejecting a God resembling a human being, supernatural events in the life of Jesus, and a factual account of an afterlife in heaven or hell; such once-heretical ideas are preached openly by ordained members of the mainline churches, as well as being held by significant minorities in the membership. I gave considerable thought to my vows of baptism and confirmation, and believe them as they have been interpreted earlier in the book.

Bishop: We liberals must be reasonably tolerant or we would not allow skeptics like you to stay in the church at all.

Bertrand Hume: The three of you are like blind people groping in an empty room, trying to describe the furniture. But there isn't any. You all build up elaborate conjectures based on some assumed preconception of God. You cannot believe that you have simply been abandoned in an empty room—there must be some spiritual furniture so your imagination makes it so. Your wishful thinking is understandable, but pathetic. All your gods are subjective; they are all made in the image of the human being, and the variants depend on the subjective experience and culture from which individuals speak.

People choose their values to reflect themselves. Holmes chooses a set that reflects himself and his experience. He props them up with fine words like "virtue," but in the end they are just his own personal collection, a typical if rather tired, old-fashioned set of male, European values.

Knox: I don't accept that there are male and female virtues, although historically males may have had more opportunity to demonstrate physical courage and women caring and nurturing. I like Holmes' emphasis of constancy and humility; many would see those as feminine qualities, wrongly in my view. There are of course differences between men and women but there is only one truth. Women display courage and men humility. Men, women, different races and ethnic groups all have different paths to truth, but there is but one God.

MH: Hume is looking through the wrong end of the telescope. When a person expresses values, they are, in his view, definitively that person's individual values, because he cannot conceive of there being an absolute. Turn the telescope around and you will find that the virtues that I have described are not "mine" in any personal sense. Hume says they are "typical";

they stem from the Greco-Roman and, particularly, the Judaeo-Christian tradition. Parts, such as the golden rule, are held by virtually every religion. I use the word virtue rather than value because the former implies something fundamental and invaluable; we all have a hundred values, some of just passing interest. Hume does not use the word virtue because he does not believe there is anything of infinite worth; everything to him is just a passing shadow.

Hume: In the end, Holmes, yours is just a stripped-down version of Knox's beliefs, but no more acceptable or believable than hers or Bishop's; *chacun à son goût*. At least, they can talk to their god and get an answer (or so they imagine) and he is there to comfort them in affliction. Your god is more remote, a god of being rather than action. What's the use of a god that cannot help you, make you well, make you happy, and help you accept misfortune? Your stripped down tooth fairy has run out of cash.

Knox: I have to agree with Hume on that last point. Holmes' version of God is not a personal God, but merely a spirit of which one cannot have personal knowledge. Holmes has not known the living Christ.

MH: Communication with God is an intensely personal affair. There is no one perfect way for everyone. While clearly the communication of a skeptic will differ from that of a devout believer who believes in a personal God, one who knows and determines everything that is forthcoming; the nature of communication differs among believers. It is accurate to say that God cannot answer the skeptic in a direct conversation, but answers to many questions are accessible. I have used the example: "Is that the right thing to do?" For every occasion when the answer is confused, there are a hundred when the answer is clear. Is my God a personal God? If by personal, one means one who has the essential human intellectual attributes (deciding, thinking, judging, choosing), then my God is not personal. If by personal, one means a God accessible to every individual person and one to whom access is difficult to sever, then my God is personal. I do not see "personal" as being a badge of merit, the more the better. I expect that Knox and Bishop, as intelligent people, do not expect God to advise them on their grocery list or choice of wine, probably not to find them a parking place; but some Christians do. Some people experience communication with God as a conversation; I do not assert that they are wrong, but there is not necessarily more truth in their conversation than mine; everything depends on the substance, not the process, of the communication. Communication with God is a mysterious experience. I suspect that those who devote their lives substantially to prayer have a different experience from those, clerics or lay people, who spend most of their time on activities that are not directly religious. I accept the validity of a range of communications with God, drawing the line where a person claims divine authority for an act that is clearly morally wrong.

Hume's belief that there is no spiritual meaning in the world is perfectly rational, as rational as the idealist belief that there is no material existence, that everything is in the mind. I cannot disprove either. But I think we know truth, beauty, courage, and justice as well as we know stars, perhaps better. No more can the all-knowing and all-powerful God to whom Knox subscribes be disproved. The search is for the most reasonable explanation of the truth we see. Hume says there is nothing beyond physical phenomena that is incontrovertibly, objectively true. Most people, with or without formal religion, say they believe in some form of God, something outside themselves, just as they believe in the physical existence of a table. That can of course be attributed to vestigial tradition. More significant to me than the majority claim to belief in God is the fact that so many thoughtful, non-church people search for something they feel is missing from their lives. According to Voltaire, "If God did not exist, it would be necessary to invent him." True in ways he probably did not intend. Many of those who do not search for a transcendental god, invest intense energy, often fanatical, in some form of hobby, work, or ideology. Coming from an atheistic family, I have seen many of those god-substitutes in action; the beliefs that accompany them have quite irrational components, no less ridiculous and usually more harmful than those of Bishop and Knox. Most of those who do not believe in God, do not believe in nothing, but believe anything. In the university, there are departments (in the social sciences and economics) full of intelligence devoted to such ephemera as free markets, postmodernism, and neo-Marxism. In addition, there are people who live dull, grey lives, as spectators, neither really believing (or disbelieving) in anything nor investing any undertaking with enthusiasm; not looking, not finding. It is possible to deny God and not depend on a substitute, but that is not a life most people admire or try to emulate.

Hume: I do believe in meaning. I just don't accept that meaning is defined by some arbitrary set of absolutes out there. Meaning is important; human beings are meaning-makers. I have my own set of values, like anybody else. I just don't defend mine on the basis that they come from God. My values are relative because there are always exceptions to any rule, as you yourself have admitted, Holmes, when you write about even murder being justifiable by circumstance.

MH: If meaning has no root in an absolute good, then one person's claim to good is just as valid as anyone else's. One cannot claim that even the crimes of Hitler and Stalin are particularly egregious; one may claim to hold superior values—

but on what basis? But I did not justify murder; murder is wrong. I argued that punishment should be meted out in terms of the harm done to the community, the need for deterrent, and the protection of the public; some circumstances provide considerable mitigation of the offence.

Bishop: You people have now moved into the other area where Holmes has things back to front. At the same time as he rejects the authority of the foundation of our faith, he tries to keep intact archaic ideas about conduct, condemning sex outside marriage, for example. The Ten Commandments made great sense in the time of small communities and the general principles are still valid today. But if the church for ever condemns the behaviour of its congregation, members will simply leave. We have to be tolerant of human wrongdoing, just as Jesus was. If we condemn every sinner in our church, we shall soon have no one left to reprove, other than seniors who have forgotten their sins or are too old to enjoy them. Sin is not a word I am fond of. We all make mistakes, and judging others for enjoying a healthy and loving relationship outside marriage is one of them.

Knox: I cannot go along with that. We must respect everyone, we must love everyone, but we do not have to love their sins. We are all sinners; we may be forgiven by a merciful God, but the sin itself must be condemned, as Holmes says.

MH: I was not condemning anyone. I write of the goodness of love and sex within marriage. There are many circumstances, but overall there are sound rules for the conduct of life. The Ten Commandments and the Christian virtues speak of right conduct, of being right with God and right with one's family and community.

I do not support the unification of all denominations precisely because there are important differences in our interpretation of the tradition. I have argued for honesty and transparency in our message; it is not even that an entire denomination should agree on everything, certainly not different denominations. It is important for different Christian factions to find common ground where they may—in the belief in a transcendental (absolute) God, in the Christian virtues, and, I hope, the Ten Commandments. There are also some things that individual denominations can agree on, e.g., the status of those whom they join together in holy matrimony and the circumstances in which marriage should take place, the nature of the church hierarchy, and the character of those who are ordained ministers.

Inevitably, there are other matters that will be determined locally by individual churches. Obviously, I, like everyone else, want to join a church which has a certain set of characteristics. Personally, I want a spiritual service that facilitates communication with God, I want sermons that relate the Bible and the tradition to conduct today, I want an aesthetically agreeable context, I want my ideas to be respected, and I want an orderly, prayerful service, where I can experience the spirit of God. At the same time, I recognize other traditions. I would not expect Pentecostals or extreme liberal mainstream churches to follow my ideas, any more than I would Muslims and Jews. There are honest differences within the Christian faith, and greater ones between religions, but God is universal. Even within churches, individual members will differ, but the differences should be small enough to permit the religious community to stand for something, to stand against some forms of conduct, and, live.

For example, although I believe that a good rule is to confine sex to marriage, that is an ideal, just as non-violence is an ideal. There are many single people, without the opportunity or desire for marriage, or divorced, who seek sex without marriage. They are very different from those who cheat on their spouse. It is one thing to accept a minister of the church who chooses to live with another person outside marriage, another entirely to condemn every adult who chooses to live by some different rules.

Knox: In the end, we have to agree to differ. Holmes thinks that loosening the church's hold on its founding beliefs will strengthen it by attracting those who feel spiritually lost, but are put off by Christian dogma. The mainline churches are already too liberal, and they lose members while the more traditional churches hold theirs.

Bishop: You people are still afraid of change—it is the dead hand of ossified tradition that turns away young people. We must embrace change. Even our modern texts are still inaccessible to young people today. We have to speak to them in their own tongue, with their own music. We must embrace new technology, television, the Net, and computer games, and meet them where they are. The constant repetition of the Ten Commandments and the use of archaic liturgy will drive them away faster than anything else I can imagine.

Hume: Nothing you do to embrace change will make any difference. The fundamentalist churches still cling to the uneducated, the ignorant, and the lost, but in time they too will be overtaken by the spirit of the age—freedom and reason. The day of Christianity has passed, except for a few spurts and flickers in third world countries which have been ripped from their own often superior culture by Western imperialism, but the excitement of freedom will eventually reach them too. Progress, freedom, individualism, and the death of supernatural religions are inevitable.

MH: You are at least partly correct, Hume; the Zeitgeist at the beginning of the twenty-first century is freedom; more important than the logical rationality that you worship, however, are materialism and self-fulfillment, which are the most readily accessible and most immediately ingratiating manifestations of freedom. Why, given the experience of the twentieth century—Hitler, Communism, violence, the profanity of popular music, the embrace of sadism and pornography, and a contemporary aesthetic divorced from beauty and harmony—would you be so naïve as to think that more freedom will lead to the acceptance of reason? Reason is a means not an end. Truth is the first casualty of chaos, disorder, and the cult of narcissism.

Bishop thinks that we can attract young people by embracing or simulating the mantras of the age, but the church will always be a pathetic follower, selling its soul for elusive chimera. Few young people are going to prefer a priest singing about himself as a butterfly to the Spice Girls. The church is and will remain for the foreseeable future the preserve of a minority. The question is whether we can make it a worthwhile, influential, and respected voice of truth. Knox thinks the traditional mainline churches can return to a higher level of belief and practice and hold or even augment their congregations. Hume again has it partly right. Most educated people leave because they simply neither believe the foundations of the dogma nor see the relevance of the church to modern life. My argument is that religion's relevance to life is the same as it has always been—the church should call us to being right with God and with our neighbours. Softening that message is to sink into secularism and irrelevance.

Hume: That's all very well, but what is left in your church, without either a fuzzy, kindly old paternal god forgiving everyone, or a fearsome one frightening the wits out of the old and innocent? Tell me, suppose there were clear empirical evidence discovered proving that there had never been a man, Jesus Christ, that he is just a pastiche put together from many sources? Would it affect your faith?

Bishop: Good question, Hume. Is Jesus really alive in your faith, Holmes? Do you claim a personal relationship with Christ as your saviour?

MH: Tolstoy was asked that question more than a century ago, when allegations were made that archaeologists had found evidence of the non-existence of Jesus. Tolstoy's answer is quoted by Wilson (*God's Funeral*, 141): "They are attacking the last of the outworks, and if they carry it, and demonstrate that Christ was never born, it will be all the more evident that the fortress of religion is impregnable. Take away the church, the traditions, the Bible, and even Christ himself: the ultimate fact of man's knowledge of goodness, i.e. of God, directly through reason and conscience, will be as clear and certain as ever, and it will be seen that we are dealing with truths that can never perish—truths that humanity can never afford to part with." That is the core of my answer. Tolstoy himself echoes the tradition that he denies. I referred before to Plato's vision of our being slaves watching shadows on the wall (today literally shadows in boxes called television and computer)—we should turn and see the light, "There is but one, and that one ever."

Knox: So you admit that Christ is a minor figure in your religion?

MH: Was George Herbert, whom I quote, not a devout Christian? I said that Tolstoy's answer was the core of my own response, that my starting and finishing point is God. Tolstoy was writing in the turbulence of late nineteenth century religious disarray. He reflects the combined force of eighteenth century skepticism and nineteenth century discoveries in geology and evolutionary biology. He implicitly accepted an essential conflict between science and religion. Today, most educated people find little if any conflict between the two modes of thought, whether they believe either in some overarching unifying factor embracing both or that science has little to contribute to the distinct entity of the spirit of God. My argument has consistently been that memory of the Christian narrative is essential to the faith; some abstract spirit of good is not enough to feed our minds, our hearts, and our souls. I distinguish between alleged historical events, which I see as, in terms of their historical accuracy, having only minor relevance to religious belief today, and the entire narrative myth (a mix of history and legend), which has everything to do with the sustenance of religious faith. Whereas to many open-minded Christians of the nineteenth century (and even in the twentieth), the new knowledge of science and historical research appeared to be crucially important to spiritual life, today it is unimportant. The story of the life of Jesus, born humbly, renouncing material pleasures of this world, preaching a universal God, dying in the name of God and our sins, despairing of God and forgiving us, his killers, in the final moments, and rising again in the faith, is the crucial allegory. But it would be just that, an interesting allegory, if there were no God to symbolize our consciousness of choice between good and evil.

Bishop: So it's just another story?

MH: Not at all. It is an expression of truth, far more important than whether water was turned to wine, or bread and fish conjured out of thin air, or corporeal bodies shot up into heaven above. Placing spiritual faith in material facts is like the child who falls in love with the picture of a handsome Jesus on the cross or sees a benign old man in white robes as a kinder, softer version of his father. If those fantasies are necessary for some to find the truth of God and the Christian tradition, so be it, but let us not substitute colourful stories, however entrancing, for the truth of God.

Hume: So, the stories, the lies, are all right as long as the end is good? You can fill children with any stuff and nonsense as long as they behave themselves according to your archaic rules?

MH: Ministers of God in particular should never lie, or pretend to believe facts they do not. At the same time, there is no need for them to separate fact from narrative every time they refer to the Bible; sufficient that they make clear on occasion that we differ in the areas of the Bible which we believe to be factual. It is the spiritual truths that they should emphasize; to get hung up on which part of the Bible is literal and total, factual truth (hardly any) is to fall into the trap of a parallel (and conflict) between scientific, empirical fact and spiritual truth. I have no problem with a minister of a mainline church who believes much of the narrative to be factual as long as she recognizes that many of her congregation do not. I have no problem with the minister who does not believe the literal facts as long as he makes it clear that mainline Christians, including himself, vary in their thoughts about the "facts." As for children, they should learn the Christian story as a beautiful tale— it would be a rare mainline Christian who thought the entire legend surrounding Christmas and Easter was factual.

Conclusion

Consider again the fundamental questions of Hans Küng, listed in Chapter 2. Why is there anything at all? I have not attempted a comprehensive explanation of the origin of the universe. I simply do not see the relevance of any plausible explanation of the physical world and its origin to the nature of God; put another way, no theory, old or new, will affect most people's (and my) notion of God. Does that mean there is no meaning in our lives? I have argued that there is reason to believe in something beyond ourselves, first in terms of essential truth and second in terms of the consequences for our lives on earth.

God represents our source of meaning. Although I see God as being external to the human being, without beginning or end, I have also suggested that the question as to whether God is immanent (from ourselves) or transcendental (from outside the human being) is not a vital question for me. I assert simply that there has to be something to be perceived and there has to be a mind to perceive it; there is an it and we nearly all know it. Secular social science has a new word for those people who have no conscience about doing wrong; they are called sociopaths. Note that they are not insane; they know the difference between good and evil, but choose evil. Our soul, defined as the uniqueness of our character, represents our sense of meaning (James Hillman, *The Force of Character and the Lasting Life*, 1999, Random House).

So the question of whether God exists before human life and after the destruction of all human life is unimportant as a spiritual issue, bound up with the concept of the nature of time and space, which we imperfectly understand. Science may well find links between our conscious and unconscious, cognitive and emotional, thought processes, between our physical development and our spiritual growth, thereby supporting the sense of some unitary explanation of human life; there are undoubtedly genetic factors influencing our personalities and attitudes (hence our values), but belief in good continues to transcend science, although undoubtedly the Humes of this world will equally continue to deny such transcendence. I have not attempted a detailed critique of empirical rationalism, but it is widely accepted that when it is used narrowly to eliminate all truths other than those with observable cause and effect, it is reduced to intellectual nihilism.

What ought we to do? That is the second important question in the book, the first being the question and nature of

God's existence; God's existence would have little import if it did not have application to morality. The Judaeo-Christian tradition, through Moses, Jesus, Paul, and the life of the church, has given a continuing message as to what we should do. Critics, including some Christians, are mesmerized by the issues of the times, but they are unimportant compared with the central areas of agreement.

Braithwaite, an empiricist who goes beyond the simplistic, scientific materialism of the nineteenth century, recognizes the spiritual aspects of religion, observable outside the material realm. He agrees with many moralists that, "unless religious principles are moral principles, it makes no sense to speak of putting them into practice" (18). He quotes C. S. Lewis writing of his conversion from philosophical idealism, "a religion that cost nothing," to Christianity, "something to be neither more nor less nor other than *done*." To Braithwaite, emotion is a key aspect of religion, distinguishing it from moral codes such as Confucianism. We talk of loving God because without an emotional attachment a dry code of conduct will soon be adjusted and then put aside (R.B. Braithwaite, *An Empiricist's View of the Nature of Religious Belief*, Cambridge University Press, 1955).

Religion is centrally attached to a moral narrative, he asserts:

> A man is not a professing Christian unless he both proposes to live according to Christian moral principles and associates his intention with thinking of Christian stories, but he need not believe that the empirical propositions presented by the stories correspond to empirical fact (27).

Religion resides in a living tradition, continuously molded, based both on a historical narrative and the code to which it points.

What deserves contempt and what love? The answer stems directly from the previous question. We love God and (in carefully defined terms) our neighbour; we honour our parents and care for our family and our community. Our contempt is for the reverse—the sins of commission and omission. The act of wilfully separating oneself from God is what deserves contempt.

What really matters for us? The answer is clear. What matters is to find meaning in our lives, not just as an abstract, academic perception, but by living a good life. I have argued that goodness is more than just being civil to one's neighbours, it is the acceptance of a standard outside oneself; one does not simply award oneself gold stars for a variety of actions one judges to be altruistic. We should recognize our shortcomings, but within context. We confess our misdoings, not in maundering self-pity and masochistic denial of self, but to move on. We should not close off our lives, but open them up to Plato's light and Herbert's sun (that one ever). There is no single path to the good life; we are gloriously different and make our own way, but every path has right and wrong turns. We all make wrong turns, but the trick is not to die by giving up, but to find a new and better pattern of life within the circumstances in which we find ourselves.

We all meet misfortune not of our own making, and its distribution is never fair; there is no human god up there giving each of us her just deserts. We should distinguish the vagaries of life from the "evil that men do." It is easy to become mired in the luxurious mud of accident, seeing all our problems as stemming from external force, and easier still to attribute all problems to others, to "them," who never treat us as well as we deserve. Christians are tempted to make martyrs of themselves, announcing their list of injuries while implicitly boasting of their ability to bear them, in place of genuine forgiveness; non-Christians are more likely to attribute their problems to the machinations of others, harbouring envy, resentment, and greed.

The Christian way is one built on faith in God, hope, and courage, always treating others as we ourselves wish to be treated.

The sympathetic skeptic may well react to this book along these lines. "There is a lot of common sense in what you say, but I still see no compelling reason why I should join a church. You agree that many churchgoers are still compelled by the facts of the Gospels and the challenge of death. What is the point of joining a community in which I shall be a minority? I live a pretty good life—I am not a terrible sinner. You say there is no point to religion if it has no influence at all on conduct. Why bother? I lead a busy life; if I have spare time, would it not be better to provide some direct community service than to become involved in the mechanics of church life, maintaining the church community and its inevitable fund-raising?"

The core answer to that question is that if you really believe in the good of God, you should want to shore up the belief and the community that shares it. Put another way, it is important to have a way to express your belief, to recognize the light outside yourself, and it is important to society that people who share a belief in God get together and announce it. Western society is essentially secular; church attendance is low and reference to religion in the media is rare and seldom flattering. Even members of mainline congregations live outside church in a secular world where their religion is hidden, perhaps denied—not directly, but inadvertently as a result of a form of shame; the same people would never hide their support of a sports team or make of car.

Our children slip even more easily into total disbelief, because the skeptics' hesitancy in announcing any form of religious belief to friends and co-workers is carried over into an avoidance of "indoctrinating" children; they may, if we are lucky, pick up our fundamental values from our behaviour, but religious understanding is left, by default, to the media and public school, both likely to be neutral or hostile.

We are afraid of admitting religious impulse because we believe we are a small minority, because we do not want to be hypocrites giving the impression that we believe the Bible as being substantially factual, because we think we shall be derided, because we do not want to appear to be priggish, intolerant kill-joys, and because, when pressed, we are not even certain we should claim to be Christians. We are also constantly told by the media that we have no business parading religion in public, although there is no such prohibition in the case of other ideologies.

It is impossible to say how many we skeptics are, but we should bear in mind that only about one-quarter of Canadians (fewer British, more Americans) are regular churchgoers. I suspect that we hangers-on, moths around the light, probably number at least ten per cent of the population, some inside, more outside the mainline churches. That may seem a small minority, but most are likely to be thoughtful people. While the number of actively hostile people may be somewhat greater, it is probably fair to say that the largest proportion of all, at least in Britain and Canada, consists of people who call themselves believers, can even name their denomination, but who live independently of the church, neither hostile nor supportive, using it for baptism, marriage, and death. I should like to reach out to some of them as well as to the self-confessed skeptics; but that can only be accomplished from the basis of a community, a religious tradition.

Francis Fukuyama (277–279) believes that the religious tradition is important to what he sees as a coming reconstitution of social order. There are signs (declining crime rates, leveling off of births outside marriage, and the recapture of some

American cities by law and civility) that he may be correct. It is important that Christians have a stake in the new order, not in the form of some extreme Puritanism, and not in the guise of a New Age religion based on politically correct ideologies.

Once one begins to think of joining a Christian church, the reasons for joining multiply. It is encouraging to meet other people who share one's values. It is good to be able to talk over beliefs without boring or infuriating friends and neighbours. It is good to find a place to channel work for the larger community, knowing it will be directed reasonably consistently with one's own beliefs. The religious service itself can be a marvellous centre for spiritual refreshment, for thought, for confession, and for aesthetic involvement. It is pleasing to have a place where family can be baptized, married and remembered after death in a decent, meaningful, and reverent way. It is good for children to meet other children who are being raised in a pattern similar to their own. It is good to be a member of a living community, with young, middle-aged, and old, all with similar commitment. It is helpful to be able to talk about issues knowing one is not entirely alone, not subjected to the scorn of the secular enthusiast. It is valuable to have a knowledgeable and faithful leader who is interested in your spiritual life, who wants you as a member of the church for spiritual as well as material reasons.

Obviously, there are some churches that do not fulfill many of those functions for anyone, and few will serve them all for every member. Unfortunately, the skeptic has to shop for a church, and that is not necessarily an enjoyable process. It does require that one think through very carefully one's reasons for joining. Although one should not want to feel too comfortable in church (the object of religious belief is not complacency), it is unhelpful to leave church upset and angry. I, for a variety of reasons, am an Anglican; there is an Anglican tradition of tolerance of differing dogma. Skeptics coming to the church today could as well find a home, depending on their own circumstances and the particularities of the church, in any of the major denominations, Protestant and Roman Catholic. There is almost as much doctrinal difference within denominations as there is between them. The culture, the liturgy, the music, the membership of the congregation, and the nature of the minister or priest are all important.

In the end, we are returned to the starting point. If there is a God, if God is good, free human beings should serve and share that truth. Christianity does not have a monopoly of God and good; those outside the faith are not lost, condemned to everlasting hell. The Christian faith happens to be the spiritual expression that is inseparable from Western civilization, and from daily life, even in the twenty-first century. That is not to assert that skeptics will be unable to find truth and harmony in, as examples, Islam or Judaism. But the further the faith is from their own background, the closer they will be to denying, separating, and opposing, rather than building—and skeptics are likely to be quite accomplished at that already.

There is a hinge between belief in the good of God and in the leadership of Jesus Christ on the one hand and a good life on the other. There is no value, beyond hypocrisy, in asserting that there is good, and at the same time, determining that the individual "I" can re-define the right choice according to my passing mood, whim, and rationalization. That is the creed of the nihilist who chooses to worship himself.

Good is interminable and constant. There are times when one is perplexed, when there seem to be only bad choices. That does not mean there is no good, that everything is relative. A hundred times one faces good and bad choices; we all sometimes choose the latter. In the hundred-and-first, there is no clearly good choice, because the circumstances and values are confused. We should no more abandon morality because it does not always help us than we should food because it occasionally makes us ill.

As an educator, I used to ask young people, often confused about a future defined in terms of jobs and money, to imagine themselves seventy years old, looking back on their lives. What would they like to have accomplished, to have been? Their answers rarely focused on material belongings and more often referred to family and moral values. It is inevitable, in the culture in which we live and breathe, that we, as adults, define ourselves in terms of our families and friends, our possessions, our age, our health, and our wants. Even so, we should regularly take the opportunity to turn away from that world and focus on the development and expression of our character, our soul.

SELECTED BIBLIOGRAPHY

Brown, Peter. *The Rise of Western Christendom*. Oxford: Blackwell Publishers, 1996.

Egerton, George (Ed.). *Anglican Essentials: Reclaiming Faith within the Anglican Church of Canada*. Toronto, Anglican Book Centre, 1995.

Frum, David. *How We Got Here: The 70's*. Toronto: Random House Canada, 2000.

Fukuyama, Francis. *The Great Disruption: Human Nature and the Reconstitution of Social Order*. New York: The Free Press, 1999.

Hillman, James. *The Soul's Code: In Search of Character and Calling*. New York: Random House, 1996.

Küng, Hans. *On Being a Christian*. London: Collins, 1977.

Lasch, Christopher. *The True and Only Heaven: Progress and its Critics*. New York: W. W. Norton, 1991.

Lewis, C. S. *Mere Christianity*. London: Fount Paperbacks, 1977.

Meeks, Wayne A. *The Origins of Christian Morality*. New Haven, CT: Yale Univeresity Press, 1993.

MacIntyre, Alasdair. *After Virtue*. Notre Dame, IN: University of Notre Dame Press, 1981.

McGregor, Douglas. *The Human Side of Enterprise*. New York: McGraw-Hill, 1960.

Metger, Bruce M., and Coogan, Michael D. (Eds.) *The Oxford Companion to the Bible*. Oxford: Oxford University Press, 1993.

Ragg, Lonsdale and Laura (Translators and Editors). *The Gospel of Barnabas*. Chicago: Kazi Publications, 1975.

Thomas, Griffith. *The Catholic Faith*. (New revised edition) London: Church Bookroom Press, 1952.

Reeves, Thomas C. *The Empty Church: The Suicide of Liberal Christianity*. New York: The Free Press, 1996.

Tolstoy, Leo. *Walk in the Light and Twenty-three Tales*. Farmington, PA: The Plough Publishing House, 1998.

Wilson, A.N. *God's Funeral*. New York: W. W. Norton, 1999.